JAILED FOR POSSESSION: I̲ ̲ ̲ ̲ ̲ ̲ ̲ ̲ ̲ ̲ ̲ ̲ ̲,
REGULATION, AND POWER IN CANADA, 1920–1961

As rates of illegal drug use increase, the debates over drug policy heat up. While some believe penalties should be harsher, others advocate complete decriminalization. Certainly, debate over the 'war on drugs' is not new. In the early 1920s, as the drive for Chinese exclusion gathered steam, Canadians blamed the Chinese for the growing use of opium and other drugs, and parliamentarians passed extremely harsh drug laws to counter this use. These laws remained in place until the 1960s.

In *Jailed for Possession*, Catherine Carstairs examines the impact of these drug laws on users' health, work lives, and relationships. In the middle of the century, drug users regularly went to jail for up to two years for possession of even the smallest amount of opium, morphine, heroin, or cocaine, often spending more time incarcerated than on the street. As enforcement stiffened and drugs became harder to obtain, drug use became an increasingly central preoccupation, making it almost impossible for users to hold down steady jobs, support families, or maintain solid relationships.

Jailed for Possession, the first social history of drug use in Canada, provides a careful examination of drug users and their regulators, including doctors, social workers, and police officers.

(Studies in Gender and History)

CATHERINE CARSTAIRS is an assistant professor in the Department of History at the University of Guelph.

STUDIES IN GENDER AND HISTORY

General Editors: Franca Iacovetta and Karen Dubinsky

Jailed for Possession

Illegal Drug Use, Regulation, and Power in Canada, 1920–1961

CATHERINE CARSTAIRS

UNIVERSITY OF TORONTO PRESS
Toronto Buffalo London

© University of Toronto Press Incorporated 2006
Toronto Buffalo London
Printed in Canada

Reprinted 2007

ISBN 0-8020-9029-X (cloth)
ISBN 0-8020-9372-8 (paper)

Printed on acid-free paper

Library and Archives Canada Cataloguing in Publication

Carstairs, Catherine, 1969–
    Jailed for possession : illegal drug use, regulation, and power in
Canada, 1920–1961 / Catherine Carstairs.

(Studies in gender and history)
Includes bibliographical references and index.
ISBN 0-8020-9029-X (bound)
ISBN 0-8020-9372-8 (pbk.)

1. Drug abuse – Government Policy – Canada – History – 20th century.
2. Drugs of abuse – Law and legislation – Canada – Criminal
provisions – Social aspects. 3. Drug abuse – Treatment – Canada –
History – 20th century. I. Title. II. Series.

HV5840.C3C39 2006   362.29′16′09710904   C2005-905129-9

University of Toronto Press acknowledges the financial assistance to
its publishing program of the Canada Council for the Arts and the
Ontario Arts Council.

University of Toronto Press acknowledges the financial support for
its publishing activities of the Government of Canada through the
Book Publishing Industry Development Program (BPIDP).

This book has been published with the help of a grant from the
Canadian Federation for the Humanities and Social Sciences, through
the Aid to Scholarly Publications Programme, using funds provided by
the Social Sciences and Humanities Research Council of Canada.

Contents

Acknowledgments

This book started as a dissertation at the University of Toronto. My supervisor, Franca Iacovetta, provided invaluable feedback, counselling, and encouragement throughout graduate school. More recently, she took time away from her own work to give the manuscript a thorough edit. I could not have asked for a better supervisor. Carolyn Strange provided wise advice, wit, and lots of smarts. Mariana Valverde maintained a keen interest in the book, and has always been a wonderful source of new readings and advice. Patricia Erickson and Paul Rutherford also provided very useful comments, as did my external examiner, Veronica Strong-Boag.

After I finished my PhD, Robin Room invited me to do a post-doc with him at Stockholm University at the Centre for Social Research on Alcohol and Drugs. My immersion in the world of drug and alcohol studies made this a better book. I am in awe of Robin's knowledge, good humour, and work ethic. I had a second wonderful post-doc supervisor in Wendy Mitchinson at the University of Waterloo.

My colleagues at the UBC History Department, especially Bob McDonald, Dianne Newell, Leslie Paris, and David Breen welcomed me to Vancouver and helped me adjust to the ins and outs of faculty life. I was lucky to have my external examiner, Veronica Strong-Boag, nearby in Women's Studies, and I continued to take advantage of her generosity as a mentor and a critic at UBC.

I was sad to leave UBC, but I am already very attached to my new home in the History Department at the University of Guelph. I am especially grateful for a first semester course release, which enabled me to finish the final revisions to this manuscript.

Many people generously gave their time to read portions of the manuscript and comment on them, including: Robin Room, Leslie Paris, Alan Gordon, Stuart McCook, Dan Malleck, Michael Szonyi, Sharon Wall, Lisa Levenstein, and members of my consumer history reading group, including Jeet Heer, Steve Penfold, Joseph Tohill, Sarah Elvins, Russell Johnston, and Daniel Robinson. U.S. drug scholar David Courtwright provided one of the most generous and useful commentaries – if I had been able to do everything he suggested, this would be a much better book. Rebecca Strung cleaned up my footnotes.

I gained a lot of experience with research agreements while writing this book and subsequently took up a lot of archivists' time. Daniel German at the National Archives ushered through my request for case files, and then he had the joy of reviewing all of my photocopies to make sure that I had blacked out the names. I also owe debts to Kerry Badgley, Cathy Bailey, and Marta Khan. At the Simon Fraser University Archives, Frances Fournier kindly dragged out box after box.

I also need to thank many agencies for financial support, including the Social Sciences and Humanities Research Council, the Hannah Institute for the History of Medicine, the Ontario Ministry of Training, Colleges, and Universities, the University of Toronto School of Graduate Studies, and the University of Toronto History Department. The Aid to Scholarly Publications Program of the Canadian Federation for the Humanities and Social Sciences provided a grant for publication. Revised versions of chapters 1 and 3 appeared in the *Canadian Bulletin of Medical History* and *Contemporary Drug Problems*. I am grateful to the editors of these publications for allowing me to include them here. Len Husband, Andy Carroll, and Barbara Tessman at University of Toronto Press also deserve thanks for taking such good care of the book along the way.

My last thanks go to my friends and family, including Sharon Wall, Carolyn Podruchny, Lisa Levenstein, Alexa King, Karen Lasser, Elena Mantagaris, Leslie Paris, Brett Bayley, Jennifer Carstairs, Paul Faulkner, and most especially Gregory Downs. My parents, John and Sharon Carstairs, have supported me every step of the way. This book is for them.

JAILED FOR POSSESSION

Introduction

What would happen if we legalized or decriminalized drugs such as cocaine, heroin, and marijuana? Would use increase? Would there be more addiction and drug-related deaths? Would the problems caused by drug prohibition, such as drug-trade violence, addiction-related crime, and the poor health of users, disappear? By decriminalizing or even legalizing drugs, could we improve the lives of users and reduce the societal costs of addiction? Or would we just make things worse?

In the 1990s, as rates of drug use increased, profits from the drug trade funded military conflicts around the globe, and HIV and hepatitis C wrecked the health of many users, this question took on a new urgency and was fiercely debated by social scientists, public policy makers, and drug users themselves.[1] This book tries to answer this question from a different angle, by examining what happened to drug users' health, work lives, and relationships after the passage of extremely strict laws against drugs in the early part of the twentieth century. Did these strict laws prevent new people from using drugs? Did they persuade existing users to quit? And did they improve or worsen users' quality of life?

This book is part of a rapidly expanding international literature on the history of drug use and drug regulation. Increasingly, drug policy experts, historians, and the public want to understand why drugs were criminalized in the first place, what impact this had on patterns of drug use and on the drug trade, and what lessons the past holds for the present. In recent years, historians have published books on the origins of the international drug trade, its links with colonialism, the international efforts to control illicit drugs, the history of 'drug panics,' the changing meanings of addiction, and the development of anti-drug campaigns around the world.[2] But with the exception of work by David

Courtwright on the United States and Frank Dikotter et al. on China, there has been relatively little social history of drug use and almost no examination of what happened to users after the passage of strict drug legislation. This book shows how the regulation of opiates, marijuana, and cocaine was carried out in one country, and the impact of this regulation on drug users and their regulators, including police officers, doctors, and social workers. Canada had some of the strictest drug laws in the world – stricter even than many U.S. states – and it kept remarkably comprehensive records on users, making it a valuable case study.[3]

American scholars have described the 1920s through the early 1960s as the 'classic' period of narcotic control – classic in the sense of 'simple, consistent and rigid.'[4] This perhaps applies even more to Canada, where drug users regularly went to jail for six months, a year, or even two years for possession of even the smallest amount of opium, morphine, heroin, or cocaine. Drug users in Canada often spent more time incarcerated then they did on the street. Over time, as enforcement increased and drugs became harder to obtain, drug users spent much of their time searching for drugs and the money to buy them. As a result, drug use became an increasingly central preoccupation, making it almost impossible for drug users to hold down steady jobs, support families, or maintain solid relationships with non-users. Few doctors wanted drug users as patients, and treatment was almost non-existent. Police, on the other hand, were almost ever-present. Enforcement personnel followed drug users on the street and could search them on sight. They invaded drug users' homes at all times of day and night without warrants, and frequently spied on them through transoms and windows. There were few sources of support for drug users, outside of their friends and families. One of the very few, the John Howard Society of British Columbia (JHS), a prison-visiting society, tried to help former convicts, including many drug users, with employment, social assistance, and counselling-oriented casework.

The drug users of the 'classic' period usually suffered from multiple problems – poverty, difficult childhoods, discrimination, and mental illness. These problems, which ensured that they lived in the most run-down sections of Canadian cities, and that they had usually spent time in jails and prison even before they used drugs, meant that they had more opportunities to try drugs than the average Canadian. Once they discovered the ability of opiates to relieve pain and create a sense of well-being, their many troubles often kept them using. But the harsh legal response to drug use then provided them with a whole new set of problems. The stories of Edgar A. and Kitty H. provide two typical examples.

Edgar A. was born in small-town Saskatchewan in 1901. He told a social worker that his earliest memories were of 'fighting and discord,' and he never learned to read or write. He started using drugs in his twenties. After a scattered career as a barber, bush worker, and circus hand, and the early death of his wife, he stole a car in 1934 and was sentenced to a year in the BC Penitentiary. Although he used drugs through much of the 1920s and '30s, he was not convicted of a narcotic offence until the early 1940s. In the 1940s and '50s, Edgar served eight penitentiary sentences (sentences of at least two years) for drug offences. He was hospitalized for tuberculosis and accidents on several occasions. By the early 1960s, he was hard of hearing and blind in one eye.[5] In 1964 he was found to be a habitual criminal and he likely died in jail.

Kitty H., an Aboriginal woman, was born in 1933. Her mother died in a drunken brawl when she was four or five, and she was raised by her grandparents. She had tuberculosis as a child and young teenager. Her grandmother was a serious drinker, and Kitty became a skilled home-brew maker as a child.[6] She started drinking heavily herself in her early teens and soon ran away from home to Vancouver where she began using drugs. After a stint in the Girls' Industrial School, she returned home, but quickly ran away again. At twenty-three, she gave birth to a premature baby that lived for only four days. Her husband blamed her for the child's death, as she was using drugs at the time. Overwhelmed with guilt and remorse, she broke down and received shock treatment. She told her social worker 'she takes drugs when she is depressed,' but she had refrained from using for long periods of time. She drank heavily as well as using drugs.[7] In the late 1960s, when her file ends, she was still using drugs from time to time, but she was not a heavy user.

A Brief History of Drug Use in Canada

The experiences of Edgar A. and Kitty H. were typical for their day, but they were markedly different from the experiences of drug users a generation or two earlier. In the nineteenth century, Canadians used opiates (including opium, morphine, and heroin) – often in the form of patent medicines – to relieve pain, reduce fevers, fight coughs, and stop diarrhoea. Invariably, some of those who started taking opiates for medical complaints, or to relieve the pain and anxiety of daily life, became addicted, but as long as the drug was readily available and could be purchased cheaply, this did not necessarily cause many problems. In addition to this quasi-medical use, many Chinese immigrants, following widespread practice at home, smoked opium, both to cure illness and for relaxation, and some white Canadians adopted the habit. Cocaine was a more recent invention, having been isolated from the coca leaf only in 1860, and it was not as widely used, but eye surgeons and dentists used cocaine as a local anaesthetic, and a few young people took it for exhilaration and energy.

It was all perfectly legal. Prior to the passage of Canada's first drug laws in 1908 and 1911, Canadians could purchase opium, cocaine, and morphine at their local pharmacy and at Chinese shops. But in the late nineteenth and early twentieth centuries, the non-medical use of opium, morphine, heroin, and cocaine became increasingly disreputable. Doctors, concerned about addiction, became cautious about prescribing opiates for pain relief, and the number of 'respectable' addicts who had become addicted through medical use began to decline. At the same time, industrialization and urbanization, the need for a disciplined workforce, and the Victorian drive for self-control led to growing unease about psychotropic (mood-changing) substances of all kinds, especially alcohol. Prohibition and temperance activists stressed the deleterious impact of 'demon rum' on work habits, home life, and morality.[8] Large swaths of the country declared themselves dry, and, in a national referendum in 1898, Canadians voted narrowly in favour of prohibition, although it was never implemented.

Despite its reputation, alcohol was widely used by people from all classes of society. How much worse was opium, used by the 'heathen Chinese,' and drugs like cocaine, associated with youth gangs and dance halls? When legislation controlling the sale and possession of opium, cocaine, and morphine came before the House of Commons in 1908 and 1911, it was seen as a necessary public health measure, needed to prevent addiction, poisoning, and recreational use, and it met with strong support.

The penalties for violating the Opium and Drug Act of 1911 were fairly minor. This changed when a huge anti-drug panic, closely tied to the drive for Chinese exclusion, emerged in the early 1920s. In chapter 1, I explore the anti-drug panic and its legal consequences. In the economically troubled years that followed the First World War, the Asiatic Exclusion League and BC politicians renewed their campaign to end all Asian immigration, and drugs became an important aspect of their campaign.[9] Newspapers, moral reformers, and parliamentarians accused evil Chinese traffickers of bringing innocent young girls and boys to ruin through drugs, providing yet another reason for keeping them out of Canada. As a result, Canada's drug laws were significantly strengthened, leading to six-month minimum sentences for possession – penalties that were removed only in 1961.

The state also put far more resources into enforcement, starting in the 1920s. The Opium and Drug Branch (renamed the Narcotic Division in 1923 and the Division of Narcotic Control in 1949) was established in 1920, as part of the new Department of Health, and it took charge of coordinating enforcement efforts and managing the licensing system. The newly created Royal Canadian Mounted Police (RCMP), formed in 1920 from a merger of the Royal North West Mounted Police and the Dominion Police, was asked to enforce the act, along with other federal statutes. Thus, in just a few short years, the state acquired the ability to fully enforce the act, and the penalties for violation had skyrocketed.

As I explore in chapters 2 and 3, these changes had a dramatic impact on the lives of users. At first, police targeted Chinese opium dens, where it was easy to make large numbers of arrests. Faced with constant raids and severe penalties, many Chinese stopped using, or switched from smoking opium, with its strong fumes and bulky equipment, to taking morphine and heroin. White working-class users like Edgar A. were not policed as intensively as the Chinese users, but they received strict sentences when they were caught. Some middle- and working-class drug users continued to obtain morphine from doctors on prescription, although it was becoming increasingly difficult to do so. During the 1920s and '30s, the high penalties for drug use and the greater difficulty in obtaining drugs seem to have led to a slow decline in use. This was not an entirely positive development, as the laws created much more dangerous conditions of drug use, including the replacement of the milder opium with morphine and heroin, and the substitution of the hypodermic needle for the opium pipe.

By the 1930s and especially during the Second World War, when smuggling all but ceased, it was very difficult to obtain drugs. Many drug users roamed the country seeking sympathetic doctors willing to prescribe. In Vancouver, where there was a more regular supply, users started injecting impure opium that was prepared for opium smoking, leading to serious abscesses and other health problems. Other users switched to codeine (a weaker opiate that was not subject to the strict provisions of the Opium and Narcotic Drug Act), Benzedrine (an amphetamine), barbiturates, or alcohol. Others grew their own poppies to make poppy tea. Despite the relative scarcity of drugs, a new generation of rebellious young people started using during the war years, attracted to drugs' pleasures and the dangers of using them.

After the war, shipping resumed, and drugs became easier to obtain and use, but users faced a vastly different situation. There were few Chinese drug users left. Instead, in the 1940s and '50s, there was a far more homogeneous group of white, working-class drug users, many of whom were quite young. These users had usually been in trouble with the law from an early age and had spent time in juvenile institutions. Surveillance of drug use by the police and the Division of Narcotic Control vastly intensified. The division carefully monitored doctors' prescriptions and quickly wrote to any physician who was prescribing more than what the division thought was normal. The RCMP and municipal police forces in Toronto and Vancouver, where most of the known drug users lived, carried out a vigorous campaign against drug users, and as the stories of Kitty and Edgar show, it was nearly impossible to be a drug user in post-war Canada and not spend a great deal of time in penal institutions. Only drug-using doctors escaped the constant cycle of arrest and imprisonment.

Illegal drug users were subject to such intensive policing and such regular incarceration that it would be fairly easy to impose a 'social control' model on the study of their lives, or to fall into the trap of painting a simple picture of drug users as heroes and regulatory agents as villains.[10] In fact, drug users wielded some power themselves, and the regulatory agents were often well-meaning. Moreover, the regulatory agents were often constrained by other forces, including the drug bureaucracy, in their dealings with drug users. Throughout the book, I have chosen to use the word 'regulation' rather than 'control' because it better encompasses the failures as well as the successes of the state's efforts at drug prohibition, and it permits a more nuanced understanding of the multiple ways in which power operates. I am very concerned with the operation of state power, given its critical influence on drug users' lives, but I have taken heed of Foucault's warning that 'we must construct an analytics of power that no longer takes law as a model and a code.' Power, Foucault explained, 'is exercised from innumerable points, in the interplay of non-egalitarian and mobile relations.'[11] In chapters 4, 5, and 6, I examine the impact of JHS social workers, doctors, and police officers on drug users, but I also explore how each of these groups of moral agents were themselves regulated by the state and by their own training and beliefs.

There is a large body of work on moral regulation that shows how regulated 'others' fought back and exerted agency, but there has been less emphasis on how the regulators themselves were governed by state and non-state institutions, by budgets, by professional associations, and by their own sense of ethics and justice. In this study, I show that power was exercised (in unequal ways) by police officers, parliamentarians, social workers, doctors, government bureaucrats, journalists, and drug users themselves.[12] I show that the doctors, police officers, and social workers from the JHS faced numerous constraints. Doctors, even if they wanted to, could not prescribe drugs for drug users without incurring the wrath of the Division of Narcotic Control. JHS social workers faced funding and institutional limitations. The nature of police work was dictated by evidentiary requirements imposed by the law and the courts, and by commands from the Division of Narcotic Control. None of these groups had unrestricted power and there were, in fact, some ironies in how power was exercised.

On the basis of their class status, we tend to think of doctors as being the most powerful of these three groups, but it was police officers, not doctors, that had the ear of the Division of Narcotic Control, and who exercised the most control over policy-making. It was police officers, not doctors, who were most preoccupied with the bodies of drug users, as they inspected their bodies for signs of drug use and tried to physically prevent their consumption of drugs. And it was social workers, not doctors, who were most interested in 'curing' the drug user. Doctors regarded drug users as difficult patients, and were, for the most part, quite willing to leave the issue of drug addiction to the criminal justice system. It was the police who had the most to gain in terms of claiming drug addiction as a particular area of expertise. They had the most personnel in the field, and narcotic policing was an interesting step up from the daily grind of police work – it was a way of gaining prestige and respect. Like doctors, few social workers took an interest in drug addiction in this time period, from 1920 to 1961, but those that did, such as the John Howard Society of British Columbia, did so out of a larger interest in advocating for the disadvantaged, and they had little to gain professionally from the field.

The chapter on policing (chapter 4) explores the growing sophistication and effectiveness of narcotic policing in Canada from 1920 through 1961. Policing caused drug users considerable stress and anxiety; it led drug users to distrust even their closest friends and their families, and to create secret (and dangerous) rituals of drug use to avoid detection. The chapter on doctors (chapter 5) shows the pressure placed on physicians by drug users who begged them to prescribe, and by the Division of Narcotic Control, which carefully monitored their prescribing practices and reprimanded them for violations. Conventional wisdom in medical history argues that the professionalization process was complete by the early part of the twentieth century, but chapter 5 shows that doctors' professional authority was questioned in the 1920s and that it was only in the 1950s and '60s that doctors gained greater autonomy in treating drug users. The chapter also demonstrates how the public looked to doctors, and especially to psychiatrists, to put forward solutions for the treatment of drug users in the 1950s, even though relatively few doctors had much interest in the field. Chapter 6, the third chapter on moral regulation, examines the work of the John Howard Society of British Columbia. It shows how these left-wing social workers were restricted in their efforts to achieve social change by their need to cooperate with the criminal justice system, and by their limited funds. Instead, social workers encouraged drug users to engage in a careful and prolonged process of self-examination and to find within themselves the reasons for their use of drugs.

The book concludes with a final chapter on policy. In the 1950s, psychological explanations of drug use and sympathy for the drug users, who were now mostly white and young, led to growing demands for treatment. In 1952 the Vancouver Community Chest and Council, which was the forerunner of the United Way, wrote a report suggesting that daily doses of heroin be provided to addicts. RCMP officers countered with the suggestion that addicts be imprisoned for life. In 1961 a new Narcotic Control Act removed the minimum penalties for possession. Instead, in Part II of the act, users could be sentenced to indeterminate periods of custody in a penitentiary for treatment. Part II was never signed into effect, because the necessary treatment institutions were never built, but because the new act made possession an indictable offence, judges still had to give prison terms, and six-month sentences remained quite common. In the mid-1960s, the use of marijuana and other drugs exploded. Suddenly, many middle-class young people appeared before the courts – a very different population from the heroin users that had dominated since the Second World War. Sentence length fell dramatically, more people were given suspended sentences or probation, and finally, in 1969, the act was amended to make it possible to proceed by summary conviction, ending mandatory prison terms. Drugs remained illegal, but the extremely harsh penalties of the 'classic period' had come to a decisive end.

One curious aspect of the 'classic period' in Canada is that drug use, especially in the period after the Second World War, was highly centralized. Drug use was largely an urban phenomenon, and it was far more common on the West Coast than it was in the Maritimes, or even central Canada. From 1922 to 1961, British Columbia had less than 10 per cent of Canada's population, but 47 per cent of all the convictions under the Opium and Narcotic Drug Act. Another 24 per cent of convictions took place in Ontario, 20 per cent in Quebec, 9 per cent in the Prairie provinces, and less than 1 per cent in the Maritimes.[13] Although convictions measure police activity better than they do actual rates of use, they are the best data available on the prevalence of narcotic use across the country, and given the intensity of policing in this period, they are quite a useful indicator of use. Most drug users who bought their drugs from the illicit market, especially from the 1930s onwards, were known to police and were arrested regularly. There were small numbers of users who obtained drugs from doctors and were able to avoid detection by police, but these seem to have been spread fairly evenly across the country. There is no indication that there was a hidden body of users in the Maritimes, the Prairies, or rural Quebec. Because of the disproportionate number of users in BC, the importance of British Columbia politicians and community activists in the drug debate, and the rich records available at the John Howard Society of British Columbia (the only social-work agency I am aware of that had a significant drug-using clientele), this book pays enormous attention to British Columbia. However, it does not neglect developments in the rest of the country – drug policy was a federal responsibility, and I trace drug-using patterns, treatment facilities, and police practices across the country.

The Problem of Addiction

It is impossible to write about drugs without addressing the complex question of addiction. The Opium and Narcotic Drug Act placed strict control over opiates (opium, morphine, and heroin), marijuana, and cocaine. There was very little marijuana use in Canada from 1920 to 1961, and cocaine was in widespread use only in the 1920s, so this is primarily a book about opiate users. Other drugs with harmful consequences, such as alcohol, tobacco, and barbiturates, were commonly used, but they were not as strictly controlled. The consequences of being an alcohol or barbiturate user were therefore very different, and these drugs are not considered in this book. With the exception of marijuana, the drugs that are controlled under the Opium and Narcotic Drug Act are generally regarded as being highly addictive, but in the words of drug scholar Ronald Akers, addiction is a 'troublesome concept.'[14] The myth that people are instantaneously addicted is just that; numerous studies have shown that the vast majority of people who try opiates and cocaine do not continue using them.[15] Moreover, many people are able to control their use of heroin, cocaine, and other illegal substances over a long period of time – out-of-control 'junkies' are only part of the total drug-using population. It is more difficult to become physically addicted than many people think. Users of opiates usually need to take them on a daily basis for several weeks before acquiring a physical dependence on the drug, although, of course, many people feel an emotional need to take the drug well before they become physically dependent.

Quitting is difficult, but far from impossible, and many users stop (or turn to other substances) as they age. Withdrawal from opiates causes symptoms similar to a bad case of the flu, with yawning, diarrhoea, abdominal cramps, goose bumps, a runny nose, and irritability, but many users find the suffering of withdrawal almost unbearable.[16] The severity of withdrawal depends partly on the extent of the drug user's habit, and his or her mental and physical health before withdrawal. Throughout much of the time period studied here, especially in the 1930s, '40s, and '50s, the drugs sold by street peddlers were fairly weak, and withdrawal may not have been that severe. But addiction is far more complex than physical dependence – long-term drug use appears to change brain structure and functioning, and the craving for drugs often persists long after withdrawal has been achieved.[17] Despite decades of extensive research, scientists do not fully understand why people become addicted and why it is so difficult for people to quit, but it is certain that it involves a complex array of factors including personality, life-history, and physiology. What is important for this study is that many people use drugs (sometimes for long periods of time) without becoming addicted, that it takes some time to acquire a physical dependence on opiates, and that quitting drugs involves far more than overcoming physical dependence.

As David Courtwright, Caroline Acker, and others have shown, ideas about addiction have changed quite dramatically over time and have had a significant impact on how lawmakers, doctors, and even members of the public viewed addicts.[18] In the early part of the nineteenth century, addiction was seen as a vice – a sinful activity that people could control.[19]

In the late nineteenth century, the disease model of addiction began to emerge, although there were conflicts between researchers who viewed addiction as a physical illness and others who believed that addiction was caused by an underlying mental disorder, usually neurasthenia, or 'chronic exhaustion.' As the number of middle-class and upper-class addicts declined, and addiction became associated with the 'disreputable' working class in the 1910s and '20s, psychiatrists and others increasingly defined addicts as 'psychopathic personalities,' whose mental and moral defects preceded their addiction. This version of the disease model did little to increase sympathy for addicts. Nor did it attract many new researchers to the field. Addiction remained understudied, and there was little unanimity among doctors as to the nature of addiction. Public opinion was similarly divided. Some regarded addiction as a vice and believed that addicts should be treated as criminals, while others saw addiction as a disease (either physical or psychological) requiring treatment.

In Canada, public support for the disease model grew in strength, first during the Great Depression, when sympathy for the 'down and out' of all kinds, including addicts, increased. It solidified in the 1950s, as faith in the ability of psychiatry and psychology to solve social problems, including addiction, expanded and the government began to assume a much greater responsibility in providing for the disadvantaged.

Theory and Methodology

In writing a social history of drug users and their regulators, I owe a significant debt to two bodies of literature. Ever since Howard Becker published his fascinating book on marijuana users, *The Outsiders,* in 1963, anthropologists and sociologists have explored drug users' motivations for taking drugs, their drug-using 'careers,' the impact of drug use on users' other relationships, and the importance of drug use in their daily lives.[20] My methodology is different from theirs, as I did not interview users themselves, but like these scholars, I wanted to take drug users' motivations and hardships seriously and convey the drama of their individual stories. I was also influenced by the many historians who have used case files in their work, including, in the Canadian context, Joy Parr, Carolyn Strange, Karen Dubinsky, and Franca Iacovetta.[21] By showing the impact of the law and the state on people's lives, this literature has brought life to the sometimes dull realms of legal history.

The sources included the extensive papers of the Narcotic Division/ Division of Narcotic Control, medical journals, and contemporary reports by psychologists and social workers. I also examined two sets of case files – 390 files from the John Howard Society of British Columbia and 159 files that were maintained by the Division of Narcotic Control. (For more detail on the case files, and on issues of access, confidentiality, and interpretation, please refer to the appendix.)

This study is grounded in social history, and the study of gender, race and class. The history of drug use in Canada is inextricably tied to Canada's history of racism.[22] Ideas about the morally degenerate but highly intelligent and cunning Chinese played a key role in the anti-drug discourse in the 1920s. Images of the 'nefarious' Chinese drug trafficker led to harsh drug laws and long sentences; Chinese-Canadian men came in for a disproportionate share of police attention for their drug use. By contrast, in the 1920s, white drug users were often seen as innocent victims and received relatively less attention from the police, although demoralized 'dope fiends' received long sentences when caught. After the Second World War, the vast majority of drug users were white, which helps to explain why there was a greater emphasis on treatment.

Gender ideologies and patriarchal relations of power also had a strong impact on the lives of drug users.[23] Stories of feminine weakness and guile were used to construct powerful anti-drug narratives that drove the campaign to increase the severity of Canada's drug laws. Ideas about appropriate female roles, as well as the structural realities of a gendered labour market, meant that female drug users experienced the world of drug use very differently from male users. Narratives of femininity meant that middle-class women were much more successful at feigning illnesses and obtaining drugs from doctors than their male counterparts. Working-class women who used drugs earned money for drugs primarily through prostitution, while male drug users more often committed theft or engaged in peddling drugs, which women drug users did much less frequently. Selling drugs gave male drug users greater access to money and power, but it also resulted in long sentences. Prostitution could be lucrative, but it was dangerous and often demoralizing. Many female drug users insisted that it was prostitution that led them to take drugs. At the same time, both female and male users were criticized for their violations of normative gender roles – women because they were out on the street and men because they failed to hold down jobs and support families. Thus, gender ideologies and gender inequalities affected the lives of male and female drug users in multiple ways.

Class also played an important role. There were undoubtedly some middle- and upper-class drug users, and there were definitely drug-addicted doctors, but these users rarely came to the attention of regulatory authorities. In fact, by the 1930s, the number of middle-class and upper-class users was probably quite small. Doctors were reluctant to prescribe opiates, and buying them illicitly would likely garner police attention. Middle-class people altered their consciousness with drugs, but they were legal drugs, such as amphetamines, barbiturates, and benzodiazepines or alcohol. The fact that most opiate and cocaine users were working class permitted the state to take a 'criminal' approach to drug use, allowed for the intensive surveillance of drug users' lives, and ensured that most drug users would spend much of their time in conflict with the criminal justice system.[24] Also, drug use is, at least in part, a response to the alienating experience of life on the margins of consumer society, as well as an escape from the difficult emotional circumstances sometimes brought about by poverty.

Most of the drug users examined in this book were poor, troubled, and the subject of considerable attention from regulatory agents. The history of drug users therefore provides an interesting case study of the state, and of professional power, in Canadian society at a time when the state's capacity for regulation was vastly increasing. It also raises important questions about the dangerous consequences of strict drug control. This book shows that a harsh enforcement approach failed to bring an end to drug use, destabilized users' lives, harmed their health, and made drug use attractive to a small community of rebellious users. A more lenient approach to drug use will undoubtedly come with its own set of harms and dangers, but the strict approach that characterized the classic years was even worse.

Chapter 1

The Drug Panic of the 1920s and the Drive for Chinese Exclusion

Opiates have been described as the world's best painkillers, as an elixir for the romantic imagination, and as a dangerous cause of moral decay. Cocaine has been seen both as a harmless 'glamour drug' and as a catalyst of inner-city violence. Drug users themselves interpret the effects of drugs differently, depending on their cultural background, their preconceived ideas about drugs, and the environments in which they use them.[1] In other words, language and practices construct the meanings of drug use for both users and non-users. Although there have been occasional celebrations of drug use, especially in the later part of the twentieth century, most researchers and commentators on the question have thought of drug use as a social problem, particularly in the period under review here. This chapter examines how this social problem was defined in the 1920s, and by whom, and what impact this had on drug laws in Canada.[2]

In the 1920s, the campaign for Chinese exclusion and fears about changing gender roles fed into an inflammatory moral panic about drug use and trafficking. Reformers and journalists described evil Chinese traffickers leading young white (and usually female) Canadians to ruin and demanded strict penalties. Politicians and the press expressed much sympathy for the plight of 'innocent' white users, and they sought the harshest penalties possible for the traffickers of drugs, especially Asian traffickers. To address public concern, Parliament passed severe legislation with very little regard for who would actually be affected by the new drug laws.

The Early Development of Canada's Drug Laws

In the late nineteenth century, Canadians grew increasingly uneasy about drug use of all kinds, including alcohol. The Victorian ideal of self-control made the use of substances that altered mood and behaviour frightening, even degrading, and organizations like the Woman's Christian Temperance Union sprung up to counter the most widely used psychotropic substance – alcohol. Their campaigns met with some success – in 1878 the Canada Temperance Act allowed any county or municipality to prohibit the retail sale of alcohol, and in 1898 Canadians voted marginally in favour of prohibition in a national plebiscite, although national prohibition was not implemented until the First World War, and then only briefly.

Canada's first law against opium was part of this reaction against alcohol and other drugs, but it had its immediate origin in an anti-Asian riot on the West Coast. In 1907, after a summer of mounting anti-Asian activity, several thousand white Vancouverites assembled for an anti-Asian parade on 7 September. During the speeches at City Hall, part of the crowd marched to nearby Chinatown, where they smashed windows with stones and bricks. Another group attacked the Japanese quarter.[3] The government sent the deputy minister of labour, Mackenzie King, to investigate the riots and the claims for compensation. Several opium manufacturers who had been operating legally in Vancouver submitted claims for damages,[4] and the members of a Chinese anti-opium league took the opportunity to ask King for help in their efforts to discourage the manufacture and sale of opium. The temperance-minded King was appalled that opium manufacturing was still being allowed. In a report, he warned that opium smoking was not confined to the Chinese in British Columbia and that it was spreading to white women and girls. He quoted a newspaper clipping about a pretty young woman found in a Chinese opium den. He also reviewed the progress of the anti-opium movement in China, the United States, England, and Japan, leaving the impression that Canada was far behind in this international moral reform movement.[5] A few weeks after King tabled his report, the minister of labour introduced legislation prohibiting the manufacture, sale, and importation of opium for other than medicinal purposes.[6] The legislation passed without debate, reflecting widespread·consensus about the dangers of opium and the need for control. That same summer, reflecting concern about addiction to and adulteration of patent medicines, Parliament passed An Act Respecting Proprietary or Patent Medicines, forbidding manufacturers from manufacturing or selling any proprietary or patent medicine that contained alcohol, or that included more alcohol than was necessary as a solvent or preservative.[7]

Another act, three years later, forbade the possession of opium and other drugs for non-medicinal purposes. The sale or possession of morphine, opium, or cocaine became an offence carrying a maximum penalty of one year's imprisonment and a $500 fine. There was no minimum penalty. Smoking opium was a separate offence and carried a maximum penalty of $50 and one month's imprisonment, and again, there was no minimum penalty. There were several reasons behind the new legislation. First, the 1908 legislation had not stopped opium smoking in Canada, and the police argued that more drastic measures were needed. Chief Rufus Chamberlain, the chief constable of the Vancouver City Police, recommended that opium smoking and possession of opium-smoking equipment become offences under the anti-opium act.[8] Second, Mackenzie King, who introduced the 1911 legislation, had attended the 1909–10 International Opium Commission in Shanghai. The commission was an American initiative meant to help China eradicate the opium traffic (and increase America's trade with China), and Canada's 1911 legislation was intended to bring its laws in line with the Commission's resolutions. The legislation also had public approval in Montreal, where a cocaine panic, initiated by the Children's Aid Society, had enlisted the support of churches and Catholic and Protestant clergymen, settlement house workers, the Montreal Council of Women, pharmacists, and the mayor.[9]

Canadian society was becoming increasingly dry at this time, and it is not surprising that opiates and cocaine also came under attack. The population of drug users was also undergoing a significant demographic shift. Regular medical practitioners had become much more restrained in their use of narcotic drugs in the 1890s, and the number of medically created addicts had decreased. David Courtwright has argued that in the United States, by the time the Harrison Act (the first federal drug legislation) passed in 1914, drug use among upper- and middle-class white females had significantly declined, while drug use among lower-class urban males had increased.[10] In Canada, Cheryl Krasnick Warsh's study on the Homewood Retreat shows that a parallel decline in medically addicted users likely took place in the late nineteenth and early twentieth centuries.[11] The fact that opium was perceived to be used by working-class Chinese, and cocaine by disreputable Montrealers, contributed to the notion that these drugs, like the people who used them, needed to be controlled and regulated. However, there was a significant difference between the 1908 and 1911 legislation and the legislation that would follow in the 1920s. In the 1910s, fines were the norm, but after the drug panic of the 1920s, drug users were likely to go to jail.

Racism and the Drug Panic of the 1920s

The anti-drug campaign of the early 1920s exhibited all the features of the classic moral panic described by Stanley Cohen: the danger was exaggerated, 'right-thinking people' played an active role, and the concern subsided after legislative goals were achieved.[12] Newspapers, women's groups, social service organizations, labour unions, fraternal societies, and church congregations all joined in the campaign to eradicate what they called the 'drug evil.' They blamed Chinese Canadians for the degradation of white youth through drugs and demanded harsh new drug legislation, as well as the total prohibition of Chinese immigration.

Their campaign produced results. In 1921 maximum sentences for trafficking and possession increased from one year to seven. In 1922 Parliament passed legislation that allowed judges to order the deportation of any aliens convicted of possession or trafficking and introduced a jail term of at least six months for people convicted of possession or trafficking offences. The legislation authorized police to search any location except a 'dwelling-house' without a warrant if they suspected drugs were present. In 1923 codeine and marijuana were added to the Schedule of restricted drugs without debate. The same legislation limited the right to appeal a conviction for possession or trafficking.[13] This flurry of law-making marked a significant turning point in Canada's approach to drug use. By the mid-1920s, drug use had been thoroughly criminalized, both by the law and in the mind of the public.

With the significant exception of work by Cheryl Krasnick Warsh and Dan Malleck on the nineteenth century, historians have largely ignored the history of drug use and legislation in Canada.[14] Sociologists and legal scholars filled the gap. Inspired by the drug debates of the late 1960s, they produced a series of articles in the 1960s and '70s that claimed that Canada's drug laws were inspired by anti-Chinese racism.[15] In recent years, this view has been challenged, most notably by Clayton Mosher, whose 1998 book, *Discrimination and Denial,* asserted that the drug literature in Canada 'has rather uncritically accepted the notion that the legislation was implemented to control the immigrant Chinese.'[16] Mosher acknowledges that there is considerable evidence to show that the laws were a response to Chinese opium smoking on the West Coast, but insists that more empirical evidence is needed to substantiate these claims. Certainly, anti-Asian racism was not responsible for making drugs illegal in Canada – there were many reasons for the 1908 and 1911 acts, including concern about addiction, and Canada's participation in the international reform movement. Nevertheless, careful examination of the links between the anti-Chinese discourse and the drug laws makes it clear that anti-Chinese racism was critical to the passage of Canada's extraordinarily severe drug laws in the 1920s, as I will show in this chapter, with particular reference to the important, but heretofore ignored, newspaper and citizen campaign in Vancouver.

In making this case, I am not ignoring the role played by enforcement officials and government bureaucrats. In *Panic and Indifference* (1991), the only book-length study of drug laws in Canada, Giffen, Endicott, and Lambert acknowledged the importance of the 'dope fiend mythology,' including its anti-Chinese elements, but they downplayed the importance of racism and stressed instead that the demands for new drug legislation came primarily from enforcement officials and bureaucrats in the Department of Health. Their study of the relevant government documents led them to conclude that the officials responsible for enforcing the legislation were the most important group influencing the development of Canadian narcotic policy.[17] Certainly, the enforcement network initiated many of the encroachments on civil liberties, but, as we shall see, these would have never passed through the House of Commons without the widespread panic inspired by the anti-drug campaign. In 1924 the chief of the Narcotic Division wrote that he never had any problem obtaining the necessary appropriations because 'of the very strong feeling in the country at the present time on this drug question, and it being an unpolitical question.'[18] The enforcement network had free rein to suggest new legislation precisely because of heightened public concern.

The effectiveness of the drug panic depended on the creation of a racial drama of drug use that featured 'innocent' white youth and shadowy Asian traffickers who turned them into morally depraved 'dope fiends.'[19] People believed this drama because it took shape in the middle of a concerted drive to exclude the Chinese from Canada, segregate their children in West Coast schools, and place restrictions on their business enterprises and land ownership.[20] Examining the racialization of the drug panic helps explain why anti-drug crusaders called for strict penalties for possession and trafficking and at the same time wished to establish treatment facilities for the poor (white) drug addicts for whom they had so much sympathy. It also explains why parliamentarians, many of whom were lawyers, were willing to overlook the negative effects on civil liberties in their desire to pass harsh legislation to counter what they regarded as a 'Chinese' menace.

Race was the driving force behind the anti-drug campaign, but the discourses of class, gender, and age were also employed to advantage. The 'victims' of the 'evil Chinese drug traffickers' were always young, and the narratives of their corruption fed into long-standing fears about the dangers posed by urban environments and unsupervised leisure.[21] For several reasons, women were usually the protagonists in these anti-drug tales. Notions of female vulnerability allowed authors to portray some women as blameless victims of 'drug addiction disease.' Many stories of female drug users were copied directly from 'white slavery' narratives – a young woman was taken in by an older person, drugged, and then forced to earn a living through prostitution. At the same time, female drug users were considered to be more dangerous than male drug users: they were prostitutes who spread venereal disease and despicable mothers who abandoned or mistreated their children. Female 'dope fiends' fit neatly into a gendered narrative of womanly weakness and guile, with which Canadians were already familiar. Masculinity, on the other hand, was linked to wage-earning and family responsibility. In the narratives of male users, the victims were almost always said to be successful young men from good families, and their downward descent in class status as a result of drug use was a recurring plot used to create a sense of drama and excitement.

Causes and Effects of the Canadian Drug Panic

The first person to write extensively about the drug question was the practised social reformer Emily Murphy, although it was the anti-drug campaign that began on the West Coast shortly after that would have a much greater impact on drug legislation. Murphy was a leading suffragist, a temperance activist, and a popular writer under the pen-name Janey Canuck. She was also a key player in eugenic debates, and a staunch supporter of the Sexual Sterilization Act in Alberta, which allowed for the sterilization of the mentally disabled.[22] In 1916 she was appointed police magistrate for Edmonton, and then for Alberta, becoming the first female magistrate in the British Empire. It was as a judge that she first encountered addicts and became interested in the question of drug use.

In 1920 Murphy published a series of five articles in *Maclean's* magazine. She followed these with two additional articles in *Maclean's* in 1922, and with her book *The Black Candle*. In 1923 she nominated herself for a Nobel Prize for her work.[23] Murphy's importance has been overstated

both by herself and by subsequent drug scholars. The Division of Narcotic Control had little respect for Murphy, and the Vancouver parliamentarians who played a leading role in drug legislation paid far more
attention to the anti-drug crusade in their own city.[24] Nonetheless,
Murphy's articles did mark a turning point, and her book, which drew
heavily on the Vancouver campaign and was dedicated to the Vancouver
drug investigators, brought the Vancouver drug panic to a larger Canadian audience.[25]

Murphy's debut article was entitled 'The Grave Drug Menace.' The
first page made clear that this was a Chinese menace, featuring a spooky
drawing of a hand with long fingernails holding a Chinese tablet, a
picture of a wizened Asian man with smoke coming out of his ears, and a
photo of an Asian man smoking a pipe. The text itself focused on white
female addicts and warned, 'all folks of gentle and open hearts should
know that among us there are girls and glorious lads who, without any
obliquity in themselves, have become victims to the thrall of opiates.'[26]
Murphy explained that drug use posed a serious threat to the white race,
as it accounted for most cases of miscegenation.[27] In subsequent articles,
Murphy accused the Chinese of continuing their nefarious activities
behind locked doors and hidden passages, despite the Opium and Drug
Act.[28] Several times she referred to her imaginary Chinese characters as
'Ah Sin,' a quick shorthand for describing the moral failures of the
Chinese, and had them engage in what was clearly meant to come across
as 'foreign' behaviour.[29]

In her 1922 book, *The Black Candle*, Murphy took care to distance
herself from what she considered to be prejudice or racism. 'We have no
sympathy with the baiting of the yellow races, or with the belief that
these exist only to serve the Caucasian, or to be exploited by us,' she
wrote. 'The Chinese as a rule are a friendly people,' she condescend-
ingly pronounced, 'and have a fine sense of humor that puts them on an
easy footing with our folk, as compared with the Hindu and others we
might mention. Ah Duck, or whatever we choose to call him, is patient,
polite and persevering.' Despite her favourable assessment of what she
viewed as the Chinese character, she assumed that it was her right to
name the Chinese, and to tell the truth of their character. As she put it,
'it behooves the people in Canada and the United States, to consider the
desirability of these visitors – for they are visitors – and to say whether or
not we shall be "at home" to them for the future. A visitor may be polite,
patient, persevering, as above delineated, but if he carried poisoned
lollypops in his pocket and feeds them to our children, it might seem

wise to put him out.'[30] By complimenting the Chinese and criticizing their exploitation, she gave greater credibility to her view that the Chinese were outsiders who threatened the well-being of Canadian children through drugs.

Evil Chinese traffickers were not Murphy's only stock character. To make her point about the dangers of drugs, Murphy told dramatic stories about the downfall of white users. White users in the early stages of drug use were cast as 'innocent addicts' – young people who had been mislead by others into trying drugs, sometimes even without their knowledge. However, over time, 'innocent addicts' could become 'dope fiends,' with no moral or ethical sense, limited intelligence, and wasted bodies marred by the punctures of hypodermic needles.

Murphy was one of Canada's best-known writers, and her monthly feature in Canada's leading news magazine garnered attention in newspapers across the country.[31] But a far more important anti-drug campaign in Vancouver dwarfed her efforts. Vancouver had the largest number of drug arrests and the biggest Chinese community in Canada. It was also the primary location for anti-Chinese organizing, which was gathering steam in the tense and economically strained years that followed the First World War. In the spring of 1920, coinciding with Murphy's campaign in *Maclean's*, the *Vancouver Daily Sun* ran a brief campaign against the drug traffic. Its editorials called for the abolition of Chinatown; one declared that it was 'absolutely necessary to prevent the degrading of white boys and girls who are being recruited into the ranks of drug addicts. If the only way to save our children is to abolish Chinatown, then Chinatown must and will go, and go quickly.'[32] The *Sun* was not alone. The Child's Welfare Association and the chief of police publicly called for more severe penalties for drug use, and the Kiwanis club began planning a home for 'drug-sufferers.'[33]

The first major citizens' campaign occurred when returned solider Joseph Kehoe pleaded guilty to eight charges of robbery with violence and was sentenced to five years in the Penitentiary and twenty-four lashes in March 1921. According to the *Vancouver Sun*, which covered the case intensively, this unlikely 'hero' was twenty-eight years old and came from a 'good family' in Nova Scotia.[34] Kehoe had been a medical student when he enlisted at the very start of the war. In April 1915 he was gassed and taken prisoner at Ypres. Kehoe reported that the Germans put him to work in a munitions factory, but he refused to take part in work that would be used to harm his fellow allied soldiers, and he eventually convinced his fellow prisoners to break his arm so that he could no longer work. He was brought before a military tribunal and sentenced to fifteen years' imprisonment in a military prison, but at the end of sixteen months his health was so poor that he was sent to England in an exchange of prisoners. He was discharged in 1919, and after his return to Canada he started using drugs.[35]

Vancouverites, especially returned soldiers, immediately began protesting Kehoe's sentence.[36] In a subsequent interview, Kehoe advised any young person who was offered 'dope' to 'hit the man who offers it to you, and if you are not big enough to use your fists, take a club.'[37] A few weeks later, a general meeting of the Comrades of the Great War passed a resolution opposing light sentences in the case of dope peddlers. As it had the previous year, the coverage quickly took an anti-Chinese turn. In a front-page article on 12 April, entitled 'Dope Peddler King Is Taken,' the *Vancouver Sun* told its readers that prominent Chinese businessman Wong Way boasted that he was turning over more than half a million dollars' worth of drugs each year and that he drove one of the 'best limousines in the city.'[38] His reported success undoubtedly added fire to business complaints that Chinese merchants were competing unfairly with whites.[39]

A week later, Vancouverites held a mass meeting to demand 'drastic federal action' to defeat the 'dope traffickers.'[40] The meeting was organized by the Returned Soldier's Council and included the mayor, the chief of police, the city prosecutor, officials from the Oakalla Prison Farm, and service club representatives. A week later, a second meeting called for minimum two-year sentences for first-time traffickers, and five years and the lash for a second trafficking offence. Participants demanded deportation for all aliens convicted of selling drugs, and that the police be given the right to search for drugs without a warrant.[41] An enormous headline in the *Vancouver Sun* proclaimed 'DEATH ON DOPE: CITIZENS PLAN BIG CAMPAIGN TO SMASH UP THE DRUG RING.'

In early May, the newspaper hired a former drug user to carry on a special investigation into the traffic. J.B. Wilson described himself as a 'successful young businessman' before he started using drugs. Now cured, he was anxious to 'devote my talents and my energies to assisting in rescuing others who have fallen victims to the drug ring.' Wilson argued that police were doing everything they could to stamp out the drug traffic, but that the 'Chinese dope peddler is about the most cunning human being and the smartest of them all.'[42] In a later article, he commended the RCMP, who 'are bending their energies to rid our Canadian soil of the Oriental filth of the drug traffic.'[43]

Several weeks after the first Vancouver meeting, the minister of health introduced legislation to amend the Opium and Narcotic Drug Act. H.H. Stevens, a Conservative MP from Vancouver South who had participated in the Vancouver meetings, proposed two new amendments to the act: increasing the maximum sentence to seven years, and adding whipping as a penalty for those found guilty of giving or distributing drugs to a minor. Stevens introduced his amendment with the announcement that drug traffickers were distributing drugs to children in high school and in the higher grades of elementary school.[44] Others shared the Vancouver MP's alarm. Dr. Matthew Blake, a Conservative member from Winnipeg, announced that 'the drug ring today is the greatest menace we have to contend with in Canada.'[45] Frontenac MP John Edwards mused, 'I can imagine no more brutal character than he who coolly and deliberately plans, for his own financial gain to absolutely ruin the lives of his fellow citizens.'[46]

Not all of the members agreed initially. Early in the debate, Dr. Peter McGibbon, a Liberal MP and doctor from Muskoka, argued that restrictions against the availability of drugs were too strict. 'While we have a few morphine and opium fiends in Montreal, Toronto, Winnipeg and probably Calgary and Vancouver,' he claimed, 'throughout the great length and breadth of this country there is practically none.'[47] Colonel John Currie, a Conservative from Simcoe, accused the 'so-called social service workers' of 'magnifying the effects of these drugs in order that they may draw good salaries.'[48] The Honourable William Fielding, a Liberal from Nova Scotia, found it difficult to believe that the 'evil of trafficking' in drugs with children could be as widespread as was alleged.[49]

In the end, the House implemented the harsher new penalties but did not include the lash. The members concurred with Dr. Robert Manion, the Unionist member from Fort William, who said that even though he was convinced of the 'great criminality of people who administer and sell these drugs,' he did not think that whipping was appropriate.[50] If the longer sentences did not succeed, Dr. Manion argued that he would be willing to consider whipping at a later date. The continuation of the drug panic ensured that he would have that opportunity the following year.

As the spring of 1921 progressed, the panic temporarily disappeared from the headlines, but activity continued backstage. The Rotary, Gyros, and Kiwanis clubs established an Investigating Committee into the Drug Traffic.[51] That summer the *Vancouver Sun* published Hilda Glynn Ward's novel, *The Writing on the Wall.* The plot featured wealthy Vancouver citizens who became addicted to drugs and subsequently cooperated with the Chinese in their drive for the domination of Canada. At the beginning of 1922, the Investigating Committee had a great opportunity to publicize their findings when the *Vancouver Daily World*, Vancouver's oldest newspaper, launched an anti-drug campaign that eclipsed the *Sun*'s.[52] The paper highlighted the drug issue on its front page for months, increasing its circulation by one-third.[53]

From the beginning, the *World* blamed Asians for the spread of the drug habit. On the first day of the campaign, the *World* featured two front-page articles under a headline banner that proclaimed 'Drug Soaked Addicts Pass on Way to Jail.' One article described the case of Yung Yuen, 'an ivory faced Chinese,' who was sentenced to a year in prison for procuring three packages of drugs for a 'white victim,' and that of Lim Gum, 'an undersized bald-headed little Chinese,' who was found with four tins of opium. These unflattering descriptions of the Chinese men drew attention to the perceived physical differences between Chinese and whites. The 'foreign' nature of the Chinese and their customs was highlighted by the depiction of Yung's trial, in which he was said to have written his name on a piece of paper and then burned it with a match while mumbling 'Chinese rigmarole to the effect that so might his soul burn after death if he failed to tell the truth.' By contrast, the two whites described in the article were both 'victims.' The 'sorriest case of all' was a young man named Fawcett whose 'white face, constricted knees and scarred limbs bear witness to his plight.'[54]

While the descriptions of the Chinese were meant to make the reader feel hostile, angry, and disdainful, the portraits of whites, who were accused of similar crimes, provoked sympathy and compassion. White drug use and Chinese drug use were being delineated as two quite separate problems. Later in the campaign this division became even more striking: newspaper estimates for the number of addicts in Vancouver explicitly excluded 'Orientals,' thereby indicating that drug use among whites was a very different issue than drug use among the Chinese.[55]

The anti-Asian discourse in Canada in this period consistently emphasized the intelligence of the Chinese and their craftiness as reasons for prohibiting their immigration to Canada. The idea that the Chinese were consummate drug smugglers, on account of their ingenuity and cleverness, would not have surprised the citizens of Vancouver. Most were already convinced that the business acumen of the Chinese posed a serious threat to white enterprise. The second article that appeared on the *World*'s front page announced that 'All Boats from Asia Bring in Illicit Drugs,' and it was subtitled, 'Oriental Crews Largely Engaged in Traffic.' It described Asian traffickers as 'wily' and claimed that innocent passengers were sleeping on top of drugs hidden under berths and 'stitched into mattresses.'[56] The following day, an article entitled 'Dying Lad Tells How Boys and Girls Are Made Drug Addicts' asserted that most of the drugs came from Chinatown. A young addict confided that one dealer had a secret code whereby the purchaser would request drugs by number, thereby lessening the chance of being caught over the phone.[57] Under such circumstances, it would not be easy to catch the 'cunning' Asian drug traffickers. The message was clear: Vancouverites needed to wake up to the danger under their beds and defend themselves against the Asian drug menace.

On the third day of the *Vancouver Daily World*'s campaign, the newspaper announced its solution to the drug problem with a headline that blared 'Deport the Drug Traffickers.' The article asserted (wrongly) that 1778 Asians were convicted of drug offences in the Vancouver Police Court in 1921.[58] Since most received fines instead of going to jail, they were free to 'commit the same sin against society.' The article concluded with the statement that 'Vancouver's first move in abolishing the drug traffic must be the absolute banishment by deportation of every Oriental who lends himself to the drug ring.'[59] Over the months that followed, the *World* encouraged organizations throughout Vancouver to pass resolutions to that effect. As a result, thousands of Vancouverites signed petitions asking for mandatory sentences for drug possession and trafficking, and for the deportation of naturalized aliens who participated in the drug traffic.[60]

On day three, the paper also announced that the Child Welfare Society was joining the fight against the 'drug evil,' despite threats against their lives. The *World* further claimed that 'actual attempts have been made on the lives of government officials engaged in the fight against the big influences at work behind the scenes.'[61] The following Sunday, evangelist C.O. Benham of the Central City Mission urged all Christians to get behind the *Vancouver Daily World* campaign.[62] Within ten days, a variety of social service clubs and fraternal organizations, including the Rotary club, the Kiwanis club, the Board of Trade, the Imperial Order Daughters of the Empire, and the Child's Welfare Association were organizing a mass meeting.

Over the next several weeks, the newspaper kept up its daily barrage of stories about white victims and Chinese villains. The oft-repeated idea that the Chinese might bring about the destruction of the white race through drug use appeared in a particularly blatant form in a front-page story about a wealthy addict who was 'dragged down by drugs.' Emphasizing Chinese 'superiority' in terms of greater will power and self control, the white addict asserted that the Chinese drug sellers 'taunted him with their superiority at being able to sell the dope without using it. Taunted him by telling him that the yellow race would rule the world. That they were too wise to attempt to win in battle but that they would win by wits. That they would introduce drugs into the homes of the Caucasians; would strike at the white race through "dope," and that when the time was ripe they would take command of the world.'[63]

On 29 January, 2000 Vancouverites attended a meeting held at the Empress Theatre, where they passed a unanimous resolution asking for the elimination of fines as a penalty for drug trafficking and the substitution of prison sentences of not less than six months and not more than ten years, with lashes, and the deportation of aliens.[64] The *World* reported that women wiped tears from their eyes, as the self-styled drug investigator Charles Royal told the audience about 'girls in their teens' who sold themselves to Chinese, Japanese, and 'Hindoos' to get money for drugs. 'They shuddered,' the newspaper continued, 'when he pointed out that many of them came from the best families in Vancouver and in the Dominion and when he told of a young boy of this city, himself an addict, who had, at the instigation of the Chinese traffickers, started his sister on the drug habit, and then had used her to pander to the passions of these self-same traffickers in order to get the money to buy drugs, women turned pale, while men clenched their hands and gripped their lips with their teeth to keep down the anger that fought for an outlet.'[65] The following day, the city council and the mayor both gave their support to the anti-drug campaign.[66]

Four days after the mass meeting at the Empress Theatre, the New Era League sponsored a successful meeting of women opposed to the drug traffic at the same locale. Mrs. James O'Brien, one of the leading Vancouver activists, 'touched on the degradation of young girls who fell into the tolls of the Orientals once they became drug addicts.'[67] O'Brien also told the story of a young boy 'who was in jail on a charge of stealing and administering drugs to a young girl.' An Asian man caught in the same circumstances would have been thoroughly vilified, but O'Brien regarded this boy's youth and race as far more important than his crime:

'I could not forget the sight of that young fellow behind bars,' she said. 'I keep on remembering his big blue eyes, filled with tears. I asked him if there was anything I could do.'

'Just tell mother I'm hungry,' he said.

'And then I went to Stanley Park and saw Orientals driving by in their big limousines, rich through the gains that had put that poor boy behind the bars.'[68]

The idea that numerous Asians could drive through Stanley Park in limousines in the early 1920s was preposterous, but it was effective rhetoric for white Canadians alarmed about Asian economic competition.

A subsequent meeting at the Colonial Theatre and a well-attended meeting of the Vancouver Board of Trade passed the familiar resolution (first passed at the Empress Theatre on 29 January) asking for the end of fines and the substitution of prison sentences for all persons convicted of illegally selling drugs or narcotics.[69]

The Chinese elite grew increasingly worried about these attacks on their community. In early February, according to the *Chinese Times*, a number of the wealthier merchants, the president of the Chinese Benevolent Association, and the Chinese ambassador got together to discuss ways to stop the drug traffic in Chinatown. Charles Royal crowed, 'I cannot say how glad I am that influential Chinese are linking up with us. It takes an Oriental to fight an Oriental with any degree of success.'[70]

The campaign's momentum slowed somewhat in February, but by early March Charles Royal and Mrs. James O'Brien had addressed dozens of smaller meetings, and numerous telegrams had been sent to Prime Minister Mackenzie King and the Liberal Party executive encouraging action on the issue.[71] In April, a coalition of members from British Columbia and the Yukon met with the minister of health and asked for compulsory sentences and deportation.[72] In May 1922, New Westminster Unionist W.G. McQuarrie introduced a motion into the House of Commons asking for the government to take 'immediate action with a view of securing the exclusion of Oriental immigration.'[73] Vancouver South Liberal-Conservative Leon Ladner, who had spoken at several of the mass meetings in Vancouver, delivered a long speech highlighting the discoveries of the Vancouver Investigating Committee. He concluded that the drug traffic was reason enough to stop all Chinese immigration.[74] While most of the members participating in this debate stressed economic issues, three members also emphasized the dangers of the drug traffic.

The government introduced a new drug bill at the beginning of June 1922. By this time, no parliamentarian claimed that the drug panic was overblown. Members from all parties urged Henri Beland, the health minister, to take even more stringent steps against the drug traffic. The minister indicated that numerous requests had reached him from 'benevolent, charitable and religious bodies' as well as parliamentarians 'on both sides of the House' to abolish the option of a fine.[75] The new bill increased minimum penalties for possession to six months. At the first reading, Progressive member Archibald Carmichael asked for an amendment to deport all Asians found guilty of trafficking in drugs.[76] Ladner advised the government to pass an amendment allowing for the lash, in cases where drugs had been sold to juveniles.[77] Both of these measures were ultimately included in the 1922 act.

The anti-Asian racism of the Vancouver campaign had a clear impact in the debate that followed. Ladner told the story of a girl of sixteen who had come before the investigation committee in Vancouver. Addicted to either morphine or cocaine, she prostituted herself with Chinese men and suffered from venereal disease. 'This traffic is carried on in a cool and calculating way,' Ladner concluded. 'The men who sell the drug do not themselves use it; they know its terrible effects, but they exercise all their resourcefulness and ingenuity to induce others to acquire the habit.'[78] Fully persuaded, Dr. Manion, who had been opposed to the lash the previous year, deferred to the members from British Columbia on the grounds that they were more 'familiar with this question than perhaps the rest of us, even those who are in the medical profession.'[79] Although there were still a few MPs, such as United Farmer Oliver Gould, who opposed the lash on humanitarian grounds, even he felt compelled to state that the traffic 'is one of the greatest evils extant in this country.'[80]

In the debate over deportation, it was clear that the 'foreigners' to be deported were Chinese. Health Minister Henri Beland pointed out that 'so far as a provision for deportation is concerned the committee will realize that it would not very well apply to Canadians. Only to Chinese who have not been naturalized could it apply.'[81] He did not even consider the possibility that citizens of other countries might be deported by this bill, although after it went into effect in 1922, large numbers of Americans were also deported.

In 1923, not long after the passage of that year's Chinese Immigration

Act, which prohibited all Chinese immigration except for a few students and merchants, the anti-drug consensus resulted in yet another set of revisions to the Opium and Narcotic Drug Act. By this time, the drug panic had also spread to Toronto and Montreal, and that spring, large meetings of prominent citizens were held at the Loew's Roof Garden Theatre in Toronto and at the Mount Royal Hotel in Montreal.[82] In the parliamentary session that followed, the government passed legislation that restricted the right to an appeal for people convicted of possessing, selling, or importing/exporting a drug without a license; it also increased the fine for smoking opium and increased the maximum penalty for being found in an opium den and for possession of opium-smoking equipment. The debate was short, but the anti-drug consensus was clear. Mr. E.M. Macdonald stated, 'we are all agreed that this nefarious traffic, which saps the mind and body of the people can only be dealt with in the strongest possible way.'[83] Dr. Manion, who opposed the measure to restrict appeals on constitutional grounds, made sure to indicate that his failure to support the amendment was not because he was 'soft on drugs.' 'I presume,' he clarified, 'there is no member of this House, whatever may be his party affiliations who is not just as eager as my hon. friend to do away with the illicit use of any of these habit-forming drugs.'[84]

In 1923 Parliament added marijuana to the Schedule of the Opium and Narcotic Drug Act. The reason behind the decision is unclear, as there appears to have been very little psychotropic use of marijuana in Canada at the time, and the anti-drug campaign paid no attention to the drug.[85] There were no seizures of marijuana in Canada until 1937, nor was there any discussion of marijuana in the parliamentary debates. Most scholars and activists have pointed to a chapter on marijuana in Murphy's book, *The Black Candle*, to explain the inclusion of marijuana,[86] but this was the twenty-third chapter in a 400-page book. It was only seven pages long and garnered no significant attention at the time.[87]

The real reason probably lies in Canada's attendance at international meetings where the drug came under discussion. The Hague Opium Conference in 1911–12, which Mackenzie King attended, called for a scientific study of Indian hemp.[88] By 1922, ten U.S. states had enacted marijuana prohibition. That said, there is no evidence of direct pressure from the United States. Although the Americans supported the restriction of marijuana at international meetings, they did not pass their own federal legislation against it until 1937. In the Geneva Convention of 1925, Indian hemp was limited to 'medical and scientific' consumption,[89] and in a 1929 memo, the assistant chief of the Narcotic Division, K.C. Hossick, wrote that Canada was required to include cannabis on the Schedule of restricted drugs because Canada had ratified the The Hague Opium Convention.[90] This was not true, as it was not until 1925 that hemp was brought under international control; Canada made marijuana illegal before that time. Hossick's reference to international concern may indicate that the idea for putting marijuana on the restricted list had come from international discussions. Much later, in 1974, Alexander B. Morrison, the assistant deputy minister of the Health Protection Branch, Health and Welfare Canada, wrote, 'it appears that Col. Sharman, then Director of the Federal Division of Narcotic Control, returned from meetings of the League of Nations convinced that cannabis would soon fall under international control. In anticipation of such action, he moved to have it added to the list of drugs controlled under Canadian law.'[91] Although the Marijuana Party of Canada, *Cannabis Culture* magazine, and other groups supporting the legalization of marijuana continue to argue that Murphy was responsible for the criminalization of marijuana, the international meetings offer a far more likely explanation for the decision.[92] Significantly, it is the international conventions that pose one of the biggest stumbling blocks to the legalization or decriminalization of marijuana in Canada today.

Although the 'drug panic' ended in 1923, the tropes that guided it had been firmly established and regularly reappeared in magazine and newspaper articles throughout the decade. In 1929 the debate over the consolidation of the Opium and Narcotic Drug Act, which added whipping to the punishment for all trafficking offences at the discretion of the judge, showed how clearly the discourse of the innocent addict and the nefarious trafficker had permeated the public mind. Mr. Edwards described a murderer as 'white as the driven snow in comparison with the low, degraded human beast who for a few dollars' profit will gradually murder his fellow-man by selling to him habit forming drugs.'[93] By contrast, the addict was described as a 'poor creature.'[94] The minister of health, James King, declared that addicts were not being prosecuted under the act.[95] But that year more than half of the convictions under the act were for smoking opium or for frequenting an opium den – two provisions that were clearly aimed at drug users, not at drug traffickers.[96] What he meant when he said that they did not prosecute the addict was that they did not prosecute the imaginary white 'victims' of drugs. They were prosecuting working-class drug users of all races.

Interestingly, in the 1929 debate there was no mention of the race of traffickers. Did this mean that the racialization of drug use was on the decline? Perhaps, although the connection between drugs and Asians was still strong in the popular press.[97] Indeed, the 1929 debate was short, and possibly by this time parliamentarians felt no need to stress the culpability of the Asian trafficker, as the image was already well established in the public mind, and the Chinese Immigration Act of 1923 had all but ended Chinese immigration. The lack of attention to race in the 1929 debate may have marked a transition point insofar as the panic over the Chinese had subsided, but the view that drug use was dangerous and that drug traffickers were immoral remained. It was no longer necessary to exploit anti-Asian sentiment to pass strict laws against drugs.

Through the 1920s and beyond, the Narcotic Division emphasized enforcement. The government made no effort to provide treatment facilities, even for the innocent young addicts who incurred so much sympathy and who inspired such a strict legislative response to drugs. Throughout the 1920s, the minister of health and the Division of Narcotic Control asserted that treatment was a matter of provincial jurisdiction and encouraged the provinces to pass legislation allowing for compulsory treatment of drug addicts in provincial mental institutions. This was in keeping with the federal government's reluctance to get involved in health and welfare in the 1920s. Only Alberta and Nova Scotia passed legislation providing treatment for drug users, and only Alberta put it into effect. As it turned out, the white drug users who came to the attention of regulatory authorities were rarely the promising young men and women of the middle classes who were featured in anti-drug campaigns. Many female drug users were prostitutes, and the men were often vagrants who had had previous encounters with the law.[98] Police officers and health officials who came into contact with these 'dope fiends' regarded them as difficult and noisy prisoners and patients. The popular press, and especially Murphy herself, who had considerable contact with drug users in her role as magistrate, condemned them as 'emaciated, non-productive, drooling parasites.'[99] Although 'innocent' white addicts served as an effective rhetorical tool for anti-drug crusaders who wanted stricter laws against the drug traffic, neither the government nor social service organizations were willing to spend money on the treatment and rehabilitation of the socially disadvantaged 'dope fiend,' whose moral senses were said to have been destroyed by drugs.

Conclusion

The link between drug use and the Chinese was a key factor in the demonization of drugs that took place in the early 1920s. It was no accident that the most important campaign against drug use in Canada took place at the same time as a concerted drive for Chinese exclusion. In this intolerant environment, an understanding of drug use emerged in which Chinese drug traffickers were vilified, Chinese drug users were either ignored or regarded as a moral contagion, and white drug users were portrayed as tragic victims. This imagery provided one more excuse for completely halting Chinese immigration for more than twenty years, and it resulted in strict drug laws that would shape the lives of drug users for generations.

Chapter 2

'Hop Heads': The Effects of Criminalization, 1920–1945

From 1920 to 1945, the types of drugs used, the people using them, and the consequences of drug use changed significantly. This was not just the result of increased penalties. Other factors, including the Great Depression, social disapproval of drug use, and changes in the Chinese population, also played a role. Nonetheless, criminalization and harsher penalties made drug use an increasingly risky and dangerous activity. After 1922, drug users, who were often described as 'hop heads,' frequently served long terms in prison for possession. The intense policing and increased cost of drugs also prompted some users to switch from smoking opium and snorting cocaine to injecting drugs, creating many more health problems for users. The difficulty in obtaining drugs meant that drug use came to assume an increasingly central and problematic position in drug users' lives and interfered with their work and relationships.[1]

There were three main periods of drug use from 1920 to 1945. In the 1920s, there was a broad range of users who came from a variety of class and racial backgrounds, including a large number of Chinese users who engaged in the longstanding practice of smoking opium to relax, improve respiratory problems, and relieve pain. There was also a large population of white users who took a diverse array of drugs, including opium, cocaine, morphine, and heroin. Some of these white users had become addicted through medical use and others were taking drugs to self-medicate, but many took them initially for the thrill they provided.

By the 1930s, there were relatively few Chinese drug users left – the result of deportations, harsh penalties, and the aging and shrinking of the population after the implementation of the Chinese Immigration Act of 1923. The white users, who were increasingly drawn from the lower classes and often had a history of crime, were finding it more difficult to acquire a supply of drugs. Many travelled across the country trying to obtain drugs from doctors. They substituted codeine, paregoric, and other drugs for hard-to-obtain opiates such as morphine and heroin.

During the Second World War, drugs were even more difficult to obtain. Theft from drugstores increased, and users turned to legal psychotropics, such as barbiturates and Benzedrine. Despite the shortages, a new cohort of rebellious young people started using drugs at this time. Their numbers would increase in the period after the Second World War.

The Prevalence of Illicit Drug Use

There appears to have been a significant increase in drug use in the 1910s. Imports of cocaine, morphine, and opium rose dramatically from 1912 to 1919. Wartime casualties did not account for the increase; many of the drugs being imported were not used by medical professionals and were obviously being diverted into the illicit market.[2] Nonetheless, the war probably played an indirect role in the increased demand. In the early 1920s, the media often told sad tales of returned soldiers (like Joseph Kehoe) who had become addicted to drugs, and in England there were accusations that Canadian soldiers were spreading the cocaine habit.[3] Given the horrors of trench warfare and the difficulties of settling back into life at home, it would not be surprising if many soldiers turned to illicit drugs for relief, but hard evidence is difficult to obtain.[4] The war also encouraged experimentation among young people, and it shook religious bonds. It softened attitudes against alcohol, leading to well-publicized drinking among young men and women in the 1920s, and it probably led some to experiment with drugs as well.[5]

In 1920 the newly created Department of Health assumed responsibility for the Opium and Drug Act. The department quickly inaugurated a system for controlling the imports, exports, manufacture, sale, and distribution of illegal drugs. All wholesale druggists provided statements of their sales to retail druggists, dentists, veterinarians, and physicians, while retail druggists provided information about the prescriptions they filled for doctors. The department removed from the market a number of preparations that contained large quantities of opium and morphine. By 1922, the legal cocaine imports were a quarter of what they had been in 1919, the legal morphine imports were a third, and the legal crude opium imports were one-twentieth, indicating a significant reduction in the amounts being diverted to the illicit market (see figure 2.1).[6]

Figure 2.1
Legal Drug Imports, 1912–30

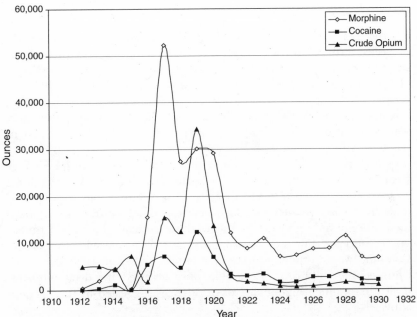

Source: NAC, RG 13 Series A-2, vol. 239, File 1919-1805; Canada, Department of Pensions and National Health, *Annual Report for the Year Ended March 31, 1931.*

By the early 1920s, therefore, it was becoming harder to obtain drugs through legitimate channels in Canada, but smuggling persisted and the illicit market continued to thrive. Opium, cocaine, and morphine were readily available in every major Canadian city, in part because there were still very few international controls on drug production and export. In 1924–5, at the Opium Conference in Geneva, participating countries agreed to more strictly control the manufacture, sale, and distribution of opium, morphine, heroin, and cocaine and to carefully monitor their import and export.[7] Within a year, the Narcotic Division reported that the International Opium Convention was already having an effect. By 1931 the League of Nations felt that legal manufacture no longer exceeded legitimate need.[8] Kathryn Meyer and Terry Parssinen show that exports of heroin, morphine, and cocaine from the principal exporting countries dropped dramatically between 1928 (the year the International Opium Convention went into effect) and 1932.[9] Certainly by the early 1930s Canadian drug users were finding it considerably more difficult to obtain drugs.

In 1923–4 the Department of Health tried to determine the number of drug users across the country. They solicited information from chiefs of police, crown attorneys, magistrates, and others. Approximately 50 per cent of doctors responded to a questionnaire that the Department of Health had sent to all registered physicians, and they identified 777 people who required narcotics for medical conditions. From its other sources, the department concluded that there were approximately 9500 drug users in the country: 2500 in British Columbia, 3800 in Quebec, and 1800 in Ontario, with small numbers in every other province except PEI, where there were none.[10] These numbers may have been low, because drug users in the 1920s could use drugs for a long time without coming to the attention of authorities, especially if their lives were 'respectable' in other respects. Moreover, the department did not indicate whether or not these estimates included Chinese opium smokers, but they probably did not, as the numbers in British Columbia would otherwise have been much higher. In 1922 alone, 519 Chinese men in British Columbia were arrested for drug offences, indicating a much higher rate of use than is suggested by the statistics above.[11]

By 1930 the official estimate of drug users dropped to 8000, including those people who were addicted as a result of a medical condition, and by 1939 it fell to 4000.[12] These estimates were little more than reasonable guesses, based on information received from doctors and police, but there was also a noticeable decrease in convictions over the time period (see figure 2.2). Convictions often tell us more about the practices of police forces and judges than they do about drug use, but in this case the dramatic decrease in convictions was not the result of a lack of zeal on the part of the police.[13] Nor was it the result of judges refusing to convict. The declining number of convictions appears to correlate with a decrease in the total number of drug users – especially occasional drug users and Chinese drug users – as well as with changes in how people obtained drugs. In the 1930s, police were also seizing much smaller quantities of drugs and supplies, and drug users were turning to substitutes – especially codeine, paregoric, and poppy heads, indicating a shortage of more desirable drugs.[14] These changes affected the two major groups of users – Asian-Canadian drug users and Euro-Canadian drug users – very differently.

Figure 2.2
Convictions of Drug Users, 1920–45

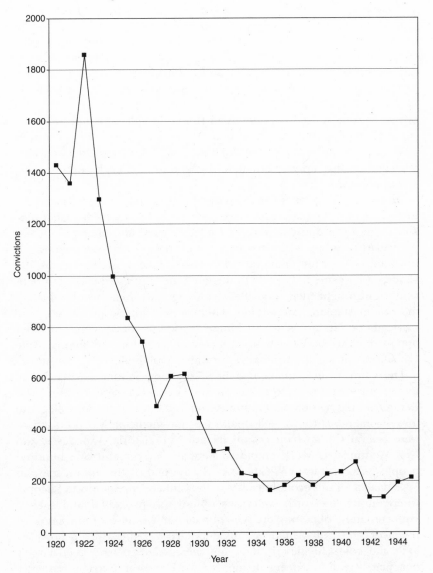

Source: Canada, Dominion Bureau of Statistics, *Annual Report of Statistics of Criminal and Other Offenses* for the years 1920 through 1945.

Asian Drug Users

The vast majority of drug users of Asian origin were Chinese. Opium had long been used as medicine in China, but its use exploded in the nineteenth century when British traders flooded China with high-quality Indian opium. The Chinese protested, but the British Treasury in India depended heavily on opium sales, and the British ultimately fought two Opium Wars to force China to remain open to foreign trade. After the Treaty of Tianjin in 1858, during the second Opium War (1856–60), opium became a legal commodity in China. Modernizers and nationalists in China opposed the trade, but effective suppression began only in 1906 with an imperial edict prohibiting opium smoking, followed by a 1908 agreement between Britain and China to restrict the opium trade and cultivation.

Opium smoking served many purposes in China: it was an elaborate social ritual for the elite, a painkiller and aid to hard work for labourers, and a medicine that countered fever, diarrhoea, and cholera.[15] It was particularly widespread in the southern coastal regions of China, which provided most of the immigrants to Canada. Like most immigrants, the Chinese who came to Canada in the late nineteenth and early twentieth centuries brought their food, their clothing, and their customs, including opium smoking, with them. There were Chinese in Canada who frowned upon it, just as many Chinese decried the practice at home, but opium smoking had much in common with alcohol use among white Canadians – it was hotly debated but widely practised.

The Chinese in Canada had been smoking opium since Chinese immigrants first arrived to partake in the Fraser River gold rush in 1858. Before the passage of the Opium Act in 1908, which made it illegal to import, manufacture, or sell opium for non-medicinal purposes, there were several Chinese-run opium factories in Victoria, Vancouver, and New Westminster, which employed between seventy and one hundred people.[16] According to Wickberg et al., the end of the opium trade in 1908 dealt a serious economic blow to the Chinese community in Victoria, where 'much of North America's opium was processed and sold.'[17] Unfortunately, obtaining information about Chinese opium-smoking practices is difficult. Anti-drug crusaders such as Emily Murphy provided long and colourful descriptions, but these seem to have been largely imaginary creations. In his memoirs, C.W. Harvison, a former commissioner of the RCMP, who spent the early 1920s assigned to drug enforcement in Montreal, offered the following description of the 'opium joints' he raided:

These were not the luxurious 'opium dens' of the movies, wherein smokers sprawl in comfort on plush divans while scantily clad maidens flit across deep oriental rugs to serve their every want ... The furnishings were simple: a wooden shelf covered with straw matting ... The premises used for smoking were usually on the upper floor of buildings, over shops, restaurants, or other business premises. Three or four of the larger and most frequented places were upstairs over gambling rooms ... The Chinese opium smokers were almost invariably peaceful and docile. Many of them were older citizens who had had the habit for years and could not understand why, suddenly, a fuss was being made.[18]

Not all smoking took place in opium dens. Many Chinese men worked in isolated communities, and they smoked where they lived and worked. At mills, canneries, and other work sites, smoking in the evening appears to have been commonplace.

Historian Anthony Chan estimates that as many as 40 to 50 per cent of the Chinese in British Columbia were addicted to the drug in the 1880s, though this seems extraordinarily high.[19] More likely, there were large numbers of Chinese men who smoked occasionally for medicine, for relaxation, or for pain relief, without being physically addicted. As R.K. Newman pointed out in his study of opium smoking in late imperial China, careful observers of opium smoking in China in the late nineteenth and early twentieth centuries divided users into 'light' or 'moderate' smokers, 'regular' users or those who had 'the yin' (craving), and at the extreme, 'opium sots' who gave up their work and family to pursue opium smoking.[20] He estimates that in China in 1906, approximately 60 per cent of men smoked for medical purposes, 70 per cent of men smoked on festive occasions, approximately 12 per cent were regular users, and only 1.8 per cent of men were heavy users.[21] This was probably true in Canada as well. Drug experts such as Norman Zinberg have shown that large numbers of people use opium, heroin, and cocaine without experiencing their use as problematic or acquiring physical or psychological dependence on them.[22] Given that the majority of the Chinese who came to Canada in the late nineteenth and early twentieth centuries worked long hours at menial jobs as servants, cooks, and labourers, very few Chinese in Canada could devote themselves fully to opium smoking.[23] Opium smokers in Canada at this time, as in other times and places, probably engaged in opium smoking as a relaxing recreational activity in their spare hours away from physical labour. Smoking opium was also a means of self-medication, relieving the symptoms of tuberculosis, rheumatism, and other disorders that were widespread among the Chinese in Canada – the result of poverty, crowded living conditions, and inadequate sanitation.

The Opium and Narcotic Drug Act affected the Chinese differently from white Canadians, partly because the act contained separate offences for smoking opium, for being found in an opium joint, and for possessing opium-smoking equipment. These offences carried significantly less severe penalties than those for possession of opium. Opium smoking, for example, carried a maximum penalty of $50 and costs, and/or one month in jail. Clayton Mosher's dissertation on narcotic enforcement in five Ontario cities shows that Chinese arrested under the act from 1908 to 1929 received shorter sentences, on average, than those received by white Canadians.[24] This was not the result of 'paternalism' as Mosher claims. It was because the Chinese were often charged with one of the lesser offences, such as opium smoking or being found in an opium joint, rather than being charged with possession or trafficking. These lesser charges had lower standards of evidence; they were easier to prosecute and served to raise revenue for the criminal justice system.

Before the drug panic of the early 1920s, most Chinese men found with drugs in their possession were fined, although some may have served time in jail if they were unable to pay their fines. In 1918 and 1919, 87 per cent of those convicted under the Opium and Narcotic Drug Act had the option of paying a fine.[25] For smoking opium, fines usually ranged from $25 to $50, which was about a month's wages for the average Chinese worker.[26] If the offender could not afford the fine, the alternative was one to two months in prison. Men found guilty of possessing or selling drugs were often given much harsher sentences, including fines of up to $500 and sentences as long as three months.[27]

As of 1922, minimum sentences of six months were imposed for all cases of possession, but the offences of opium smoking and being found in an opium den were still on the books and remained punishable by fine. Moreover, especially in the first year, many magistrates interpreted the new legislation to mean that they could still give fines for possession.[28] Often possession charges were reduced to opium smoking in the case of Chinese addicts.[29] Over the course of the decade, however, it became more common for Chinese men to be charged with possession and to receive harsher sentences. This meant that more Chinese men started serving prison time for offences against the act. They included Dai Y., a market gardener outside of Saskatoon. When the RCMP raided his shack in 1924, they found a complete opium layout including a lamp, pipe, and opium pills. Dai Y. claimed that these belonged to his previous partner, who had already been convicted under the Opium and Narcotic Drug Act. At his trial, the sheriff testified that Dai Y. was a 'hard working, industrious man.' The judge responded that this did not throw 'much light on his smoking proclivities' and sentenced Dai Y. to six months, $200, and costs.[30]

Despite the growing severity of the drug laws, many Chinese men still managed to escape with fines rather than imprisonment – either because they were charged with one of the lesser offences or because magistrates showed sympathy for their situation. Despite the ferocity of anti-Chinese sentiment in the early 1920s in Canada, there were some elites who felt that opium smoking was a relatively harmless practice, similar perhaps, to their own drinking habits.[31] Lawyer Tom MacInnes wrote in *Saturday Night* that 'one may smoke opium to old age, and come to no great harm except from sudden and complete deprivation of it.' He condemned the drug laws for driving people to morphine and cocaine instead.[32] Some judges appeared to agree. Police raided Joe L.'s laundry in Montreal in 1932, and in the closet they found an opium pipe with traces of stale opium. Joe L. insisted that the pipe was old and that he no longer smoked opium. The RCMP took the pipe but did not press any charges at the time, although Joe L. was later arrested and charged with having opium-smoking apparatus in his possession. He pleaded guilty, explaining that another Chinese man had left the pipe at his place several years ago and that it had not been used since. The judge apparently took this story into consideration as well as the 'age, frail health and poor financial condition' of Joe L. and sentenced him to pay $5 and costs.[33]

That judges could be quite lenient with Chinese opium smokers was cause for concern at the Narcotic Division. In 1924 the deputy minister of health complained that Chief Justice Decarie in Montreal took it upon himself to reduce a number of charges from possession or trafficking to opium-smoking offences. These cases included that of Tam G. in Montreal, who was arrested with forty-three decks of opium and another tin partly full of opium, indicating that he was probably a peddler. Justice Decarie reduced the charge from possession to opium smoking so that Tam G. could avoid deportation, and sentenced him to $50 and costs.[34] In British Columbia, Chief Justice Hunter of the Supreme Court liberated seventeen Chinese men serving sentences from six to eighteen months on the grounds that the papers of commitment were irregular, and he dismissed another five Chinese men on the grounds that the complaints did not show the year of the statute[35] –

Hunter's attention to detail may have reflected his views on the drug law. The Narcotic Division condemned these developments and responded, in part, by employing specially appointed narcotic prosecutors who could bring a greater degree of expertise to the process.[36]

For Chinese Canadians, even more important than the increased fines and prison time in the 1922 changes to the Opium and Narcotic Control Act was the provision that allowed the government to deport any alien convicted of possessing or selling narcotic drugs.[37] For example, Sui T., a man who had lived in Canada for forty-four years, was deported after serving six months for having drugs in his possession.[38] Between 1923 and 1932, 761 Chinese were deported as a result of this section, or almost 2 per cent of the total Chinese population in Canada.[39] On average, those deported had been in Canada for almost seventeen years.[40] People who had previously smoked on a recreational or casual basis may have stopped in the face of such serious penalties, while many of the most devoted users were ultimately sent back to China.

Determined to enforce the new acts of the 1920s, police regularly raided opium dens, and many Chinese were convicted. In 1922 nearly 3 per cent of the total Chinese population was convicted under the Opium and Narcotic Drug Act, and in some cities, the conviction statistics were even higher. In Vancouver, 4.5 per cent of all Chinese were convicted for narcotic offences in 1922, and in Montreal in 1923, 6.3 per cent of all Chinese were convicted. Police in Windsor reported raiding a Chinese opium den on a weekly basis, and Harvison raided opium dens in Montreal nightly in the early 1920s.[41] These exceptionally high rates of conviction show the extent to which the Opium and Narcotic Drug Act was used against the Chinese population of Canada. Moreover, as many Chinese did not smoke opium, these high conviction rates show that drug use was becoming an increasingly risky activity. After several years of extremely high conviction rates in the early 1920s, the number of Chinese found guilty of narcotic offences began to fall. In the nine-year period from 1922 through 1930, there were 4900 convictions of Chinese Canadians under the act, but in the nine years from 1931 through 1939, there were only 825 Chinese-Canadian convictions – less than a fifth as many in the same number of years (see figure 2.3).

In response to the high conviction rates, Chinese Canadians, like other Canadian users, began to switch from easily detectable opium smoking to taking drugs by injection or orally, as these techniques create no smell and require smaller and more easily disposable pieces of equipment,[42] and by the late 1930s, the RCMP seized very little opium-

Figure 2.3
Convictions under the ONDA by Racial Origin, 1921–45

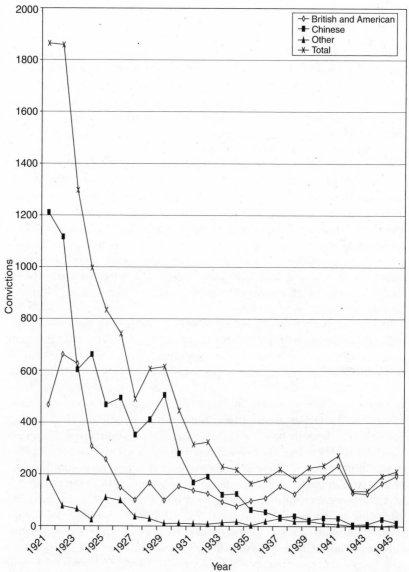

Source: Canada, Dominion Bureau of Statistics, *Annual Report of Statistics of Criminal and Other Offenses* for the years 1921 through 1945.

smoking equipment.[43] This is not to say that opium smoking disappeared altogether; some Chinese opium smokers found clever ways of enjoying their drug without being caught by police. One way was to board ships docked in Vancouver harbour, where opium prices were cheaper and the risk was less. In 1927 C.H.L. Sharman, the chief of the Narcotic Division, and the RCMP conducted a raid of the *Empress of Russia*. They saw seventeen men smoking and seized a large number of pipes and 'a good deal of opium.'[44] A month later, Sharman reported that 'conditions in regard to opium smoking on the CPR liners, while in port, were approaching a scandal.' When the *Empress of Asia* was in port for a brief stay, he claimed that more than a thousand people visited the ship, including a well-known trafficker.[45]

Another source of opium was Chinese medicine. Police found opium pills in the Lethbridge room of Jim L. in 1921. Under oath, Jim L. admitted that he used to smoke opium, but that these pills were for stomach pains and 'they are to stop you from going to the toilet too much.' If Jim L. had stopped smoking recently, he may have gone into withdrawal, one symptom of which is loose bowels. Opium pills certainly would have cured his stomach pains, although as the ingredients were not listed, Jim L. may not have known their contents. Alternatively, he might have been clever about putting together a plausible, although ultimately unsuccessful, defence.[46]

In China, 'red pills' containing morphine or heroin became a common opium substitute during the Republican era (1911–49). The pills were smoked much like opium, but they created less smell, were cheaper, and could be smoked far more quickly – aiding secrecy.[47] In 1929 the RCMP seized red-coloured 'anti-opium tablets' or 'anti-smoke pills' from at least five Chinese stores in Vancouver. These pills contained morphine, but the Department of Health did not prosecute the shop owners since they apparently had not known what the pills contained. Five years later, the RCMP seized over 350,000 red pills, advertised as 'cough pills,' from Chinese stores. These pills contained morphine or heroin but had been legally imported into Canada. Again, the vendors were not charged.[48] In 1937 there was another investigation into Chinese pills; this time the offending pills were Dr. Tang Shih Yee Pills. In Lethbridge, a Chinese shopkeeper and his son claimed that the pills in question were purchased by older Chinese men in the winter months for $11 per bottle to stop their coughing.[49] In another case, police found 102 boxes of Leung Poy Kay Pills under the bed of the owner of a fruit store on East Pender Street in Vancouver. The pills analysed positively for morphine, but the other medicines found in his shop all tested negative. The RCMP suspected that the man was a supplier of opium to 'white woman addicts,' but the man claimed he did not know the pills contained morphine, and he was acquitted on appeal.[50] Afterwards, the Chinese Benevolent Association sternly warned its members that 'it is imperative not to have in possession or for sale any of these pills, in order to avoid prosecution.'[51]

Notwithstanding these attempts to get around the drug laws, it seems clear that Chinese opium use had declined significantly by the early 1930s. The Chinese in Canada were extremely hard-hit by the Great Depression. More than a hundred starved to death in Vancouver in the early 1930s – there was little money to spend on opium.[52] Also, the Chinese population was aging, and like most drug users, they probably smoked less, or gave it up entirely, as they grew older. By this time, many drug users and sellers had been deported, and the second generation of Chinese rarely continued the habit. The conviction rates of Chinese under the Opium and Narcotic Drug Act began to drop quite dramatically in 1930, and by the end of the decade, only a handful of Chinese were arrested each year. A 1936 RCMP report from Saint John, New Brunswick, noted that there were no known opium smokers, and there had been no opium den operating in Saint John for five or six years. It added, 'all Chinese known to be connected with the narcotic drug traffic are either deceased or located outside the district.'[53]

Still, a few users remained. When Constable Price of the RCMP compiled fifty-two case histories of addicts in Vancouver in 1945, he interviewed seven Chinese drug users. Six of the seven had been born in China. None had any education, and all were working class (Price said 'coolie class'). Price reported that the Chinese users were reluctant to give information to police, but he concluded that 'none of them appeared to regard narcotic addiction as unusual, as even their fathers or friends in China were addicts, thus to them Opium was accepted in common usage.'[54]

The Chinese were not the only Asians in Canada who used opiates. Some South Asians in Canada ate opium, a practice largely ignored by police until they discovered large numbers of poppy heads being sold over the counter of retail drugstores to Asians in British Columbia in the early 1930s. They also discovered that many South Asians were growing poppies, often hidden behind trees or within a crop of corn, and were harvesting poppy heads, which had a morphine content of 0.25 per cent.[55] On 1 January 1933 the department brought opium poppy heads under control. The new rules meant that poppy heads could 'only be imported by licensed narcotic wholesalers and sold by retail druggists on a physician's prescription.' At the same time, the department took out advertisements in Canadian Asian-language newspapers to announce that people who harvested poppy heads would be prosecuted for the illegal possession of morphine. That year, three South Asians were charged with possession of morphine and given six months' imprisonment.[56] For the remainder of the decade, small numbers of whites and Asians were found in possession of poppy heads and sentenced to prison.[57]

Given the dismal working conditions and virulent racism faced by Asian immigrants to Canada, it is not surprising that more than a few of them took solace in habits that had been common in their home countries, such as smoking opium or drinking poppy-head tea. The penalties for their indulgence could be severe, including fines, long prison terms, and deportation. As Clayton Mosher's work has shown, they received shorter sentences for drug offences than did whites, but this should not be seen as a paternalism that operated in their favour, since the police targeted their communities for enforcement. The Chinese frequently faced charges that were easier to prosecute but resulted in less severe penalties. Moreover, they often received shorter sentences with the knowledge that, many would be deported after their release from jail. In response, some Chinese and other Asian Canadians attempted to find ways of working around the law, while others seem to have put their opium pipes aside. It must have been extraordinarily difficult for some to give up a habit that they had had for much of their adult lives. For many in the Chinese community who were used to being targeted for gambling and public health offences, it must have seemed disappointingly familiar.[58] The police campaign against Asian drug use was yet another example of the Canadian state targeting minority groups for intensive policing and surveillance.

White Drug Users

White users in the 1920s found it easier to avoid detection than Chinese users, although they generally received longer sentences when caught. There were two broad groups of white users. The first, and probably largest, group of people obtained their drugs, including cocaine, opium, morphine, and heroin from the illicit market. These users started using drugs at a young age and often had criminal records. They were largely, but not exclusively, male (see figure 2.4), had little education, and were often employed as racetrack hands and circus and show people. They

Figure 2.4
Convictions under the ONDA by Gender, 1920–45

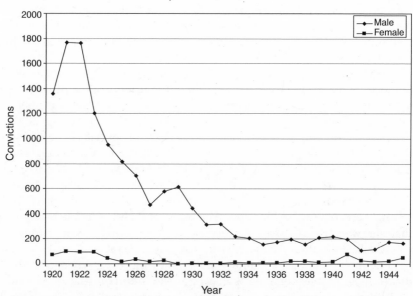

Source: Canada, Dominion Bureau of Statistics, *Annual Report of Statistics of Criminal and Other Offenses* for the years 1920 through 1945.

often started their drug use by smoking opium or sniffing heroin or cocaine. In the early part of the decade, there appears to have been more users, both male and female, who were better off, and who may have enjoyed drug use as part of the excitement of 'slumming.' The second group obtained morphine from doctors and was older, wealthier, and better educated. They generally took their drug by injection, and few had criminal records. This group included many women who successfully complained of 'female' ailments, especially kidney problems. These groups were not completely separate; some 'criminal addicts' occasionally obtained drugs from doctors, and some 'respectable' addicts obtained drugs from the illicit market when necessary.

Montreal, Canada's largest and most cosmopolitan city, was the biggest centre of white drug use in the 1920s. Drugs could be purchased from pool halls, restaurants, and clubs. In 1922 the RCMP officer commanding the Quebec District estimated that as many drugs were consumed on a daily basis in Montreal as in the rest of the country put together. Police knew of more than a dozen peddlers who sold large amounts daily in small quantities.[59] Young people held drug 'parties,' and certain clubs were well-known centres of the drug trade. In Montreal there were many white peddlers, while in British Columbia it was more common for whites to purchase their drugs, including morphine and cocaine, at Chinese establishments.[60]

According to police reports, many white drug users were young people out looking for a good time. Kid B., one of the leaders of the drug trade in Montreal, regularly took 'Gayety' show girls out to what the police described as 'slumming' parties, which could include going to Chinatown or smoking opium at 'Jean's place.'[61] In 1921 a special agent of the RCMP met two young women on Granville Street in Vancouver. The women had been out all night and told him, 'Gee, I would like to get some more junk.' They took him to an opium joint on Granville St., and then to G. Wong's place, which the police described as a 'snow shed' for 'young girls and boys of the white race.' One of the women later testified that she went there partly for the cocaine, and partly because 'other young folks went there.' It is not clear how regularly the two women used cocaine, but they were certainly familiar with the drug sellers and the drug-selling establishments.[62] Similarly, at the Montreal trial of Yvonne P., witnesses testified that young people in Montreal occasionally attended crowded 'drug parties' in downtown rooming houses, where they gave each other shots.[63]

In the early 1920s, drugs were fairly inexpensive, at least compared to the astronomical prices in the years after the Second World War. The RCMP estimated that regular drug users in Vancouver spent between $1 and $15 per day on drugs. A conservative average would be $3 per day. A half-grain deck of morphine, cocaine, or heroin sold for approximately twenty-five cents in Vancouver, about the same price as a bottle of beer (a grain is 64.8 milligrams).[64] In Toronto, where the RCMP estimated that addicts consumed approximately ten grains daily, decks contained from three to five grains and cost $1.[65] Working-class people could afford drugs – common labourers in Montreal and Vancouver at this time made approximately $20 per week, which meant that drugs were expensive, but not completely impossible for the occasional user.[66]

Police reported that there were many recreational opiate and cocaine users. In 1922 the RCMP reported that in Edmonton there were approximately '175 confirmed morphine addicts, 200 confirmed cocaine addicts, and another 300–400 "party addicts"' – people who indulged in drugs perhaps twice a week.[67] A special agent of the RCMP reported in

1923 that 'the entire underworld uses it,' but emphasized that not everyone had a 'habit.'[68] Like Chinese opium smokers, many of these occasional users probably stopped using in the early 1920s when it became harder and more dangerous to obtain illegal drugs. Case files and police data from the 1930s onwards show little evidence of 'party addicts' – people who used regularly in a controlled fashion. Once these people left the drug-using community, the only role model for new drug users were people who were often heavily addicted, either mentally or physically, and were thus unable to pass on to new users methods of controlling their own drug use. Work by doctors, anthropologists, and sociologists shows that drug users learn how to use drugs within a community of other users, and that this learning environment influences how the new user manages his or her use. By driving 'controlled' users out of the community with strict enforcement and severe penalties, drug enforcement decreased the likelihood that new users would learn techniques for managing and controlling their drug use.[69]

White drug users were less likely to be arrested than their Chinese counterparts, but they were more often convicted of possession rather than opium smoking or being found in an opium joint and thus served longer sentences. White drug users frequently had previous criminal records. Sydney C., for example, had many theft convictions before he was convicted on a drug possession charge in 1927 and sentenced to six months. Two years later, he was convicted of possession for a second time and given one year. His previous convictions for theft (a very common pattern among drug users) may or may not have been connected to his drug use.[70] Seventy per cent of the drug users studied by Dr. A.R. Richards at Burwash Industrial Farm in 1928 indicated that they had started their criminal careers because of drugs, but since drug users were keen to make the case that all of their troubles stemmed from the criminalization of possession, this should probably be regarded with a degree of scepticism.[71]

Richards's 1928 study of one hundred drug users incarcerated at Burwash Industrial Farm provides an interesting portrait of what the Narcotic Division called the 'criminal addict.' The vast majority were white (84 per cent), although 11 per cent were Chinese Canadian, and 5 per cent were African Canadian. By comparison, Chinese Canadians accounted for less than 1 per cent of the total population of Canada, and African Canadians accounted for less than 0.5 per cent of the total population in 1931.[72] They were working class, with the most common occupations being race horse hands, circus and show people, salesmen,

and chauffeurs – occupations confirmed by the case files of the National
Archives and the John Howard Society. Most had little education: 72 per
cent had a primary education, 23 per cent had a secondary education,
and 3 per cent had a university education. The vast majority (84 per
cent) started using before the age of 25, and 30 per cent had started
under the age of 20. They bought their drugs primarily from peddlers
(84 per cent) rather than doctors (14 per cent).[73] Even heavy users
stopped using frequently; over half of the subjects had quit voluntarily at
least once.[74] As a result of incarcerations and other impediments, 80 per
cent of them had stopped using twice or more. Thirty-three per cent had
stopped using five or six times. Today, most people who quit addictive
substance use usually do so many times before they succeed,[75] and
Richards' study suggests this pattern was true in the 1920s as well.

For both white and Asian users (although evidence for white users is
easier to obtain), the illicit and uncontrolled drug market led to adulteration of drug supplies and an increase in fatalities.[76] The superintendent of the Montreal General Hospital reported that there had been 128
cases of narcotic poisoning at the hospital in 1922, including 14 deaths.[77]
In 1925 the provincial coroner in Quebec told the *Montreal Star* that the
number of fatalities was increasing and that many deaths occurred when
a user unexpectedly came across a purer supply than he or she was used
to.[78] The Dominion Bureau of Statistics did not keep data on deaths
resulting from overdoses of illicit drugs, but several sensational trials
involving overdose deaths in Montreal in the mid-1920s, as well as a
number of inquests in Vancouver, suggest that this was a growing problem.

White users, like Chinese drug users, began using stronger drugs and
making greater use of the hypodermic needle during this time period.
According to police, the main drugs used in the early 1920s were opium,
morphine, and cocaine. Seizures of heroin began to increase in the late
1920s, and by the mid-1930s, it had become one of the most common
drugs used (see figures 2.5 and 2.6). As the price of drugs increased due
to scarcity and drug-law enforcement, drug users also switched from less
efficient, but less harmful, modes of drug transmission, such as 'sniffing,' to taking drugs by injection. At Burwash, Dr. Richards noted that
drug users frequently had abscesses and ulcerations from administering
drugs with equipment that was not sterile. Richards recounted the case
of one user whose left leg was 'double the circumference' of his right
'due to thrombosis (blockage of the veins) of practically every superficial
vein of the limb.'[79]

Drug users' profiles show many other health problems, both mental

Figure 2.5
Convictions for Drug Possession by Type of Drug, 1921–45

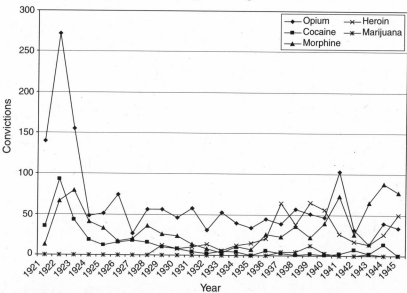

Source: Canada, Dominion Bureau of Statistics, *Annual Report of Statistics of Criminal and Other Offenses* for the years 1920 through 1945.

and physical. Richards reported that self-mutilation was common among drug users, especially during withdrawal. The poverty and dismal living conditions endured by many users also contributed to other health problems, such as tuberculosis and Bright's disease (kidney disease). More than half had venereal disease.[80] It is unclear whether these health problems were the direct result of their drug use, or whether the health problems contributed to patterns of problematic substance use as people used opiates to relieve their pain and anxiety.

Users who successfully obtained drugs from doctors used purer drugs and suffered from fewer health problems than people who bought from the illicit market. These users, who were frequently middle or upper-middle class, often received their drugs from the same doctor for years, and could remain invisible to the law for long periods of time. In 1943 a man turned over a quantity of morphine to the Sault Ste. Marie detachment of the RCMP, explaining that the drugs belonged to his recently deceased mother. She had used drugs for almost forty years – they were

Figure 2.6
Convictions for Drug Possession by Type of Drug, Including Non-Specified
Drugs, 1921–45

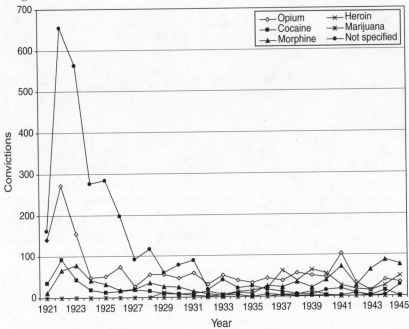

Source: Canada, Dominion Bureau of Statistics, *Annual Report of Statistics of Criminal and Other Offenses* for the years 1921 through 1945.

first provided by her physician husband and then by her son, who was also a doctor. After the son passed away, she managed to obtain drugs from two local physicians until her death.[81]

Although the Narcotic Division made some efforts to go after doctors in the early 1920s (see chapter 5), the division was not generally anxious to prosecute middle-class users or the doctors who prescribed for them. The division divided drug users into three categories. The first category included people who were inadvertently addicted as a result of a medical condition. The division had 'nothing but sympathy' for these people, who were usually terminally ill. The second category included 'professional addicts,' such as doctors, pharmacists, and veterinarians. The Narcotic Division described them as people who occupied 'a decent position in the community' but became addicts because of 'over-work, nervous strain, dissipation.' In cases where the person had 'something to lose such as family ties or the right to practice a profession,' the division felt that there was much that could be done and they dealt with such cases in the 'strictest confidence.' Finally, the division identified 'criminal addicts.' These were working-class people who obtained drugs illicitly. The division characterized them as a 'dangerous menace to society.'[82]

In the 1920s, the drug-using scene was more diverse than it would be for at least another forty years. There were a variety of users from different economic and social backgrounds. Although middle- and upper-middle-class users existed, they appear to have been on the decline. They were usually able to obtain a regular supply from doctors, and they rarely interacted with the court system. Chinese use was also on the decline, as their communities were targeted for enforcement efforts and many hard-core users and suppliers were deported. The majority of users, both white and Chinese, who came to the attention of authorities were working class. Many of these were probably occasional users, who stopped as they aged, or as the penalties for breaking the law grew ever more severe. The increased difficulty of obtaining drugs led to more health problems for users as more of them began using the hypodermic needle and stronger drugs, such as heroin. As drugs became more expensive and took more effort to obtain, drug use caused greater disruptions to their lives.

The Great Depression

In the 1930s, the disruption in international shipping, the greater control over the international production of narcotics, and the low incomes of working-class users made it harder for them to buy drugs from the illicit market. In response, many users, especially those outside of British Columbia, travelled the country obtaining prescriptions or stealing drugs from doctors while others turned to codeine and paregoric, stopped taking drugs, or used only occasionally. A typical case was that of Alphonse B. He reported that he began smoking opium in Toronto in 1929. His supply dried up after three months, so he switched to morphine, which he took hypodermically for the next two years. By the early 1930s, he was unable to obtain morphine, so he went to the country for a gradual withdrawal.[83] Some people used irregularly. George W. reported that he started using heroin in 1937, but took it only when he could get it. At the height of his habit, he claimed he took the rather low dose of thirty to sixty quarter-grain 'pops' every month.[84]

Another option was obtaining drugs from doctors – addicts could be extremely persuasive. In his memoir of practice in rural Nova Scotia in the 1930s, Edmund Brasset explained:

One evening when I was finishing office hours, a stranger came in, a thin, stooped, shabby man. His clothes were old and thin and worn and did not fit him well. The coat was too large and his trousers were too small and he wore a bowler type of hat. It was hard to tell from looking at him whether he was thirty or fifty years old. His face was lined and anxious and it was obvious that he was under great mental stress. What attracted my attention were his eyes – bright, quick and intelligent.

He said immediately 'Doc, give me a shot of morphine. I need it very badly, I know you don't know me, but I can pay and I need it the worst way.'

'Sit down,' I said 'and tell me about yourself.'

He sat down but immediately got up again and began pacing the room.

'I can't sit still,' he said. 'I'm an addict. I have to take three grains twice a day. I haven't had any this morning. Please, Doc, I can pay.'

Brasset refused to give him the drug, saying that it was against the law:

> With this he started to plead again and then all of a sudden slumped down into a chair, put his two hands to his head and began to rock it back and forth. His eyes shut and his face went into a contortion of agony. I felt sorry for him. Perhaps a quarter grain would give him some relief.
>
> 'No more good to me than a drink of water,' he said, 'please let me have twelve tablets, Doc, please, please, please.'
>
> Suddenly he went down on his knees and began to wring his hands with an expression of despair. I was filled with embarrassment just looking at him – never before had I witnessed such a scene.
>
> 'Very well,' I said, 'here it is.'

There were limits to his sympathy; when the patient came back for another shot the following morning, Brasset refused him. Two other users later visited Brasset – Brasset thought that the first user had told the other users about him, and he did not prescribe to either: 'I did not want my office to become known as a way station for unfortunates of this kind. But I was sorry for them.'[85] Doctors across the country faced similar dilemmas throughout the Depression.

Two groups of women drug users were particularly skilled at obtaining drugs from doctors: women with previous illnesses and registered nurses. Women who had once had a legitimate illness that required narcotics were often able to play on doctors' sympathy (especially if they could show evidence, such as kidney scars). June W. became well-known among Toronto doctors for simulating a kidney ailment. Dr. J. told police that he first encountered June W. when a car stopped at his office one night, and a woman screaming with pain had been brought in. He gave her a hypodermic of morphine and sent her home. Two weeks later he was downtown when he heard a woman crying in the middle of a crowd. He discovered June W. and gave her an injection of water, whereupon she got extremely angry. A second doctor reported that he had first seen June W. in her home in downtown Toronto. She had symptoms of kidney trouble and was apparently in severe pain, so he gave her morphine by injection. Her urine tests were negative, and he became convinced that she had memorized the symptoms to obtain prescriptions. She acquired a long record for forging cheques, but she was not convicted under the Opium and Narcotic Drug Act until 1957.[86]

Registered nurses were able to draw on their professional authority to assert the legitimacy of their need for narcotics. Some users called this the 'foreign nurse game.' Vivian S. was a private nurse who first came to the attention of the RCMP in Montreal for raising a prescription from three to twenty-five tablets in June 1933.[87] In 1937 she apparently had a legitimate kidney complaint, and a doctor made arrangements for her to enter hospital. In the meantime, she forged several prescriptions under his name and raised the amount of drugs prescribed in others, while obtaining prescriptions from several doctors at once. The doctor emphasized that he had given the prescriptions with the 'emphatic warning to Vivian S. that she was a *nurse* and ought to be well *aware* that in procrastinating she was running a danger of addiction as well as other complications following renal calculi.' As the investigation continued, Vivian S. quit her job without notice, stole some goods from her employer, and fled.[88]

Drug users travelled widely in their attempts to obtain drugs, in part because they found that rural doctors were more willing to prescribe than city doctors were. The chief of the Narcotic Division, Colonel Sharman, regularly reprimanded doctors for prescribing to these users. 'There is,' he wrote to one doctor, 'a great Freemasonry amongst these gentry, who, for example, in the course of a trip across Canada "riding the rods," habitually stop over at certain points, frequently at the smaller places, to the complete exclusion of others, because they, by means of information exchanged amongst themselves, know just where they will meet with the reception they desire.' Sharman claimed that most doctors provided drugs out of sympathy rather than out of the desire to make money. He believed that there were many doctors 'who, I am sure, would be horrified if they knew the extent to which their names were bandied around amongst the travelling addict fraternity as being "good for a shot."[89] His story was confirmed by drug users such as Abel N., who told police that 'it was very easy for anyone in possession of money to obtain narcotics from physicians in the interior [of British Columbia].'[90]

Drug users sometimes resorted to theft. One Winnipeg drug user went to a doctor in 1931 complaining of gallstones and asked for morphine. The doctor refused, giving him a prescription for a non-narcotic pain reliever, but the drug user stole a prescription form and forged the physician's signature. After taking the prescription to two druggists, both of whom were suspicious of the forgery, he was caught by police who charged him with having morphine in his possession. He was sentenced to eighteen months.[91] It was also very common for users to steal doctors' bags, often from their cars, which were easily identified with special licence plates.[92]

Drug users who were unable to obtain morphine or heroin sometimes turned to codeine, a much milder opiate that had briefly been on the schedule of the Opium and Narcotic Drug Act but was removed in 1925.[93] Imports of codeine increased from 9000 ounces in 1927 to 36,000 ounces in 1933. In 1934 the Department of Pensions and National Health reported that codeine was being used as a 'carry-over' drug by addicts who could not find a supply of morphine or heroin.[94] The Royal Victoria Hospital in Montreal showed that people taking codeine in massive doses experienced withdrawal.[95] In 1934, with the cooperation of wholesalers and pharmaceutical associations, the Narcotic Division limited the amount of codeine some retail druggists could sell and entirely prohibited some druggists from selling it. As a result, by 1935 illegal peddlers were selling codeine at high prices.[96] In British Columbia in 1935, amendments to the BC Pharmacy Act restricted codeine to prescription.[97] According to the Narcotic Division, the illicit codeine market had noticeably decreased by 1936,[98] but that same year the *Vancouver News Herald* reported that one drugstore in Vancouver was buying more than 200 ounces of codeine per month. The store was frequented daily by known users, who admitted to police that they were injecting the drug hypodermically.[99]

The department also believed that the use of paregoric, a medicinal beverage with as much as 40 per cent alcohol, and a quarter grain of morphine per ounce, far exceeded legitimate medical need in the 1930s.[100] One retail drugstore in Toronto purchased seventy-five gallons of paregoric in a single month. Although paregoric was exempted under the Opium and Narcotic Drug Act because of its low morphine content, the department took the matter up with the Canadian Pharmaceutical Association, which recommended that no retail druggist should be allowed to obtain more than half a gallon per month. In March 1933 the Excise Division of the Department of National Revenue brought paregoric under control on the grounds of its alcohol content, and prohibited retail druggists in Canada from obtaining more than half a gallon per month. This did not entirely end the use of paregoric; in 1939 the RCMP reported that the twenty-seven drug users residing in Edmonton were finding it very difficult to obtain supplies. Three doctors would apparently provide drug users with injections in their offices, but they would not give them anything to take outside. The users were taking trips to the country where they were trying to obtain drugs from country doctors. They were also separating morphine from paregoric by boiling it on the stove.[101]

Users were flexible and creative in the search for drugs in the 1930s, but even the most successful users often went without supplies. In 1929 Sydney C. told police that he obtained large amounts of morphine – an ounce at a time – from a peddler who operated from a taxi stand in Toronto. By the 1930s, he was getting drugs from doctors, although he appeared to be travelling widely in his search for drugs. In 1931 he received morphine from a doctor in Manotick, Ontario. Later that year, he raised a prescription for twelve tablets of morphine to twenty-five tablets in Campbellford, Ontario. In 1939 he was arrested in Coburg, Ontario, for having passed a worthless cheque. The police searched him and found an empty bottle of paregoric, a hypodermic syringe, six capsules of white powder, and twelve small white tablets, but an analysis of the capsules and tablets showed that they contained no narcotics. Sydney C. told police that he had left Toronto, where he was living, because he was finding it difficult to obtain drugs and was on his way to relatives in rural Ontario.[102]

Montreal still had a high rate of convictions in the early 1930s, but by the late 1930s the largest centre of illegal drug use in Canada was Vancouver, where opium continued to arrive, in contrast to the drug shortages that prevailed elsewhere. It was in Vancouver that drug users originated the unhealthy practice, which may have been unique to Canada, of injecting smoking opium, leading to severe abscesses and other health problems because of the impurities in the smoking opium.[103] Because the illicit market functioned better in Vancouver than anywhere else in the country, drug users in Vancouver honed their techniques for hiding drugs and avoiding the police. Vancouver drug users were able to stay in the same location for longer, which also meant that they had a sense of community unavailable to the transitory users who travelled across the country 'making doctors.' Because of the friendship networks and a more secure supply of drugs, Vancouver remained the most popular centre for drug use in Canada throughout the 1940s, '50s, and beyond.

The difficulties of obtaining jobs and drugs in the 1930s also made it difficult for drug users to work steadily. Common occupations for drug users included salesman, logger, clerk, cook, waiter, and barber. The women tended to report that they were waitresses or housewives. Realistically, though, most users combined legal and illegal activities, and some probably derived most of their income through illegal activities, including theft, false pretences, and housebreaking. Peter B., for example, first began serving time for housebreaking in 1921. In the 1920s and '30s, he was sent to prison four times for false pretences, once for shopbreaking, once for breaking and entering, and three times for offences under the Opium and Narcotic Drug Act. At various times he gave his profession as cook, Pullman conductor, and salesman, but he spent so much time in prison that it is hard to imagine that he worked full time for any extensive period.[104] By the 1930s, the need for many drug users to move around on a regular basis, both to obtain drugs and avoid police, meant that few of the users who came to the attention of narcotic authorities had steady work records. Looking for drugs had become their full-time occupation.

The Second World War

The war further increased the difficulty of obtaining narcotic drugs for illicit use. Codeine became much harder to obtain in 1939, when regulations under the War Measures Act prevented the use of straight codeine in the manufacture of preparations containing other medicinal ingredients, without a special license. It also prohibited the sale of straight codeine, except by prescription, and made possession of codeine an offence under the Opium and Narcotic Drug Act, meaning that people found in possession of codeine were subject to the same penalties as those found in possession of morphine, heroin, opium, and cocaine.[105] By 1944 the Department of Pensions and National Health was finding it extremely difficult to import enough codeine to meet medical needs. There were also shortages of morphine, making doctors much more reluctant to supply drugs to addicts.[106]

Smugglers were thwarted by the war, and by 1940 the Narcotic Division reported that there were no narcotics available through illegal channels.[107] By 1941, though, Colonel Sharman modified this statement to admit that drug users on the West Coast were obtaining smoking opium.[108] Drug users turned to doctors or robberies to obtain their drugs. Thefts increased from 46 in 1938 to 143 in 1942 to 285 in 1943, and thefts became more professional as non–drug users realized the potential profit.[109] Prices, which had increased over the course of the Depression, skyrocketed during the war. In 1942 a can of smoking opium was selling for $950, compared to $300 before the war and $100 a decade before. Morphine reached the unbelievably high price of $20 per grain.[110]

Drug users became increasingly desperate. Neil C. was so successful at obtaining drugs from doctors in the 1930s that police believed that he was peddling these drugs in addition to using them himself. During the war, he had no such luck. In September 1942 police reported that Neil C. and a friend had tried to obtain drugs from Dr. W. in High Prairie, Alberta, but they were refused. Later that evening, the doctor discovered the friend in the act of breaking into his office. Two weeks later, the pair tried to obtain drugs from a doctor in McLennan, Alberta. They were unsuccessful, but they robbed a drugstore early the next morning. They were caught and given two years for theft.[111] Yves G., a resident of Edmonton, also lacked regular supplies during the war years and immediately thereafter. He resorted to a variety of means to obtain drugs. In January 1945 police believed that he and several friends were responsible for the theft of narcotics from a drugstore and that he was peddling Nembutal (barbiturate) capsules. In October 1945 he persuaded a farmer friend to buy laudanum for him from his veterinarian by saying it was for his horses. That same month police caught him collecting poppy heads.[112]

Yves G. was not the only user who turned to other substances. In the early 1940s, the Department of Pensions and National Health became quite concerned about the use of barbiturates and amphetamines, both by drug users and by the public at large. An order-in-council was passed in October 1941 making these drugs and some other non-psychotropic drugs available by prescription only. Initially, the regulations made an exception for the Benzedrine inhaler, produced by Smith, Kline, and French, which was widely used to relieve nasal congestion. But desperate drug users began taking apart the inhaler, extracting the racemic amphetamine and injecting it. Reports from the RCMP in Vancouver indicated that a number of alcoholics (alcohol was rationed during the war) and drug users were selling shots of Benzedrine out of their rooms. In

1943 another order-in-council put the Benzedrine inhaler on a prescription basis, much to the dismay of Smith, Kline, and French, who then offered to change the inhaler in order to make it impossible to misuse. Eventually, the company developed an inhaler without psychotropic effect and removed the Benzedrine inhaler from the market.[113]

The decision to make barbiturates and amphetamines available only by prescription made it more difficult to obtain these drugs, but persistent drug users readily obtained prescriptions from doctors. These drugs were controlled under the Food and Drugs Act, rather than the Opium and Narcotic Drug Act, and the Department of Pensions and National Health lacked the same authority to go after doctors, so drug users seem to have obtained these drugs without much trouble. Benzedrine and Nembutal were comparatively cheap at fifty cents per shot. In 1946 when opiates were still in short supply, the chief of the Narcotic Division, K.C. Hossick, went on several evening drug raids with the RCMP Drug Squad in Vancouver. In one room, they found fifteen men lying on the floor, including several known addicts. There were no narcotics, but police found several dozen bottles of 'Woodbury's After Shave Lotion,' two or three shoe polish tins, and numerous Benzedrine inhalers.[114]

The army had a policy of discharging drug users, but some joined anyway. When a drug user or former user came to the attention of military authorities, he was investigated by the RCMP and given a medical and psychiatric examination.[115] In some cases, drug users may have exaggerated or even invented their drug use in order to be released from the army – police reported that some recruits learned from older addicts how to doctor their arms to make it look like they used the hypodermic needle. One such soldier was caught when friends told police that he was right-handed, but all of his needle marks were on his right arm, making it unlikely that he had created the needle-marks himself. Users reported using a broad range of drugs, including opium, morphine, heroin, cocaine, laudanum, codeine, Nembutal, marijuana, Benzedrine, and so on. Many claimed that they started using in the 1930s, indicating that the shortages did not stop new users from starting, although there is little indication that people sustained heavy habits. Quite a few reported that they had stopped using before joining the armed services, but had started using again after enlisting. Thefts from dispensaries may have made it easier to obtain drugs in the armed services than elsewhere. Nearly all of the discharged users had long histories of criminal involvement, and their work experiences before joining the army were often in circuses or racetracks or involved unskilled labour. The 'addicts' attracted little sympathy from army psychiatrists, who dismissed them as 'psychopathic personalities' who were of little use to the army.[116]

At the end of the war, Constable Price of the RCMP did a survey of fifty-two drug users in Vancouver. From the forty-five white addicts, Price determined that the 'average' addict was male, 34.8 years of age, had attained Grade 8 in school, had worked for 3.5 years, was first arrested at 21.8 years, first started using drugs at 21.9 years, and had subsequently been convicted of 8.6 offences, such as possession of drugs, breaking and entering, retaining stolen property, and vagrancy. This average addict had been sentenced to 5.9 years imprisonment. He had used drugs for 10.5 years and his habit had been cut from a pre-war figure of 4.45 grains of morphine per day to 0.78 grains per day. Price reported that the older the addict was, the more likely he was to select smoking opium as his preferred drug (paralleling the trends discussed earlier this chapter). Price did not indicate how many of his subjects were female, but he did report that all of the women he interviewed were prostitutes, with the exception of a nurse.

Price was hardly an impartial observer, being a member of the RCMP Drug Squad in Vancouver, but he provided some interesting case histories. Price remarked that 'A' was 'well spoken and intelligent.' He was forty-two years old, had used drugs for thirteen years, and had only quit once. 'A' had attended private school, and his home life was comfortable, but his father died when he was a boy. According to Price, 'A' believed 'the lack of a father's discipline and too much freedom and money' was responsible 'for his seeking out of poor companions.' Since he started using, he had been convicted of nine offences, including breaking and entering, living off the avails of prostitution, retaining stolen property, and possession of drugs. 'B' was a woman, twenty-one years of age. She began working as a prostitute as a young teenager and had been addicted to drugs since she was seventeen years old. She was the child of Russian immigrants on the Prairies and came to Vancouver's East End with her father as a child, after her mother left the family. Her father worked as a bootlegger and a fence, and her stepmother was a prostitute. Price noted that her attitude to police was 'resentful and rebellious.'

Price's case histories were coloured by negative accusations, providing a vivid example of the disdain with which police officers treated drug users. He referred to 'B' as a 'sullen foul-tongued girl, mentally dull and utterly lacking in any moral sense.' Nonetheless, his article also marks a transition. First, Price identified the existence of a growing number of young drug users in Vancouver. This new generational cohort of users would dominate the drug scene in the post-war period and would experience a world of drug use that was very different from its pre–Second World War peers. Secondly, Price's study of drug users was an early example of the far more careful record-keeping of the post-war period. Drug users in post-war Canada would be regularly queried and surveyed by a variety of regulators who wanted to find reasons for their use of drugs, and who hoped that their investigations would reveal the means by which they could make the users quit.[117]

Conclusion

Class and race played an enormous role in determining whether or not a drug user would come to the attention of the state in the years from 1920 to 1945. Some middle- or upper-class white users who obtained drugs from doctors undoubtedly escaped state scrutiny, whereas Chinese drug users, who usually lived in small and crowded accommodations, found such scrutiny difficult to avoid – their communities were intensively targeted for drug enforcement. Chinese drug users were frequently arrested for drug offences and were forced to pay large fines that they could ill-afford, or to spend time in Canadian prisons. In addition, over a thousand Chinese men were deported to China as a result of drug offences from 1922 to 1940. Working-class white drug users were better off than Chinese users in that they were policed less intensively, but the police did make efforts to counter street peddling. When caught, white users received long sentences for possession.

In the 1930s, as drug supplies declined, some white users roamed the country 'making doctors.' This made for a hard and solitary life, but it helped users avoid police, as it was difficult for police to enforce laws against prescribing narcotics. These users often avoided possession charges, although they frequently served time for vagrancy, theft, and other offences.

Those who continued to buy from the illicit market faced prison terms. Nonetheless, drug users continued to defy the state. Chinese drug users obtained drugs on board ships in Vancouver's harbour or in Chinese medicines. Smugglers continued to bring opium into British Columbia in the 1930s and early '40s. Drug users pled with doctors, found clever ways of extracting drugs from over-the-counter preparations, and made connections with peddlers.

Public policy decisions by the state, including harsh drug laws, strict enforcement, careful monitoring of licit supplies, and the end of Chinese immigration, greatly changed the experience of drug use from 1920 to 1945. Due to the initial successes of international drug control, the Great Depression, and increased enforcement, it became increasingly difficult to obtain drugs. Patterns of drug use also became much more harmful. Users moved away from the less harmful practices of smoking opium and sniffing heroin and cocaine to the more dangerous practices of injecting opium and heroin. By making drugs increasingly difficult to obtain, the state ensured that drug use became an increasingly central part of users' lives – users were forced to devote enormous time and attention to obtaining new supplies, and they had to pay more for these supplies, meaning that it became more and more difficult for them to hold down steady legal employment. A greater proportion of users became involved in criminal activities other than drug use. Moreover, as recreational use declined, users were less likely to learn techniques for managing and controlling their drug use from users who were able to keep their drug use under control. Thus, the number of users was almost certainly smaller, but they were a far more troubled and problematic group. The costs of reducing use were high in terms of drug users' health, their employment, and their freedom.

Chapter 3

'Hypes': Using and Quitting, 1945–1961

From 1945 to 1961, the harsh drug laws of the early 1920s remained in place, and the state put even more resources into policing. Users spent much of their life in prison. The relative prosperity of this period and its homogeneous social norms meant that few people were attracted to the risky life of drug use. The few who did become users, or 'hypes' as they were often called, were drawn from the troubled and the poor. Users started young and had usually spent time in juvenile detention homes or in prison before they started using drugs. For these rebellious young people, drug use provided the excitement of participating in a highly criticized and deviant activity, and promised increased subcultural status and a sense of community within the criminal world. In the long run, however, drug use and addiction generally worsened people's lives and narrowed their already limited options.

There were relatively few drug users (probably fewer than 4000 steady users) in the first twenty years after the Second World War. This was far fewer than there had been in the 1920s, or than there would be after 1965.[1] The cohort included people who had been using before the war and had experienced the life of the transient, doctor-shopping addict of the 1930s. When drug supplies regularized after the war, most of these users settled into Vancouver or Toronto and began buying their supplies almost exclusively from the illicit market. They were joined by a new generation of users who first began to emerge during the war. Like the older generation of users, these new users were primarily working class, but there were several important differences. Far more of the early post-war users in Canada were female. Until 1937, female drug offenders consistently represented less than 10 per cent of people convicted under the Opium and Narcotic Drug Act, but by 1946 this figure had increased to 21 per cent, and by 1961 to 37 per cent. (There were more female addicts in Canada than there were in the United States, where female users accounted for approximately 20 per cent of the addict population in the mid-1950s.)[2] The presence of women changed the economic infrastructure of heroin use, since many women were successful prostitutes who supported their partners' habits as well as their own. Another difference was that the geographical concentration of drug users in major cities was much more pronounced after the Second World War. From 1946 to 1961, more than 50 per cent of all narcotic convictions took place in Vancouver, while another 24 per cent took place in Toronto.[3] Although convictions are a better indication of policing practices than they are of drug use, most drug users who bought their drugs from street peddlers (as opposed to doctors) had contacts in one of these two cities.

As in the 1930s, users in the early post-war period were primarily white. The Dominion Bureau of Statistics stopped publishing racial statistics in 1947, but my analysis of the case files of the John Howard Society and the Division of Narcotic Control shows a vast predominance of white users. At the Division of Narcotic Control, my sample of 159 cases turned up three African-Canadian drug users (1.9 per cent), two Aboriginal users (1.2 per cent), and one Asian user (0.6 per cent). At the John Howard Society, where I examined 390 case files, fifteen of the users were Aboriginal (4 per cent), three were African Canadian (0.7 per cent), and ten were Asian Canadian (2.5 per cent). The racial differences between the two sets of case files are the result of there being proportionately more Asians and Aboriginals on the West Coast, and of the small sample sizes. However, even though relatively few drug users were black or Asian, they were slightly over-represented compared to their proportion of Canada's total population.[4]

The very small numbers of non-white users meant that there was no separate community for users who were from racial minority groups. Users who were members of visible minority groups intermarried with white drug users and spent their time on the street with white users. This pattern differed significantly from the situation in the United States, where heroin users in this period were mostly African American or Hispanic.

The Changing Drug Market

Before the Second World War, most users took a wide variety of opiates, including opium, morphine, heroin, and codeine, depending partly on availability and individual preference. From 1945 to 1947, the drugs on the illicit market (usually morphine) were obtained from drugstore robberies, often by professional non-users.[5] As the illicit market gathered steam after the war, break-ins declined, and by early 1949, the RCMP reported that the bulk of narcotics on the illicit market entered the country illegally. On the West Coast, opium use remained common in the years immediately after the war, but by 1948 it had been replaced by heroin (Mexican Brown, an inferior type of heroin that was brownish in colour), which first reappeared on the West Coast just after the end of the war (see figure 3.1). The first seizure of high-quality heroin was made on the West Coast in December 1948, and by the 1950s, only high-grade 'white' heroin was available. Heroin had been common in Winnipeg, Toronto, and Montreal before the war, but it seems to have been a rarity on the West Coast, where opium had been the dominant drug. Nonetheless, users adapted quickly. The habit of injecting smoking-opium had all but disappeared by 1946, and West Coast users responded with enthusiasm to the white heroin that replaced Mexican Brown. After 1948, heroin was virtually the only opiate available in the illicit market. The RCMP claimed that it usually came from the eastern United States via Europe, so Vancouver's status as the largest centre of drug use had nothing to do with it being a port town.

Marijuana use was rare, especially on the West Coast. According to psychiatrist George Stevenson, who carried out an extensive study of drug use at Oakalla Prison Farm from 1953 to 1956, very few drug users from the West Coast reported that they had ever tried marijuana, and only six people were arrested for marijuana offences in British Columbia from 1946 to 1961.[6] In Winnipeg, Toronto, and Montreal, marijuana was more common, and users may have started with that drug, although marijuana was the substance seized in only 2 per cent of all drug arrests in Canada in the years from 1946 to 1961.[7] This may have been a question of enforcement. A number of the marijuana users listed in the case files of the Division of Narcotic Control Division were better off, financially and socially, than the average heroin user.[8] It may be that marijuana use was more widespread than statistics indicate, but that it was used primarily by a more 'respectable' class of users, who were not subject to the same kind of police surveillance. Indeed, a 1965 study of marijuana users in Toronto suggested that a majority of the 'swingers' who used marijuana had been using it for ten years or more. 'Swingers' were well-dressed people who worked in service occupations, or in entertainment, and were generally between thirty and forty-five years of age.[9]

Figure 3.1
Convictions for Drug Possession by Type of Drug, 1946–61

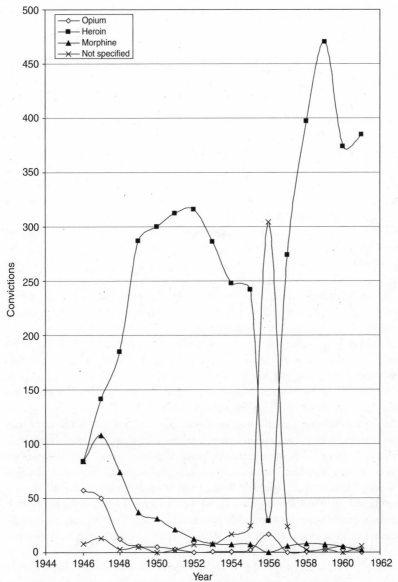

Source: Canada, Dominion Bureau of Statistics, *Annual Report of Statistics of Criminal and Other Offenses* for the years 1945 through 1961.

There were also drug users whose favourite drug was alcohol, not heroin. They used drugs occasionally, but often abstained from heroin for long periods without difficulty. Earl F., for example, went on long drinking binges and experienced periods of alcoholic blackout. He used drugs occasionally, but his main problem was alcohol.[10] Heavy drinkers sometimes turned to heroin because it caused fewer health problems than extensive alcohol use. Others used heroin to sober up or as a hangover cure.[11] Heroin users also supplemented their heroin use or replaced it with Benzedrine (a type of amphetamine), barbiturates, and methadone, in addition to alcohol, and they were occasionally found in possession of these drugs.[12]

Users bought their drugs from peddlers, and many users, especially men, peddled occasionally. Female peddlers were less common; it may have been harder for them to gain the trust of higher-ups, or perhaps they chose not to peddle because they could more easily earn money through prostitution. Being a peddler was not a steady job, and it was very risky. Peddlers served long sentences, ran the risk of being robbed by other users, and could face violence from higher-ups. In Vancouver, where most users lived in residential hotel rooms in the Downtown East-side, peddlers often congregated in the cafés and beer parlours at the corner of Hastings and Columbia. The Broadway Beer Parlour seems to have been the most popular place to buy drugs, but the White Lunch, the New Zenith Café, the New Fountain Hotel Beer Parlour, the Common Gold Café, and other places were also common. The corner's reputation was so well-known that *Maclean's* described it as 'Canada's most notorious underworld rendezvous' and claimed that 'as far east as Montreal the drug racket knows this spot simply as the Corner, and makes sure nobody undersells anybody.'[13]

In Toronto, drug peddlers were more likely to sell out of their homes or apartments, but the drug trade was centred at the corner of Jarvis and Dundas, especially around Shuter and Mutual streets. In Vancouver, sellers generally staked out a location and sold to small numbers of users at a time, whereas in Toronto the practice of arranging 'meets' with a large number of addicts seems to have been more common. In Montreal, the drug trade was much smaller, but it appears to have been in approximately the same location as the 1920s – on the 'Main' (rue St. Laurent) near rue Ste. Catherine.[14] In all locations, sales were made as secretly as possible.[15] Peddlers only sold to known users. To buy drugs, undercover officers first needed the assistance of a known drug user and had to purchase drugs several times before being trusted enough to make a purchase on their own.[16] Contrary to sensational media stories, there is no evidence that peddlers sold to schoolchildren.

There were a few people who obtained drugs through licit channels, although this was much less common than it had been in the 1930s.[17] Morphine remained the preference of most people who went to doctors for their drugs, but approximately one-third also obtained Demerol.[18] Many of these users were nurses and wives of doctors, or were doctors themselves, but a few were middle-class or working-class people who were able to persuade doctors that they had a medical condition that required the use of narcotic drugs. An unusual case was that of a young woman from Winnipeg who successfully received drugs from several doctors in a prosperous neighbourhood in 1961. She was well-read and well-connected: one of the doctors admitted that he had known her since she was a girl; one of her companions was the son of a nurse. Her familiarity with Aldous Huxley's pro-drug classic, the *Doors of Perception* (1954), may indicate that she was a forerunner of the counter-cultural drug users who would transform the drug-using scene in the 1960s.[19]

The Post-War Users

A striking feature of the drug users in the early post-war period was their youth. From 1946 through 1961, 67 per cent of the men and 78 per cent of the women convicted under the Opium and Narcotic Drug Act were in their twenties and thirties, while 35 per cent of the men and 56 per cent of the women were under thirty.[20] The John Howard Society case files indicate that, on average, women started using at 19.1 years of age, and men at 22.4 years of age. Some reported that they started using when they were as young as twelve.[21]

Most users came from economically disadvantaged backgrounds. A study of drug users at Oakalla Prison Farm in the mid-1950s found that only a third of drug users grew up in homes that the study's designers described as economically comfortable. Almost a quarter lived in homes that needed welfare assistance at least some of the time. A study of consecutively convicted users at the prison farm showed that 56 per cent of addicts who were raised in Vancouver grew up in 'the deteriorated section' of Vancouver's East End.[22] In several cases, workers at the John Howard Society noted that clients had been malnourished as children, which is not surprising, given that many of the post-war users had grown up during the Great Depression.[23]

Very few users attended church or were otherwise religious, although most reported that they were Catholic, Protestant, or Anglican.[24] In the Oakalla Prison Farm study, nearly 80 per cent of drug users reported that their parents were 'indifferent or antagonistic to religion,' or that their parents came from different religious denominations.[25] Stevenson wrote that 'they usually stated that they seldom thought about God or religion, and they had little belief in an after-life.'[26] The few drug users at the John Howard Society in Vancouver who expressed interest in organized religion tended towards the Salvation Army, which provided much-needed charity services to the Downtown Eastside and took a particular interest in the needs of alcoholic men.

Many drug users had family problems.[27] In the Stevenson study, only 42 per cent of drug users at Oakalla said that they had a 'satisfactory home life.' Only 40 per cent had both parents alive and living at home by the time they finished school.[28] Over 30 per cent reported that their father's outstanding characteristic was 'overly aggressive, quarrelsome, irritable,' while another 10 per cent complained that their father's outstanding characteristic was 'alcoholic.'[29] The case file records show that some users had endured extraordinarily troubled lives.

Adopted when she was ten months old, Sharon M. was put in the Convent of the Good Shepherd when she was nine. She repeatedly ran away from the convent to her foster home and started using drugs at age twelve. She was placed in the Girls' Industrial School, where she set an Industrial School record by running away sixty-eight times. She was released from the Industrial School just after her sixteenth birthday.[30]

Cameron G. told penitentiary officials that his parents separated when he was seven years old. His two brothers went to live with his father, who was reported to be a steady drinker and a stern disciplinarian, and he was placed with his aunt, whom he described as 'excessively strict.' Cameron G. first appeared in juvenile court at age thirteen. At fifteen, his aunt could no longer afford to keep him, so he was given to the Children's Aid Society, who sent him to a ranch north of Edmonton. At sixteen, a welfare agent advised him to join the army, set up a meeting with the recruitment officer, and told Cameron to tell the officer that he was eighteen. Within a year, Cameron was wounded by shrapnel in his left side, causing damage to his lung, and had contracted venereal disease. Returned home and honourably discharged at eighteen, he started using drugs sometime thereafter.[31] Cameron was a fairly typical user in having lived in foster homes and having had substance abuse problems and serious health problems at an early age.

Many users had experienced physical or emotional violence. William

W.'s father reportedly did time in Oakalla for assaulting him and his brother. Eventually, the boys were found living in a shack 'inadequately clothed and fed,' and were committed to the Children's Aid Society.[32] Johnny R. reported that his mother and father fought a great deal, that his father abused him and his mother, and that he found his mother too emotional to talk to. 'Under narcotics,' he confessed, 'I don't worry about nobody screaming about anything – dad used to be always screaming.'[33] It is not surprising that young people with such difficult memories would find solace in heroin use and in the community it provided.

Despite the tragic childhoods of many heroin users, few identified this as a direct explanation for their drug use. When asked why they had first started using, over 90 per cent of users in a study at Oakalla Prison Farm indicated that 'curiosity and desire for a new thrill' was at least part of the reason. Eighty per cent added that it was because they had been associating with addicts.[34] Sixty-eight per cent of users in the Oakalla Prison Farm study said that they had seen someone else take a fix before they first tried heroin.[35] Thus, it was the possibility of pleasure and excitement that led people to take their first fix, but once the initial excitement was over, heroin's ability to relieve their pain and obliterate their problems kept them using.

The Pleasures of Consumption

For many users, heroin was an intensely pleasurable drug. Veronica S. reported that her greatest joy 'was to be able to coast under the influence of drugs.'[36] But she also reported that she liked the life, suggesting that her enjoyment went beyond the drugs themselves. First experiences of drug use are not always pleasant, however; many first-time heroin users become violently ill, and it often takes a certain persistence to become an addict.[37] Gretchen R. started playing around with drugs at fifteen or sixteen years of age. Her social worker wrote that Gretchen told her that 'she didn't know why the addicts felt they were just floating on the 7th cloud when they were under the influence of narcotics as she had never really felt good yet and the drug made her desperately ill. She claims that she really doesn't like it and she really doesn't want it but it just seems to be when she gets under the influence of rounder friends that she is unable to stand on her own feet.'[38] Over 50 per cent of users who took part in the Oakalla Prison Farm study said that their first injection produced 'nausea and vomiting, sometimes with prolonged "blackout."'[39] Nonetheless, more than 60 per cent of the people studied at Oakalla took another fix within a week of the first, indicating that they were seeking something more than just the pleasures of the shot. They were prepared to work at drug use because they admired other users, and they wanted the exciting life of a heroin user – they wanted the thrills of evading the police, the kick of the forbidden, the pleasures of the drug, and the prestige on the street.

Many users, especially in the early stages of drug use, enjoyed having access to specialized knowledge and insider status – what Sarah Thornton would call 'subcultural capital' – such as knowing where to buy, and gaining the trust of a dealer.[40] Heroin users had to know what they were buying, what price they could expect to pay, and what to do with the heroin afterwards. Peddlers cut the heroin with sugar of milk and other substances, and sold it in gelatin capsules. A capsule generally contained anywhere from a tenth of a grain to slightly more than a full grain of heroin.[41] Individual capsules of heroin were usually double-wrapped in silver paper from cigarette packages, and users normally carried these capsules in their mouth, so that they could swallow them if police appeared. Larger numbers of capsules were wrapped in balloons, condoms, or fingerstalls (pieces of latex shaped like fingers), which could also be carried in the mouth, the vagina, or, in a few cases, the anus. The cost varied over time and from city to city, but capsules usually sold for $3 to $6 each.[42] Heroin users were diligent about ensuring that their capsules were appropriately wrapped in foil before placing them in their mouths, and users monitored each other to ensure that the drugs were being carried as safely as possible.

Heroin was almost always injected. A few drug users took 'skin shots,' meaning that they injected it just beneath the skin (subcutaneously), but most 'mainlined,' meaning that they injected the drug right into the vein. An 'outfit' of drug-injecting equipment – also known as the 'works' – consisted of an eyedropper, a hypodermic needle, a gee (thin paper or absorbent cotton), and a spoon. The contents of a capsule and some water were placed in a spoon, which was heated to help the substance dissolve. The contents of the spoon were drawn into the needle, which was placed on the end of the eyedropper with the aid of the gee. To shoot up, the drug user tied something around his or her arm, inserted the needle into a vein, and released the eyedropper contents into the needle. After use, the syringe was cleaned with water to ensure that police could not analyse it.[43]

In many American states in the 1950s, renting an 'outfit' was a common way of gaining money to buy drugs.[44] In Canada, the items in an 'outfit' were legal; drug users were sometimes arrested with more than one outfit, and there were accusations that some pharmacies actually sold them in kits. But it was common practice for users to share outfits, probably because one outfit was easier to clean, hide, or throw away if the police broke down the door. While people occasionally received shots from others, most heroin users shot up themselves and had to be familiar with all of the stages of preparing a shot, finding an appropriate vein, and using the needle effectively. These complex rituals, which took some effort to learn, lent a prestige and status to heroin use.

It was not just specialized knowledge and pleasure that gave heroin its status. Young people with experiences of crime and institutional life looked up to older users in prison and on the street, partly because drug users had a reputation for being hardened 'cons,' had some power within the prisons, and had a strong sense of community. Becoming a heroin user allowed young 'rounders' (delinquents) to identify with a group that was regarded as the most rebellious and, in many ways, the most cohesive group in Canada's prisons.[45] In 1958 Rebecca R. told a social worker that 'it is because the person wants to feel part of a group that they usually become an addict.' She said that non-addict rounders were 'half baked' rounders, and that unless drugs were taken, 'he or she does not feel part of the group ... and it is because they want this sense of belonging that many of them turn to the use of narcotics.' 'To many it was like a game,' she revealed, 'almost like winning a war, and the war was won when they were able to score and take a fix successfully ... It was somewhat this thrill of being able to win ... that made the whole idea of using drugs attractive to young teenagers.'[46]

Rebecca R. was not alone. A matron at the Oakalla Prison Farm confirmed that the young inmates were 'greatly enamoured of the exciting, glamorous life of the narcotic addict. They frequently aspire to membership in the addict group.'[47] Like the 'lads' described by Paul Willis in his book *Learning to Labor: How Working Class Kids Get Working Class Jobs*, who looked down on their fellow students for their lack of knowledge about sex and life, young heroin users could feel superior to 'square johns,' who knew nothing about the joys of heroin or the excitement of crime.[48]

Drug use was usually part of a long pattern of 'deviant' behaviour, and heroin use was another step in becoming a bona fide 'rounder'; most users had already spent time in juvenile institutions or in prison before they started using drugs. Case files from the Division of Narcotic Control reveal that it was unusual for someone's first conviction to be a narcotic offence, although it was more common for women than for men, perhaps because women often started using when they were younger and because women's primary illegal activity was prostitution, which was not always policed intensively. The Oakalla Prison Farm study indicated that only 22 per cent of male drug users and 43 per cent of female drug users had no convictions before they started drug use.[49] In Vancouver, most people who later became drug users were already hanging out on the 'corner' and had come to the attention of police and social workers as juveniles. In other words, they were outsiders to mainstream society before they started using drugs, and within their world, using drugs could provide them with important contacts and companionship.

The relatively small number of drug users ensured that many users knew each other and thought of themselves as a community of sorts. This feeling of community was partly created by enforcement officials, who forced users to be very cautious in their dealings with non-users and created a sense of siege among users. But the community was also created by users, who had a great deal in common, including an enjoyment of heroin, sexual and marital patterns that deviated widely from the norm, sporadic work experiences in low-status occupations, and shared experiences in jail and prison. When Stevenson asked users at Oakalla whether they preferred the company of addicts and felt a sense of loyalty to them, those who answered in the affirmative said that 'addicts help and understand each other'; 'they are the only group I can feel natural with. I am self-conscious with square-johns'; 'we're all the same – all fighting a common cause, the police and drugs'; and 'we talk the same language. We live the same life. We are all looked down on because we are addicts.'[50] John Turvey, who later became a Vancouver social worker and was a user in the late 1950s and early '60s, recalled that there was a 'lot of loyalty on the street' and 'a strong sense of ethics in the community.'[51]

While users also fought with each other and informed on one another, the idea of users standing up for one another was not just a myth. Drug users were frequently arrested in groups of two to four people, and they tried to ensure that only one person would serve time for the offence. In a situation that was typical, Norman M. was smoking and drinking in a hotel room with a female companion when the police broke in. The police found two capsules. The woman announced, 'well it's my room and my coat, everything in the room is mine, he knew nothing about it.' The police decided that they did not have enough evidence to warrant laying a charge against Norman M., even though they knew he was an addict.[52] Users outside of prison also often tried to make life a little more bearable for those inside prison. In 1954 Robert K. dropped off a package of phonograph records at the John Howard Society for the East Wing at Oakalla (where male drug users served their time).[53] A couple weeks later he dropped by again and asked the John Howard Society to inquire why the 'boys' in the East Wing 'only heard the records once' before the records were taken to other wings. More commonly, drug users tried to send drugs to their friends on the inside. In 1961 Dorothy T. sent a postcard to a friend in the Women's Institution in Kingston. The card read, 'Thought you would like this one. Your Friend.' She had inserted a cigarette paper containing heroin into the compressed cardboard of the postcard.[54]

The tight community of users also had a shared language, although many social workers, police officers, and prison officials were conversant with the argot. Common expressions included 'boosting' (shoplifting), 'bum beef' (a false legal charge), 'bulls' (the police), 'pony boys' or 'harness bulls' (the RCMP), 'score' (a purchase of narcotics), and 'yen' (a strong desire for narcotics).[55] Chief George Allain of the Montreal Police Department told a 1955 Senate committee that if an ordinary person heard a 'pusher' and a client conversing, 'he would not know they were talking about drugs, because they use some kind of a code.'[56] In an article published in 1968, a former undercover agent for the police noted that his addict subjects spoke at an average rate of approximately 47 words per minute, and that 11.7 of these words were argot, making it difficult for outsiders to understand the conversation.[57] The language played an important role in identifying users to one another, and making them feel as if they were part of a community with a highly specialized knowledge.

The Life of Drug Use

Many drug users thought, when they started, that they could enjoy the fast and exciting life of heroin use without its costs. They believed that they could use heroin without becoming addicted. This was not completely unrealistic; there were drug users who used only irregularly and never acquired serious habits. This was particularly true of men who worked in resource jobs in the interior of British Columbia. Many used while they were in town, and stopped using and returned to the bush when their money ran out.[58] Others maintained control until life tragedies intervened. Ron S. was unusual in that he began his drug use in the United States by smoking marijuana cigarettes. After being deported to

Canada in 1947 at thirty-two years of age, he began using one cap of heroin a day, but stopped when he began working, and only took occasional shots until his mother's death in 1953. He then stopped working, began shoplifting, and his habit rose to ten caps per day.[59]

Once people started using heavily, drug use began to transform every aspect of their lives, including their relationships, their work lives, and their health. The effects of the drugs themselves were only a small part of the change. Strict enforcement meant that drug users spent their lives cycling in and out of prison. It meant living a very stressful life when they were on the street: drug users were constantly staving off withdrawal, they engaged in dangerous work to raise enough money to score, their personal relationships were often in disarray (threatened by their incessant need for money and their preoccupation with drugs), and they needed to be constantly alert for police.

Relationships

Perhaps the most significant change that distinguished drug users' lives in the inter-war years from the post-war years (1945–61) was the amount of time spent in jail. Unless you were a significant trafficker, or one of the few who obtained a regular supply from doctors, it was extremely difficult to use heavily for any length of time in the post-war years without ending up in prison. Many users spent far more time on the 'inside' than they did on the street. Typical was Gene F., a pipe-fitter and logger, who first went to jail for a drug offence at eighteen years of age. He spent twelve of the next sixteen years incarcerated for theft, possession, housebreaking, and selling drugs.[60]

The constant imprisonment was one of the reasons why it was difficult for users to maintain long-term romantic relationships, either heterosexual or same-sex. While most users married at least once in their lives, many of their relationships were common-law, sometimes because they had not obtained a divorce from their previous partner.[61] Divorces in Canada were difficult to obtain before 1968. In the Consecutive Conviction Study at Oakalla, 60 per cent of users had been married at one point in their lives, although only 14 per cent were married at the time of the study. More than one-third were living in a common-law relationship when they were admitted to Oakalla.[62] Seventy-five per cent of male users and 95 per cent of female users said that they had lived in a common-law relationship at some time.[63]

Users often had relationships with other users. Richard T. told a

British Columbia Penitentiary psychiatrist that 'it is better for one drug addict to marry another person who has used them because he has never known "mixed marriages" to work.'[64] According to both social workers and users, non-users found it very difficult to live with users, who were often unreliable and could be imprisoned at any time. Charles and Mary T. made a mixed marriage work for a number of years, but as Mary explained to a social worker,

> I have never been able to live with drugs but through all the separations I have always clung to the belief that if he went logging the battle would be over. And Charles was the only thing in my life that mattered. Anyway, after seven years he finally got a job and I guess I let my hopes build up too much. I let myself believe that all the dirty filth and fear was over and we would be a normal family. Instead of us joining him at camp he came back and started right all over again and I went fruit.[65]

Some non-using spouses ended up using themselves. One man told his social worker that he had started using drugs because his wife was an addict, and 'he found it impossible to live with her unless he took drugs too.'[66]

Imprisonment, economic pressures, and emotional problems ended many romantic relationships, yet many users, especially female users, expressed a strong desire to make these relationships last. Cheryl L. wrote her imprisoned husband ten-page letters every day after she was released from jail, and told her social worker that she prayed nothing would happen to her before his release. But he stopped responding to her letters.[67] A few couples did succeed in staying together, though. Harold and Vivian T. were married for at least sixteen years, although they both started using drugs within the first few years of their marriage. They had separated at least once, but they described their marriage as happy, although the John Howard Society social worker described them as a 'truly tragic couple, both wish to break the drug habit, both are ineffectual to cope with living, deeply dependent one upon the other and they have taken to drugs when hurt or upset.'[68]

The state sometimes placed additional barriers in the way of drug users who wished to resume their relationships. In 1955 Raquelle R. had her visiting privileges with her fiancé cancelled after he kissed her.[69] When Dot S. was in Kingston Penitentiary, she resumed correspondence with her husband, Clifford T., whom she had married twenty years earlier. Clifford had been serving time as a habitual criminal and was released on parole while she was in Kingston. They were planning on getting back together but the parole board would not agree to them reuniting.[70] It was relatively rare for drug users to be granted parole, and it was even less likely if they were involved with a fellow user, as remission officials believed that their chances of rehabilitation were poorer, even though some users did get off drugs together.

Female users often had romantic relationships with other women, especially in prison. At least 13 per cent of the female clients at the John Howard Society were involved in romantic relationships with other women at some time, although the numbers were probably much higher, since the John Howard Society did not necessarily know or note very much about their clients' sexual behaviour. In Vancouver, the New Fountain Hotel Beer Parlour was well known as a centre for lesbian addicts.[71] In Toronto, Elise Chenier has noted that the lesbian community appeared to have high rates of drug use in the late 1950s and early 1960s.[72] Within jail, female users often had relationships with other users, and some women had a reputation for being 'popular with the girls.'[73] Although some relationships only lasted as long as the two women were incarcerated, others lasted a long time. Nancy's M.'s relationship with another woman survived prison terms for each of them.[74] Men undoubtedly had homosexual relationships in and outside of prison as well, but there is surprisingly little discussion of it in the files.

The cycle of arrest and imprisonment, as well as other barriers put in place by the state, similarly made it all but impossible for users with children to care for their children themselves, unless they had a female partner who was a non-user. More commonly, they left them in the care of parents, siblings, or the Children's Aid Society, and sometimes they gave their children up for adoption.[75] Female users often expressed a desire to have their children with them, and felt guilty about their inability to care for their children, but they were strongly urged by prison workers, Children's Aid Society officers, and John Howard Society staff to have others parent their children. No one ever raised the idea that taking their children away might have negative repercussions for both parents and children.

It was not easy to have a drug user as a family member. At the John Howard Society, some people expressed despair and frustration over the fact that a family member's drug use kept them hungry and in debt. Brian P.'s wife complained that she had no money for food for herself and their two children since he spent it all on drugs. She wanted to see if his Unemployment Insurance cheque could be made out to her, but the social worker found that it was impossible.[76] In a few cases, drug users admitted, or families complained, that the user stole money from their parents and partners. Catherine D. falsely endorsed some of her mother's cheques to get money for drugs, while Edward W. was sentenced to three years for the violent robbery of his stepfather. Cheryl L. and her husband regularly took money from her mother-in-law for drugs, and Cyril S. hocked most of his wife's belongings.[77]

One of the most detailed examples of family hardship is that of Thomas F., a well-educated man from a wealthy family, who started using in the early 1930s. By 1947 his father was paying him $25 each week on the condition that he stay away from the family's residence in northern Ontario. In 1949 his brother reported to the RCMP that his family was 'under a nervous tension at all times because of threats made by his brother.' The family had sent him to the privately operated Homewood Sanatorium in Guelph for a cure on several occasions, but Thomas F. returned home, uncured. The brother complained that Thomas F. stole from his family and threatened them. He beat up his elderly father, perhaps contributing to his death six months later. After his father's death, in retribution for being left out of his father's inheritance, Thomas F. threatened to burn his brother's home and business, and stole many of his possessions. His brother subsequently pleaded with authorities to confine him for life.[78]

Being a drug user in early post-war Canada meant that one's life was constantly disrupted by prison terms and by the often-desperate search for drugs and the money to buy them. Not surprisingly, this had a very negative impact on relationships with romantic partners, children, and other family members. It was a downward spiral. Relationships often ended because of prison terms and financial worries. Then, the stress and despair of having important relationships fall apart gave users even greater reason to take drugs.

Work Lives

Drug users' work opportunities were limited. Male drug users usually worked as labourers, loggers, and truck drivers.[79] Few had the education to do much else, as many dropped out in the early years of high school, and a significant portion left before completing elementary school. Moreover, drug users often had poor employment records, partly because they spent much of their time in prison, partly because they needed more money than legitimate work could provide, and partly because they faced job discrimination. A study of fifty-three male drug users at Oakalla Prison Farm in the mid-1950s showed that on average they had been employed for 7.8 years, had spent 4.6 years in prison, and had been unemployed for 3.2 years.[80] However, it is likely that much of their employment took place before they started using drugs, or at a time when they were off narcotics. The physical effects of heroin use do not preclude full-time employment, but the high cost of drugs and the time involved in scoring meant that most steady drug users could not afford to take the types of jobs that were generally open to them.

Still, most drug users worked at some point in their lives. A common pattern in British Columbia was to work in the interior and then return to Vancouver and drug use. For example, the classification officer at British Columbia Penitentiary reported that Eddie T. was 'usually employed as a kitchen hand in labouring and logging camps in and around Prince Rupert, Prince George, and Quesnel. When the bank roll is heavy he returns to haunts of the drug addict and uses the effect of drugs to alleviate his tensions, trials and tribulations.'[81] He used for decades. More unusually, a few drug users acquired other skills. Richard T. began using drugs at age seventeen, but worked as a logger, labourer, and union activist for almost seven years. At twenty-six years of age, he completed his high school diploma and entered the University of British Columbia.[82] Another user, Rick H., studied law for two years in the United States in the 1940s, and frequently represented other inmates. When released from Oakalla in 1960, he did occasional work for two Vancouver lawyers.[83]

Although labouring jobs were plentiful in the resource industries of post-war British Columbia, employers were often reluctant to hire former prisoners, especially drug users. In the fall of 1952, Ryan K. and another male drug user paid union fees to work at the Alcan aluminum smelter at Kitimat, but when the doctor noticed the needle marks on their arms, they were not allowed to start work.[84] Some police officers also deliberately hounded drug users. Gene F. testified that he had been released from jail in the summer of 1959 and gone to work in a logging camp on Queen Charlotte Island. About a month before the job was finished, the RCMP arrived on a complaint that Gene F. was using drugs and took him from the camp and placed him in jail for a twenty-four hour medical observation. The doctor could not say whether or not he was using drugs, and Gene was released, but he lost his job.[85]

There were also users who worked even while using, a pattern that was more common outside the large centres of drug use. Charles D. started using in 1939, and in 1942 he was working as a beer agent, supplying bootleg joints in southern Ontario with beer, and reputedly doing some peddling on the side. In 1947 he was reported to be a truck driver with two trucks. In 1952 he was operating a taxi. In 1958 he was unemployed, but told police that he made some money from bootlegging. His habit seems to have been fairly controlled. He told police, 'I am on heroin but I don't think I am really hooked. The amount I take varies with the amount of money I have.' Charles D. had not had a conviction in six years, and there may well have been more users like him who managed to avoid contact with narcotic officials.[86]

A labourer in British Columbia or Ontario could expect to make $65–$70 per week in the late 1950s, which meant that a $5 capsule of heroin was a very expensive proposition.[87] Drug users in the larger centres usually 'hustled' to make or sometimes supplement their living. Hustling included prostitution, theft, breaking and entering, shoplifting, and a variety of other illegal activities.

Nearly all female users worked as prostitutes at one time or another. Of ninety-eight female drug users studied at Oakalla, only two women told investigators that they had never engaged in prostitution, while thirty-six of seventy-seven said that they had started prostitution before they began using drugs.[88] The anecdotal evidence suggests that some women were quite successful at it. One sixteen-year-old girl told social workers that she worked as a call girl and was always contacted by phone. She claimed that she never fixed with others and had the drugs brought directly to her room. Her story was backed up by the fact that she had $150 to pay for a lawyer and an additional $190 in cash.[89] A John Howard Society worker wrote about another woman, Rachel B., that she had been 'operating rather prosperously for several years as a prostitute and a drug trafficker as well as an addict. She had her own car, an attractive apartment and a physically pleasant environment, one of the elements of which had been a plentiful supply of money and of the things it provides.'[90] In Toronto, female drug users who worked the 'tenderloin' district (Jarvis and Dundas), could expect to make $10 a trick in the late 1950s. Working the tenderloin was the lowest form of prostitution in the city; call girls undoubtedly made much more.[91] Many female sex workers raised money for their male partners as well as themselves, although a matron at Oakalla wrote that 'the "old man" who is able and willing to support himself and does not expect his wife to "work" for him is highly prized.'[92] Although it could be very lucrative, most women expressed a strong hatred of prostitution and preferred other methods of raising money for drugs. One woman told social workers that she lived with a drug trafficker so that she would not have to work as a prostitute as much as other female drug users.[93]

Many women blamed prostitution for their drug use. As one inmate explained to an Oakalla matron, 'when I get out of gaol I have no money and no place to go if I want to go straight and stay off drugs. The only way I know of in which I can make the money I need to get a start in life is to prostitute. I hate prostituting, so I take a "chippy fix" to keep from hating myself too badly, and then I'm off on drugs again.'[94] Anna W., another Oakalla inmate, told a John Howard Society worker, 'you know what a girl does when she has no money and no job ... I had to live, so I became a prostitute and that leads to dope – that has been the story for the last four or five years – and always only to get in here!'[95]

Few male drug users admitted to prostitution, but records catch glimpses of it. Richard T. told a British Columbia Penitentiary psychiatrist that he had engaged in two acts of 'passive fellatio' when he first started using drugs, for which he was paid $5.[96] John Turvey said that he turned quite a few male tricks when he was using drugs in the late 1950s and early 1960s.[97]

In his ethnographic study of American heroin users in the 1980s, Charles Faupel discovered that most drug users had a 'main hustle' that they were very good at.[98] Many Canadian drug users had criminal records that revealed patterns of breaking and entering or shoplifting, but it is hard to know if these represented their 'main hustles' or not. Faupel found that drug users were usually arrested for crimes other than their 'main hustle,' since they were highly skilled at their main crime. Nonetheless, prison and social work reports occasionally mention that someone was well known for a certain type of crime. Russell M., for example, was a noted pimp. The British Columbia Penitentiary classification assistant noted, 'rumor has it that he treats them pretty rough,' and in 1951 his wife pled for a two-year sentence for herself so that she could go to Kingston Penitentiary rather than Oakalla – perhaps to get away from him.[99] In another case, British Columbia Penitentiary officials noted that Victor C. 'implies that he followed his previous pattern of obtaining merchandise from local stores by means of "no account" cheques and selling the merchandise for whatever he could get.' Victor C. had served nine jail terms and six penitentiary terms, mostly for false pretences.[100] Chuck G., a musician who repeatedly failed to stop using and eventually faced a habitual criminal charge apparently had no hustle. His John Howard Society worker learned from other addicts that 'he is probably the most incapable of all addicts in regard to hustling to get money to support his habit. Short of pushing, he is not able to do anything about it at all.'[101]

Edward Preble and John Casey's 1969 article about heroin users in New York City, entitled 'Taking Care of Business,' asserted that heroin use was only a small fraction of drug users' daily lives; 'the rest of the time they are aggressively pursuing a career that is exacting, challenging, adventurous and rewarding.'[102] The article spawned a large ethnographic literature that emphasized drug users' adaptability, skills, and talents.[103] While this literature painted a rosy view of drug users' lives, and ignored the social structures or the suffering that often lay behind substance use, it did correctly point out that drug users were active, busy people. They needed to be hard-working in order to continue using. However, whether they worked in prostitution, crime, or physically demanding manual labour, the hardships of their working lives often contributed to their drug use.

Health

The trying lifestyle of the drug user did little to heal the emotional or physical scars of people who had often had a difficult youth. Some users became seriously disturbed, and self-violence was not unusual. One twenty-seven-year-old drug user came to see a John Howard Society worker after she slashed herself below her elbow. She told the worker that she had four children, her first born when she was fourteen years of age, that she hated her husband, and that she couldn't remember bearing three of her four children. She had frequent blackouts and apparently abused at least one of her children.[104]

Another user, Ruth K., grew up in a very religious family in small-town Alberta but ran away to Vancouver as a teenager. She reportedly slept in the railway station for several days and was gang-raped. She left Vancouver for Edmonton, where she participated in a violent robbery, was charged with attempted murder, and was incarcerated while awaiting trial. She was transferred to the Oliver Mental Institute, and a psychiatrist there helped her beat the charge. When she returned home, she felt rejected by her parents and fell in with a male drug user who was kicking his habit; she moved to Vancouver to be with him. She eventually landed in Oakalla for drug offences, but matrons believed that she was suffering from a serious mental disorder. Tests at the provincial mental hospital at Essondale revealed serious damage to her brain, and the matrons reported that she was given to violent spells, during which she ripped her sheets and went into temper tantrums. As a result, she had been placed in the 'hole' on several occasions, and when she refused to cooperate with the prison psychiatrist, he decided to have nothing to do with her. Less than a month later, she slashed her wrists but did not succeed in killing herself.[105]

John Z. also attempted suicide. He told the John Howard Society social worker that 'he can't stand being locked in, can't sleep, nightmares and intends to commit suicide. Showed wrist scars of last attempt.' Four days later the social worker reported that John Z. was 'perched on a Bible on a very hot radiator, shivering and crying.' He tried to commit suicide again several weeks later.[106]

Overdose was not a common cause of death in this time period, probably because the drugs were fairly dilute, although it did happen. The city pathologist in Vancouver recalled five overdose deaths in the years from 1950 to 1955, and the John Howard Society files occasionally made mention of an overdose death.[107] Most overdoses were not fatal, but their effects could be frightening, as Vickie A. noted when she told a social worker that her husband had passed out from an overdose soon after they both started using.[108] Sonia L., age nineteen, suffered from a much more serious overdose in February 1960. She told her social worker that she was in a coma for four days; her toes had become paralyzed, and she had had three operations on her leg to straighten them out.[109]

Overdose was not the only risk. Dirt at the site of injection left many users with permanent tattoo marks over their favourite veins, and many also had thrombosed veins from years of repeated use. They also had health problems associated with street life. The vast majority of users studied by Stevenson had serious dental problems, and 81 per cent of female users and 58 per cent of male users admitted to having had venereal disease, usually gonorrhea. They also had very high rates of tuberculosis, compared to other prisoners and to the population at large.[110] Many users died young.[111]

In addition to health problems, they also experienced considerable violence, much of which was police-initiated (see chapter 4), but not all of it. Peddlers sometimes faced dangers from their suppliers, and serious accidents and assaults were not uncommon. In 1957 someone called police for assistance when they saw John F. walking down Pender Street with a serious wound to the top of his head.[112] The police report does not indicate how he was injured, but while the police were looking at his wound, a silver-wrapped capsule fell out of his mouth, and the police arrested him for possession. John Howard Society files indicate that female drug users frequently experienced violence in their relationships. An Elizabeth Fry worker in Kingston informed a John Howard Society worker that Lila was scared of her husband, and 'she hated him for his beatings and quarrelling.'[113] In 1954 Rita S.'s husband served a three-month sentence for beating her up.[114]

As drug users grew older, many of them got tired of 'hustling,' of the constant search for drugs, and of the multiple prison sentences. Some quit using drugs altogether, while others switched to alcohol, which at least stopped the constant police harassment and long jail terms, though down-and-out alcoholics frequently served short terms for being intoxicated in a public place. But a few users kept on using into their old age.

One couple, Brad and Pauline M. (he was born in 1906; her birth date is unknown) started using drugs in the 1930s. In 1947 Brad hurt his knee while working as a logger, and twelve years later he still needed crutches or a wheelchair to get around, making logging or labouring impossible. By the late 1950s, neither was using steadily, and they were both experiencing serious health problems. In 1960 Pauline served thirty days in Oakalla for prostitution – according to the social worker, Pauline was 'terribly embarrassed' and 'ashamed,' and explained that she 'had never been unfaithful to Brad while he was on the street at any time.' She had a niece on staff at Oakalla in the Women's Unit and found this very embarrassing, as well as being ashamed about the fact that she was a grandmother and was still prostituting. She weighed only eighty-three pounds when she entered Oakalla.

When the social worker visited Pauline at home two months later, she found her 'in a dingy little room and really quite ill.' Pauline admitted that she was using, and claimed that the police were hounding her. She wanted to stop using, but the Narcotic Addiction Foundation of British Columbia felt that she was too weak to undergo withdrawal. Several months later, when Brad appeared in the John Howard Society offices to see about his social assistance cheque, he told them that Pauline was quite ill and seemed to be suffering from epilepsy. Brad came in again around Christmas after walking out of the Emergency Ward of the Vancouver General Hospital. His social worker reported that 'his hands and lower limbs were very badly swollen' and he 'was somewhat jaundiced.' In 1964 Pauline had an operation on her brain and consequently suffered memory lapses and confusion. She was sentenced to fifteen months in Oakalla on a narcotics charge later that year.[115]

This is not to suggest that all drug users who injected experienced critical health problems. Fred S. started using in 1911 at seventeen years of age and apparently was still in good health in the early 1960s. A British Columbia Penitentiary readmission report in 1963 noted that 'it was obvious that old age had not yet attacked his mind for he spoke very intelligently. The man expressed some degree of concern about his drug problem and even volunteered to offer information which he thought might assist in eradicating the problem as a whole.'[116] Nevertheless, for many long-time drug users, the combination of poverty, adulterated drugs, unclean needles, and violence all contributed to a variety of physical and mental health problems. In some tragic cases, this led to suicide, but for others the pain of illness undoubtedly led to renewed substance use. Heroin is, after all, one of the greatest painkillers known.

Quitting Drugs

The hard life of a drug user meant that after a few years 'in the life,' many people were anxious to quit using. Nearly all drug users quit occasionally. Of one hundred consecutively convicted drug users at Oakalla, only twenty-five had never quit voluntarily, while forty-three had stopped using voluntarily on three different occasions.[117] All hundred reported that they had stopped using while in prison, although incarcerated drug users were unlikely to tell prison researchers that they were still using.[118] Nonetheless, the evidence suggests that only well-placed drug users with trafficking or other connections could keep up a habit while incarcerated.[119] Drugs were extremely expensive, sentences were long, and wages in prison were low. People took drugs in prison, but it was fairly sporadic.

People expressed to social workers and doctors a variety of reasons for quitting – the reasons that they gave to friends, families, or themselves, may have been different. Thirty-two (46 per cent) of the consecutively convicted drug users in the Oakalla Prison Farm study indicated that they quit because they were '"fed up" with drug addict life and wished to live a normal life,' twelve (17 per cent) quit to take up regular employment, and eleven (16 per cent) quit because of fear of the police and imprisonment.[120] Malcolm N. Brandon, head of the narcotic addiction treatment unit in Oakalla, wrote that most drug users wanted to quit so that they would stop landing in jail: 'It seems very difficult to convince them that there should be other reasons for abstaining.'[121] The John Howard Society files indicated complex reasons for quitting. In a letter to his social worker, Rick H. explained that he had gone to Victoria to 'straighten myself out with both my family and my own mind.'[122] Another woman complained (perhaps for the benefit of the social worker) that 'taking drugs or alcohol doesn't really solve problems, you still have your depression left, only after taking drugs you are left with a feeling of guilt which makes your problems worse.'[123] According to his John Howard Society worker, Arnold T.'s main motivation for quitting in 1963 was his fear that he would be 'habitched' (charged with being a habitual offender).[124]

Quitting often involved getting away from Vancouver, or other major urban centres, and forming relationships with non–drug users. A common catalyst for starting again was losing a job or ending a relationship, or even more importantly, returning to Vancouver where drugs were readily available. Edward L., of Vancouver, began using drugs in the early 1950s but regularly worked outside of the city, and he stopped using when he was out of town. He told his John Howard Society worker, 'I didn't have it and I didn't think about it.' After serving two jail terms, he decided to stop using. He ended his relationship with his wife, who had refused to quit, and began living with another woman who did not use drugs. He found a job and apparently stopped using until 1958, when he was once again sent to Oakalla on a drug offence. Upon release, he found work as a logger, and during his contact with the John Howard Society through the early 1960s, there is no indication that he went back on drugs.[125]

Very few drug users received any sort of specific help with quitting.[126] There was an attempt (by non-users) to establish a Narcotics Anonymous in Vancouver in the mid-1950s, and the Narcotic Addiction Foundation of British Columbia began providing some aid in 1958, but users had to rely primarily on their own resources. In Montreal, two female former addicts established a Narcotics Anonymous that ran for two years in the 1950s. They met once a week at Loyola College and established a branch group at the Mimico prison, which had opened a treatment program in 1956.[127]

Most users quit on their own, using a variety of methods. Some went cold turkey, others used barbiturates, methadone, or alcohol to help themselves through the withdrawal, others put themselves on a gradual reduction program, and some were admitted to hospital, although in BC the hospital insurance did not cover withdrawal.[128] A few users voluntarily committed themselves to prison for the purpose of quitting, but this was rare.[129]

Drug users often had poor work histories, low levels of skill and education, weak relationships with people outside the drug-using community, and serious emotional problems. Many drug users found it difficult to quit because drugs gave them considerable pleasure and allowed them to forget, if only briefly, their other problems. But it was not the love of drug use alone that made it difficult to quit. Drug users feared isolation. The same desire to be part of a group that led many into drug use in the first place made it extremely difficult to leave that world. Few drug users had much contact with square johns, and they frequently told social workers that they felt uncomfortable around people who did not use. Ben Maartman, the parole officer for the Special Narcotic Addiction Project (SNAP),[130] which was the first parole program designed specifically for drug users, wrote about his favourite parolee:

> The idea of living with squarejohns was too much [for him] – as it was with most of the snappers ... Be that as it may the only way I have ever known a heroin addict leaving his drugs behind is by forming a meaningful relationship in the squarejohn world – particularly with a person of the opposite sex. With old time addicts this is the nub of the problem. It wasn't until I met Benny and the rest of the snappers that it sank into me just what a tremendous problem this was. Despite my previous correctional jobs, for the first time I was beginning to comprehend what it means to be a member of the addict world. It automatically makes all other strata of society as alien as a village in Outer Mongolia. Benny, like most of the snappers, was convinced that he was so different from the squarejohn world that he could never fit into it and be accepted by it. Heroin was nothing compared with this problem. The drug was merely the way out from worrying about it.[131]

Drug users continued to use because their friends used. The busy life of the drug user gave them a focus and a community. Stopping drug use was as much about leaving behind a way of life and friends, as it was about withdrawing from drugs and their effects.

Some users tried to replace heroin with alcohol and prescription drugs, with varying degrees of success. Michael P. told British Columbia Penitentiary officials that he stopped using drugs in the early part of 1962 but turned to drinking 'and found it much more debilitating.'[132] Ron S. alternated between drink and drugs and had served numerous one-week terms for being intoxicated in a public place, as well as several terms for drugs. He found that 'drink makes him ill' and preferred drugs.[133] Others made the switch more successfully: Alan R. used drugs in the mid-1940s, but did not appear in the records of the Division of Narcotic Control again until 1966, when they reported that he had advanced cirrhosis of the liver – a disease usually caused by alcohol consumption.[134] Ben Maartman reported that thirteen of the sixteen SNAP parolees, who were subjected to drug tests to ensure that they were not using heroin, became 'serious problem drinkers, if not out and out alcoholics.'[135]

Conclusion

Too often, drug use is seen as a problem that resides in individual pathology and inadequacy. Many studies, though by no means all, ignore the social and economic factors behind drug use and do not see drug users within the context of their community and relationships. This chapter has shown that the social norms, economic circumstances, and state structures of 1950s Canada gave rise to a distinct culture of drug use.[136] Using heroin allowed marginalized young people to identify with a community that had access to special knowledge and certain risky pleasures. Drug users enjoyed a certain status in penal institutions and had a reputation for standing up to the police. It is not difficult to see why rebellious young people who often already had had experiences with police and institutional life could find the drug-using community both exciting and comforting.

At the same time, the legal framework that had been established in the 1920s, and the growth of the police and the state apparatus for controlling the supply of drugs, made the life of a drug user extremely difficult. Being a drug user in post-war Canada meant spending much of one's life cycling in and out of prison, working difficult, low-paying, and sometimes dangerous jobs, and having few opportunities to improve one's lot in life. Family and romantic relationships were constantly disrupted, and few drug users with children were able to care for them themselves. Many drug users suffered from serious health problems, and many died young. Heroin consumption had its pleasures, but its costs were extraordinarily high.

Chapter 4

'After a Short Struggle': Police Officers and Drug Users

The leading role in enforcing Canada's harsh drug laws fell to the police, and they exerted tremendous power over drug users' lives. Other regulators, including doctors and social workers, were also involved in drug users' lives, as I will discuss later, but drug users often had the option of seeing a doctor or a John Howard Society social worker. They had no choice when it came to police officers who raided their homes and assaulted them on the streets. From the early 1920s to the early 1960s, the number of police increased enormously relative to the number of users, and they became increasingly sophisticated in their techniques. This chapter explores the impact of policing on one of the most disadvantaged groups in Canadian society and contributes to contemporary debates about the utility of narcotics policing. It also contributes to the small body of scholarship on the social history of policing, especially drug enforcement.[1]

Narcotics policing was higher status than most police work, and it attracted many articulate and upwardly mobile officers. The most important police organization involved in narcotics work was the highly regarded Royal Canadian Mounted Police (RCMP), which was created from a merger of the Dominion Police and the Royal North West Mounted Police in 1920. Narcotics policing became one of its key tasks.[2] The RCMP worked in close cooperation with other police forces (some of which also had dedicated drug squads), with the Division of Narcotic Control, and with specially appointed narcotics prosecutors to ensure a high rate of conviction for narcotics offenders. They also played an important role in advising on drug policy. In the 1950s, RCMP officials were involved in top-level policy discussions about treatment in the Department of National Health and Welfare. Drug bureaucrats and the media acknowledged the police as the leading authorities on drug use and drug users, and the police played a key role in disseminating information about drug use. They were also responsible for ensuring that drug users were arrested and convicted.

Policing deeply affected the way that drug users interacted with one another, forcing them to be cautious and suspicious of their peers. It created certain secret rituals of drug use and contributed to the stress, danger, and violence of users' lives. Since police officers wanted to control physical consumption of the drug, they often used invasive and violent techniques to search drug users' bodies. Police also played a role in creating the image of drug users, and to a much lesser extent their identities, by constantly seeking and compiling information about their lives and activities, information that then circulated to the media, social workers, and politicians, as well as to curious non-users. However, police were not infallible. In the 1920s they often bumbled in their enforcement efforts. And drug users were not passive victims – many fought back against arrest and invented new ways to hide their drug use.

Like gambling, prostitution, sodomy, and other so-called 'vice crimes,' narcotics offences have no victim, unless one counts drug users themselves. Except in rare circumstances, police have to rely on strategies other than obtaining information from the victim. As Peter Manning pointed out in his book *The Narc's Game*, vice officers must '"make crime happen" or construct circumstances in which evidence can be obtained.'[3] In Canada, from 1920 to 1961, this meant carefully surveying drug users, engaging informants, going undercover, and employing violence.

Recent literature on present-day policing has emphasized the role of police in compiling and relaying information about crime.[4] The police also played a critical role in information management in the middle of the century. The RCMP wrote detailed reports on every narcotics arrest and sent copies to the Narcotic Division (later the Division of Narcotic Control), and they were entered in the case files of users. Prosecutors (who were appointed by the division, and who specialized in narcotics cases) relied heavily on these police reports during trials, and the police depended on them in giving testimony. The division considered police officers to be the most knowledgeable source of information about drug users, and they were disparaging of others, such as the Vancouver Community Chest and Council, which purported to have an alternative knowledge about users and their habits. The police also supplied stories on drug use and drug policing to journalists and politicians, playing a critical role in constructing the 'image' of the drug user.

There is a small body of literature on the successes and failures of present-day narcotic policing, and I have drawn on this scholarship in evaluating the successes and failures of drug enforcement in Canada.[5] Most studies emphasize that enforcement, whether aimed at the higher-level trafficker or at the street peddler and user, is only effective for a short period of time. Captured high-level traffickers are quickly replaced by others and, as Mark Kleiman and Kerry Smith point out, busting a highly organized monopoly might even serve in the long run to lower prices, as the cartel is replaced by more open competition.[6] Another insight coming out of these studies is that effective street enforcement often moves drug use out of one community and into another.[7] Moreover, while street-level enforcement can increase the price of drugs, the relatively inelastic demand for drugs means that the increased price can result in more crime by users as they struggle to obtain enough money to make their purchases.[8] It can also result in greater profits for traffickers. Finally, these studies show that there is a tremendous temptation for corruption in narcotics policing. Police can turn a blind eye to offences if they so chose, making bribes an attractive option for violators of the law. Police can also easily plant drugs on known traffickers or users. Moreover, undercover operations often involve participating in or even initiating criminal activities, including the very activities the police are supposed to suppress.

The Structure of Drug Enforcement

Although Canada's first drug law was passed in 1908, drug enforcement was not the responsibility of any federal department until 1920, when the Department of Health took charge of the act. When the Dominion Police and the Royal North West Mounted Police were merged to create the Royal Canadian Mounted Police that same year, this new force assumed responsibility for enforcing federal statutes, including the Opium and Narcotic Drug Act, and the RCMP organized its first drug squad. During the 1920s, the RCMP asserted that they were primarily interested in pursuing the higher-ups and would leave the street peddlers and addicts to municipal and provincial police forces, but in fact they regularly raided Chinese opium joints and arrested smokers.[9] Other police forces continued to play a large role, though. In 1928, provincial and municipal police forces made 72 per cent of convictions under the act. But by 1940, provincial and municipal convictions accounted for only

29 per cent of all drug convictions, and by the 1950s, the RCMP were involved in virtually all arrests under the act.[10]

Various factors explain the increased involvement of the RCMP. First of all, rivalry between the various enforcement units in the early 1920s led to some scandals and to working at cross-purposes. Narcotics officials were keen to have greater cooperation, and because the two chiefs of the Narcotic Division from 1927 to 1959 were former RCMP officers, they favoured strong connections with the RCMP.[11] Second, during the Great Depression, municipal police forces decreased in size, while the RCMP, having entered into contracts to carry out provincial policing for the Maritime and Prairie provinces, continued to grow. Third, and probably most importantly, in 1929 the Opium and Narcotic Drug Act gave a new and extremely valuable power to the RCMP in the form of writs of assistance, which were permanent search warrants given to 'carefully selected RCMP officers' across the country. They allowed the RCMP officers (and any other accompanying police officers) to search any-where at any time, provided the officer had grounds to believe that narcotics were on the premises. The writ of assistance was not entirely unprecedented; there were similar provisions in the Customs Act. More-over, since 1922 the Opium and Narcotic Drug Act had given the police the right to search places other than a dwelling house without a warrant and, since 1925, the right to search people without a warrant, but the writ of assistance still gave the RCMP considerable power over other police forces.[12] As a result, narcotic raids increasingly involved coopera-tion between city police forces and at least one RCMP officer who held a writ of assistance.[13]

From the 1930s onwards, there was close cooperation between the RCMP and other police forces. In Vancouver, members of the city police worked out of the RCMP offices and vice versa. In Montreal in the 1950s, police did not pick up any drug users or peddlers on the street until they had contacted the RCMP, so that they would not ruin any case the RCMP was working on.[14] In Toronto in the 1950s, all drug arrests were made in cooperation with the RCMP.[15] Close communication between the RCMP and the Division of Narcotic Control allowed for the exchange of infor-mation about users across the country, and new drug-selling or drug-using practices in one place were quickly communicated to officers in other regions, increasing the intensity and effectiveness of enforcement.

Narcotics enforcement was a mixed blessing for the RCMP. On the one hand, the force had come close to being abolished in the early

1920s, and the important task of enforcing Canada's drug laws gave them an additional raison d'être.[16] On the other hand, the gritty work of narcotics enforcement clashed with the carefully constructed image of the upright and manly mounted police officer.[17] In 1922, the commissioner complained that the work was 'repulsive ... entailing as it does contact with peculiarly loathsome dregs of humanity; our men greatly dislike it and it is undertaken only in accordance with duty, and because of the knowledge that while unpleasant it is a service to humanity.'[18] Such queasiness about narcotics policing can also be seen in the RCMP annual reports, which regularly highlighted northern patrols over narcotics enforcement.

There may have been some corruption in narcotics policing in the 1920s. Certainly, it took the RCMP some time to develop standard and professional procedures in policing the narcotic drug trade. In Montreal and Vancouver, the two largest centres of the trade in the early 1920s, the RCMP were accused of irregularities in their policing practices. In 1922 the Department of Health strongly urged the force in Montreal to investigate the activities of its own officers who, it was rumoured, were accepting bribe money from traffickers.[19] In British Columbia, drug squad operations were suspended in August 1923 after several members of the drug squad were arrested and charged with possession of opium. A formal Commission of Inquiry established by Ottawa fully exonerated the police, but the commission nonetheless revealed that, at the very least, the police needed to do much more to ensure that their officers did not succumb to temptation.[20] The Narcotic Division believed that the allegations of corruption, at least in British Columbia, stemmed partly from rivalry among different police forces over the enforcement of the act.[21] By the mid-1920s, allegations of corruption had ceased and never arose again in the time period under study, although this does not mean that corruption did not exist.

Probably the most important change in the nature of policing between 1920 and 1961 was its intensity. In the early 1920s, arrests were high partly because it was easy to raid opium dens and arrest large numbers of people, not because policing was intensively focused on individuals. Individual drug users could escape detection for long periods of time. By the 1950s, however, when virtually all policing was being done with the cooperation of the RCMP, the police knew the addicts and the addicts knew the police. There were a few minor exceptions – those who obtained their supply from doctors, a few wealthy people who were able to buy drugs with great discretion, and some users in rural areas where policing was less intensive – but these were rare.[22] In his testimony to the Senate Committee on the Traffic in Narcotic Drugs in 1955, Vancouver's police chief, Walter Mulligan, was asked if he thought that the Vancouver police knew the 'full number of suspected addicts':

> Mr. Mulligan: Oh, yes, on account of surveillance, you are bound to see them moving around.
> Senator Hodges: Yes, but they might move in circles not known to the police necessarily. I am not talking of the criminal addicts or suspected addicts, but do you think there are a number that have not yet been suspected?
> Mr. Mulligan: No, I would say that shortly after the arrival of such a person in Vancouver he would be noticed very quickly.[23]

In Vancouver from 1955 to 1961 there were thirty-four full-time narcotics officers to police what were likely fewer than 1500 addicts, about a third of whom were incarcerated at any given time.[24] The same situation prevailed in other cities. In 1955 the Montreal drug squad of the RCMP had eight members policing the estimated 337 criminal and professional addicts in all of Quebec.[25]

As drug policing grew much more intensive and came under the control of the RCMP, it also became considerably more professional. The actual techniques of enforcement – surveillance and raids, the use of informants, undercover work, and the policing of individual bodies remained the same from 1920 through 1961, but the police became far more adept at them. At the same time, users improved their techniques of concealment. However, given the number of police officers relative to users in the period after the Second World War, it was largely a losing battle for the users, who were regularly caught and incarcerated.

Training

Between 1920 and 1961, police in Canada received very little education or training. Municipal police forces generally received some drill and physical exercise; according to historian Greg Marquis, the 'unwritten rule' was that 'the policeman learned on the beat.'[26] The more prestigious RCMP was slightly more advanced. T.E.E. Greenfield remembered receiving four months of training in the mid-1920s, including lectures on the 'criminal code, federal statutes, the police manual and the history of the force.' This was interspersed with physical training, especially equitation.[27] R.S.S. Wilson, who later became head of the Vancouver

Drug Squad, recalled that his training consisted primarily of riding and foot drill 'rounded out by a goodly measure of fatigues coupled with strict discipline.' 'The general idea prevailing in the Force,' he added, 'was that the only way one could learn anything about police work was by getting out of the Depot and doing it.'[28] As far as narcotics policing was concerned, this view started to change in 1929, when the RCMP introduced a Narcotic Drug Training class in Vancouver.[29] The course involved practical work, such as 'raiding opium joints, keeping observation on suspected premises, trailing drug addicts and peddlers,' and lectures by the head of the Criminal Investigation Branch in British Columbia.[30] The first class had eight students. By the mid-1930s, the RCMP had upped its educational requirements for admission, and the general training course had been increased to six months.[31]

Even the longer course did not allow time for specialized teaching in matters such as checking narcotics records. Since the 1920s, the RCMP had been in charge of inspecting drugstore records to ensure that there were no irregularities in dispensing, and in the mid-1930s the Narcotic Division was alarmed by police errors in checking these records. In one case, a police report had led the division to conclude that a doctor was prescribing too much cocaine, but in fact the amount was small, and the Narcotic Division was forced to send a letter of apology.[32] In another case, the RCMP had inspected a drugstore six times without noticing that the stores had not been keeping a narcotics register as required by law.[33] In 1947 the Narcotic Division established instructional classes in the inspection of narcotics records.[34]

While the RCMP increased its training over time, city police force training remained slack. In 1956 the Vancouver City Police implemented its first three-month training course, reporting that a 'dangerously large percentage of members of the Force, some with as much as ten years of service, had had no formal training whatsoever.'[35] The Metro Toronto Police inaugurated their Police College in 1959. The nine-week course included academic studies and training in armed combat and in the proper handling of weapons.[36]

Nonetheless, it is clear that police officers did learn a great deal on the job. By the 1930s, RCMP techniques were fairly standard across the country, and experienced narcotics officers knew what they needed to do to obtain a conviction. RCMP officers were regularly transferred, which meant that they shared information and standardized techniques. They also often recognized drug users from other cities and could share information with their new colleagues about drug users and drug-using practices in different locales.

Discrimination

Class, race, and gender played an important role in determining whom the police targeted for enforcement. In the 1920s, much enforcement activity was centred on the Chinese – in their homes, workplaces, and opium dens. Chinese drug users were often charged with opium smoking, or with being found in an opium joint. Such charges raised revenue for police forces (as they kept part of the fine), and they were subject to less scrutiny in the courtroom, because the penalties were small. At the opposite end of the spectrum, middle- and upper-class whites were treated much more leniently. Addicted doctors rarely faced prosecution. Nurses fell somewhere in-between, depending on their 'respectability' and their persistence in obtaining narcotic drugs.

Connections, youth, and gender could also make a difference. In 1941 a twenty-year-old woman was arrested with a well-known drug user who was known to be a pimp. The head of the Vancouver Drug Squad knew the young woman's family and reported that they were 'of unquestionable character and reliable citizens.' He spoke to the father, who promised full cooperation in rehabilitating his daughter. Despite the fact that she had been using drugs for almost a year, the judge took pity on her and dismissed the charge.[37] Most drug users who interacted with police officers were working-class men and women who had had previous encounters with police. Anyone who did not fit this stereotype was given extra chances and consideration by police.

Surveillance and Raids

In the early years, one of the most popular enforcement techniques was raiding Chinese residences to search for opium. From June 1921 to May 1922 the RCMP made fourteen raids on what they described as Chinese 'headquarters' at the Fraser Mills in British Columbia, resulting in twenty-eight arrests.[38] Former RCMP Commissioner C.W. Harvison recalled that in the early 1920s, when he participated in narcotics work, the police were able to make large numbers of arrests at raids. The Chinese responded by posting lookouts, barring doors, and requiring smokers to pick up their 'decks' at other locations.[39] Nonetheless, the constant police presence made it more difficult for the opium dens to operate. Similar techniques were used against white sellers and users of drugs. In 1922 the commanding officer in Montreal reported that he simply posted informers or spotters in locales where peddling was taking place. Of course, peddlers responded by moving to another location, but he

believed that they were cutting down on the trade by making the peddlers' job more difficult.[40]

The policy of frequent raids worked only for a short period of time, as
demonstrated by the drop in arrests in the mid-1920s. As drug users
became more cautious, police found it difficult to learn where drugs
were being sold and to arrest drug users in large groups. They rarely
made large numbers of arrests in single raids after this time. Moreover,
police harassment probably did decrease the number of users by mid-
decade. Just as prohibition appears to have decreased drinking in the
United States, drug enforcement probably stopped a number of casual
users from using, as they were unwilling to go to jail for their drug of
choice.[41] This left a core of users whose decision to use was not significantly affected by drug law enforcement.

By the late 1920s, surveillance and raids were painstaking, time-consuming work. In Vancouver's Downtown Eastside, narcotics enforcement
from 1939 onward focused on the residential hotels where most drug
users lived, inspecting them for drugs and paraphernalia, and then
waiting for people to return to make arrests.[42] For example, in October
1957 the police were searching the bathroom of a residential hotel when
they found a capsule secreted above the ladies' toilet. They took a
sample of the capsule and they watched the bathroom for two and a half
hours until Daniel F. went to the toilet. After he left, they checked the
spot and found the capsule missing; one officer forced the door of
Daniel F.'s room while the other kept watch on his window.[43] It worked
exactly as planned – Daniel F.'s companion threw an eyedropper and
spoon out the window, while the officer who had forced the door located
a piece of silver paper that had been used to wrap the capsule. The
exhibits tested positive for heroin, and Daniel was convicted of possession and sentenced to fifteen months. Such cases took considerable
persistence and long hours on the part of police officers, but they were
extremely successful at yielding convictions.

Another common technique was to follow drug users from popular
drug-buying locations. In 1956, three Vancouver City Police officers saw.
four known users in front of the New Zenith Café (a well-known drug
centre) and followed them to their hotel. Two officers forced the door.
They seized one of the men and found a capsule of heroin in his hand.[44]

Police often kept observation on individual rooms through the transoms. In 1960 the police learned that Betty M. lived in an apartment on
Bay Street in Toronto and that she kept her 'works' in a washroom
on the same floor. They watched her pick up her works and then spied

on her through the transom of her door. When they saw her preparing her injection, they forced the door. She was sentenced to six months for possession.[45]

They occasionally kept observation from inside the room itself. In 1961 the police followed Sally H. and another woman to a Sherbourne Street hotel in Toronto. When the women left the hotel, one of the officers hid in their closet for two hours. When she arrived home, Sally H. checked the closet. Seeing the officer, she attempted to get rid of the eyedropper and hypodermic needle. The two women were arrested, and Sally H. was sentenced to two years.[46]

Bar owners and other local business people helped police with their surveillance by providing them with space, and one bar owner even redecorated to make it easier for the police to make their observations. The owner of the Broadway Hotel Beer Parlour told *Maclean's* in 1958 that he had taken down heavy drapes and created a secret entrance to help out the police.[47] Rooming house operators also regularly assisted by providing passkeys and allowing police access to adjoining rooms for observation.

Police also regularly checked addicts on the street and kept detailed reports of the cars they were driving, how much money they had where, with whom they were living, and their future plans for employment and travel. In Vancouver it was not uncommon for addicts to be checked several times over the course of a month.[48]

Police also maintained observation from above the corner of Hastings and Main. In a 1960 case, police learned that Horace A. was selling drugs from Victoria Square, a memorial park a few blocks from Hastings and Main. Police stationed in nearby buildings kept an eye on him with binoculars and maintained telephone contact. Several times that afternoon, police saw Horace A. remove a green object from his mouth, take something from it, and hand it to someone else. In return, customers handed him a $5 bill. Later, Horace A. wrapped the green object in a maple leaf and threw it on the ground. The police seized him in the park later that afternoon and found the green bundle, which contained seven capsules. At his trial, Horace A. was sentenced to five years.[49]

Police made keen use of new technology in their surveillance operations. Photography was in use in Vancouver for crime detection by the late nineteenth century.[50] By the 1940s, the Division of Narcotic Control collected mug shots of every convicted addict in the country. The *RCMP Gazette*, distributed to police forces across the country, occasionally published photos of drug users. When the RCMP suspected Leo B. and his partner Kay B., a registered nurse, of stealing morphine from hospitals and forging cheques, they published their photographs, a description of their modus operandi, and their criminal records in the *RCMP Gazette*. Two weeks later, the St. James, Manitoba, police department reported that a woman had gone to a doctor's office requesting narcotics for a sick patient. The police used the *RCMP Gazette* to verify Kay B.'s identity with the doctor and confirm that she had also passed a cheque at the Hudson's Bay Company.[51]

Police also used film and walkie-talkies. In the early 1950s, the RCMP installed a motion picture camera at a busy intersection in downtown Vancouver, focused on an establishment that was frequented by addicts, and in a week approximately ninety drug users were photographed.[52]

Identification of users was eased with the introduction of fluorescent powder, which was used to dust drugs or money. For example, in June 1957 a Vancouver City Police drug officer discovered a cache of narcotics behind a house, and they dusted it with fluorescent powder. After two hours, they observed two men pick up the cache in a car. The men were taken to Vancouver City Police offices, where their hands and clothing were examined under a fluorescent lamp. Archie W.'s hands and clothing had several spots. The twenty-five-year-old labourer was given two years and six months for possession.[53]

The constant cycle of surveillance and raids added enormously to the stress of drug users' lives. Users who participated in a study at Oakalla Prison Farm in the mid-1950s said that their most common dream concerning drugs had them preparing a fix when the RCMP suddenly broke down the door.[54] They did what they could to minimize the risk: drug users regularly blockaded their doors with furniture, to give them extra time in case of a police raid, and they kept all of their drug-using and selling activities as secret as possible.

In a study on the policing of homosexual activity in Toronto, Steven Maynard stressed that one of the effects of 'police surveillance and the arrest of men, was to bring the subculture of public sex to the attention of a broader public.'[55] Certainly, the policing of drug use led to the growth of knowledge, as the 'evidence' of drug use was produced in police reports, courtrooms, and newspapers. As a result, in 1950s Vancouver most citizens would have known where the drug trade was centred. Although users were often reticent about introducing others into the drug culture, curious people with the appropriate underworld credentials were able to obtain a 'fix.' Moreover, as discussed in chapter 3, the strict enforcement actually made drug use attractive to people who were already involved in an oppositional subculture. In a roundabout way, therefore, surveillance could actually produce deviance.

Informants

A quicker way of making cases was for police to work through informers, who could provide critical information on when and where people would be selling and using.[56] RCMP drug squad veteran Sergeant Fripps told the Chief Constables Association of Canada in 1943, 'You have to use them [stool pigeons]. If you get a good one, he is worth his weight in gold.'[57] Within the drug-using community, informants were strongly condemned, and informers could be ostracized and punished. In 1937, police were developing a case with an informer in Winnipeg when the informer's cover was blown. The police reported that 'everyone on the Main St. about the Central Pool Hall, the Exchange Café and the Stay Pool Hall were calling him a rat and a stool and had threatened to put the boots to him if he continued coming around.'[58] Similarly, John W. helped the police with a big drug bust in 1960; when he was imprisoned fourteen years later, he still had to be placed in protective custody.[59]

Nonetheless, drug users regularly served as informants. Former Vancouver Drug Squad leader R.S.S. Wilson, putting a good face on police activity, reported that 'third-degree measures' were not necessary, as drug users feared 'the physical agony associated with the abrupt withdrawal of the drug' and would 'go to almost any lengths to keep out of jail.'[60] T.E.E. Greenfield, who served on the Toronto Drug Squad in the 1930s and '40s, also remembered that large numbers of addicts acted as police informers.[61] People informed for financial gain or reduced charges or sentences, and were apparently paid well.[62] Offences under the Opium and Narcotic Drug Act were almost always punished with a fine ranging from $50 to $200 (often in addition to a prison sentence.) Half of the fine was not an uncommon payment to informers in the early 1920s.[63] Other informers wanted revenge. In a 1938 case in Edmonton, a woman reported that she had a grudge against a particular peddler and was willing to act as an informant, but she became ill (or so she said), and the police needed another informant to complete the case.[64]

Informers could be unreliable. In later years, the RCMP rarely, if ever, brought informants to the witness stand, but they often attempted to do so in the 1920s, with mixed success. Drug users often promised to make cases and then disappeared. Others were more manipulative. A few weeks after agreeing to act as an informer, Polly M. told police that she would try to have the trafficker deliver the drugs to her room. She called the trafficker, but he was out, so she asked police to drop her off at a party and pick her up two hours later. The trafficker refused to make a delivery later that evening or the next day, and the police gave up, but a few months later they tried to use her to make a case against another woman. After carefully observing her movements, the police decided that Polly D. was 'double-crossing them.'[65]

Just as police refined their techniques of surveillance, they also became more sophisticated in their use of informants. In the early 1920s in British Columbia, the RCMP did not record how much money they gave to informants or keep track of their names – a system that begged for dishonesty.[66] Inexperience and unfamiliarity with the drug trade also led them into some potentially disastrous situations. In 1923 Detective Sergeant Salt, the head of the drug squad in Montreal, met with informer Frank Brown. Brown took him to a tavern where Brown offered two men cocaine at less than the market price. Looking at the bottle, Salt suspected that it was not cocaine, but Brown was so insistent that the two men try it that Salt began to think that there must actually be some cocaine in it. Salt, Brown, and the two men went to have the sample analyzed, but it turned out to be flour. With tempers rising, the four men went for a beer, where they were joined by two men and two women who were 'about 40 years of age, toothless, dirty and only half-clothed.' One of the women propositioned Salt, but he refused to go upstairs with her, incurring her wrath, and one of the men suggested calling in 'Ike and Bill.' Salt 'suddenly formed the opinion that I was not at all anxious to meet "Ike" and "Bill," especially as they would be between me and the door,' and made a rapid exit. Brown went with him, explaining that the location 'was known as a joint where one could get a shot of "C" and "M."' Salt retorted 'that I might get shot very easily there, but did not think that I would be able to do much arresting afterwards, and that in future I would rather he consulted me in detail about his "big" deals instead of playing the rush act.' Brown did not appear in the files again. The fact that they had employed him in the first place, and that they went along with his half-baked scheme for as long as they did, showed how little experience the police had with drug informants in the early 1920s.[67]

In a more sophisticated piece of police work in 1940, police learned from an informer that Wally C. was peddling drugs in Vancouver. The informant made two purchases from Wally C. to obtain the modus operandi, and on 4 March the informant reported that Wally C. would be in the White Lunch Café from noon until 3 p.m. Three police officers kept watch on the café, and at 2:30 p.m. the informant gave a signal, and the police officers arrested Wally C.[68] He was convicted of possession and sentenced to nine months.

Informants could also play a critical role in undercover operations. An undercover case by the Mounties in 1957 relied on the introduction of an informant who told small-scale peddlers that the undercover officer 'was okay.'[69]

The extensive use of informants by the police added to the difficulties of drug users' lives. Drug users who wanted to reduce their prison terms or needed to make money felt considerable pressure to inform on fellow users and peddlers. This undoubtedly contributed to a great deal of mistrust and unease within the addict community. Since drug use is sometimes a response to anxiety, policing may have ironically increased drug use within the community, at least by some individuals. Moreover, the use of informants contributed to the ambiguities and futility of policing narcotics use. People facing possession charges were able to inform on street peddlers who were users themselves, but the chain rarely extended much higher. Thus, police were placed in the situation of protecting one set of users in order to make cases against another set of users, without ever reaching the large traffickers.

Not all informers were drug users. Police occasionally received complaints about drug use from members of the public. The best of these usually came from apartment owners or superintendents. In 1937 the Windsor City Police received a phone call from a landlady who stated that she thought that one of her roomers, Ernest D., had drugs in his possession and would be leaving her house within a few minutes. The RCMP arrived just in time to intercept him. In his bags, police found a small quantity of heroin, a teaspoon, and three hypodermic needles, but Ernest D. escaped before he could be charged.[70]

Doctors and druggists were also a source of information, particularly with regards to robberies and forged prescriptions. In 1941 a Calgary drugstore owner reported a possible forged prescription, and when police presented him with a photograph of Daniel F., he identified him as the man in question. Daniel F. was given six months for possession.[71] Druggists also sometimes warned police when people purchased 'works,' even though the purchase of these items was perfectly legal. In 1947 the manager of a drugstore in Chilliwack telephoned the BC Provincial Police to tell them that a man had just bought an eyedropper and a small vial and had entered the Empress Hotel. The police accosted Barry M.

when he left the hotel and found him in possession of an eyedropper and a hotel key. Upon searching his room, they found eighteen tablets of morphine. In court, he was sentenced to six months.[72]

Some youthful drug users were turned over to police by their parents. In 1960 John Burton found a hypodermic needle and blackened spoon in his seventeen-year-old son's room. He contacted the police and two detectives arrived, woke up the young man, and charged him with possession. He was sentenced to one year.[73] Similarly, in 1961, Bill T., in the hope of getting his stepdaughter some help, told police that he suspected she was an addict. They arrested her and charged her with possession. To Bill T.'s relief, the charge against his stepdaughter was eventually dismissed.[74]

The police often received valuable information from people who were close to drug users, such as family members, and from people who interacted with them on a regular basis, such as landlords, druggists, and doctors. Again, this contributed to the uncertainty and unease of drug users' lives. By constantly searching for information about drug users' lives and activities, the police deprived the users of privacy and autonomy, and promoted distrust even in the users' closest relationships.

Undercover Operations

Undercover operations took a great deal of time and effort but could secure large numbers of arrests. Police work in undercover operations became much more professional by the 1950s. In the early 1920s, individual police officers operated with a great degree of independence. A former RCMP commissioner, C.W. Harvison, began his RCMP career by going undercover in Montreal. He made several purchases before other officers began to observe him in his activities. The Commission of Inquiry into allegations of irregularity in British Columbia revealed that both police officers and special agents operated without being covered by other members of the force, and this, of course, led to the strong possibility of officers engaging in illicit activities. More than one officer went astray. In 1922 Assistant Commissioner Cortlandt Starnes wrote an underling that 'the temptation for men engaged in this work to go wrong is great,' and that the Opium and Narcotic Drug Act has 'been the downfall of several of our promising non-commissioned officers.'[75] By the late 1920s, police were taking more precautions. Ideally, an officer of the RCMP who planned to make a drug purchase would be 'thoroughly searched' before the purchase by another officer to ensure that he had no narcotics in possession before meeting the peddler. The RCMP recorded the serial numbers of the bills and had the undercover officer sign for the money before receiving it. Finally, the buyer would be kept in sight from the time the money was handed to him or her.[76] In practice, however, undercover officers occasionally made purchases without being covered, in order to build trust with a peddler.

Going undercover entails long hours, deceit, fear, and the potential for corruption. Nonetheless, it was a common practice for drug squad officers. In 1930 R.S.S. Wilson posed as an 'out-of-work logger' and obtained a small room on Hastings Street in Vancouver's Downtown Eastside. Wilson recalled the difficulties of being undercover in his memoir:

> I visited the numerous beer parlors and bootlegging joints which abounded through that part of town and met all kinds of people. I realized that somehow I was able to pass myself off as one of them, talk their language and fit in as if that was the way it had always been ... But it is a lonely life to have to associate with people who are not your friends and whose ways and values are not your own. Pretending you are what you are not, and remembering all the lies you have told so you won't get tripped up, is not easy.[77]

By 1940 users were highly suspicious of users they didn't know, out of fear that they might be informants or undercover officers. T.E.E. Greenfield went undercover in 1940 after the RCMP transferred him from Vancouver to Toronto. Some users took him to a flophouse where they stripped him of clothes from the waist up to take a good look at his arm. Fortunately for Greenfield, 'he had "fixed" his arm that morning,' so that it looked as if he had the needle marks of a regular drug user.[78]

In the 1950s, the RCMP made considerable use of undercover operations, especially in Vancouver. In 1955 Constable Price of the RCMP reported that the Vancouver Drug Squad had undertaken twelve major undercover operations in the past six years. Going undercover had advantages over the use of informants, because once the operation was over, the undercover officer assumed the witness stand to make cases against the people who had sold him drugs. Price emphasized that the greatest danger was that of exposure 'which can ruin months, and even years, of careful preparation and work.'[79] The drug-using community in Canada was small, and just as narcotics officers recognized drug users from other parts of the country, the drug users sometimes recognized the police officers, occasionally ruining many hours of police work.[80]

Some of these undercover operations resulted in large numbers of arrests. A 1951–2 RCMP undercover operation in Vancouver led to the arrest of twenty-two men and five women.[81] An RCMP undercover operation in July 1961 resulted in thirty-eight people being arrested and charged with trafficking and conspiracy. After these arrests, the price of a capsule increased from $5 to $10.[82]

Men were often assigned to undercover duty when they were young recruits, enabling them to fit in with the users and not be recognized as police. Likely the most promising men were selected for this work. In 1955, two Vancouver City Police force members, twenty-five-year-old Ken Scherling and twenty-seven-year-old Bob Devente went undercover for several months. An underground resistance fighter in the Netherlands during the war, Devente immigrated to Canada in 1948 and started a contracting business. He joined the police force in January 1955 and walked a beat for a month before being assigned to undercover work. Scherling had done graduate work in science and zoology at the University of Washington.[83] After serving undercover, some officers put their knowledge of drug users to work by joining the regular drug squad.

Ideally, undercover work involved careful surveillance of the undercover officer. Throughout a 1955 operation, Vancouver City Police officers were stationed in a hotel that provided them with a good view of the Broadway Hotel Beer Parlour, where most of the drug selling was taking place. When the undercover officers made a successful purchase, they would signal to the police officers in the hotel, whereupon they would meet at a prearranged location and turn over the drugs.[84]

After observing six narcotic units of police departments in the United States in the 1970s, Peter K. Manning and Lawrence John Redlinger concluded that the use of drugs, particularly by undercover officers, was quite common, as 'it is virtually impossible to work undercover without having to weigh the danger to oneself of refusal to use,' although it was officially denied.[85] Canadian police undoubtedly used drugs as well. In a 1948 *Maclean's* article, the experienced RCMP officer T.E.E. Greenfield asserted that 'even some members of the RCMP drug squads have been addicted.'[86]

Members working undercover often experienced pressure to use. In 1955 Constable M. of the RCMP was undercover in Winnipeg when his drug-using companions insisted that he 'fix' with them so that they could see for themselves that he was, in fact, a user. Constable M. reported that he had a hard time getting away, but he did manage to turn a capsule over to police.[87] Constable M. claimed to have spent $10 on one capsule, which was somewhat high. He explained that his female companion probably bought two and kept one for herself, but since he was not covered during this buy, it is impossible to know for certain whether or not he might have used the other capsule himself.

'Works' were more readily available in Canada than in the United States, where they were often illegal, and police reports indicate that it was fairly common for Canadians to shoot up alone. American oral histories reveal that Americans made much wider use of shooting galleries and other places where 'works' could be shared.[88] This may mean that in Canada there was less suspicion placed on the undercover officer who said that he wanted to shoot up by himself.

In practice, it was hard to maintain tight surveillance over undercover men. Police regularly 'fixed' their arms to make them look like users, but nothing would engender confidence like actually using the drug. Moreover, like other people who came in regular contact with users, at least a few police officers were probably curious about the drugs' effects.

Undercover officers actively created 'crime' by asking drug peddlers to sell to them. Although street-level undercover operations could result in a large number of arrests of street-level peddlers, they rarely resulted in the arrest of higher-ups, and the street peddlers were quickly replaced. The deception involved in undercover operations did nothing to improve relations between users and the police, and since undercover officers often served as narcotics officers in the same cities where they had gone undercover, they developed antagonistic relationships with drug users who felt that they had been betrayed by people they had trusted.

Policing Bodies

As policing became more intensive, so did users' and peddlers' efforts to conceal the drug. In the 1920s it was common for peddlers to carry their drugs in pockets with slits in them. When approached by police, they would let the decks fall to the ground and kick them away. If the police found the deck, the peddler would deny any knowledge of the drug that was lying some distance away. When capsules replaced decks in the 1930s, it became more common for peddlers to carry them in their mouths. At roughly the same time, female drug users and peddlers began carrying drugs in their vaginas, although this practice was not nearly as common as carrying drugs in the mouth.[89]

Police often used violence to extract drugs from users. In a raid on Fraser Mills in the early 1920s, RCMP Constable W.L. Smith testified that he hit one of the Chinese men 'over the head with a searchlight.'[90] Chinese informants working for the RCMP in the early 1920s regularly complained of violence by Vancouver City Police officers. One informant stated that Detective Sinclair of the city police fired two shots at him as he was running away. The informant stopped, and Sinclair 'called me a bastard – son of a bitch-cocksucker. He then took me ... into the alley that leads toward the Police station. When we got into this alley he hit me on the side of the head and called me more bad names.'[91]

After drug users started carrying the drugs in their mouths, the violence increased. Police officers grabbed drug users by the throat to prevent them from swallowing the drugs, and they put their hands into the mouths of the users to dig out the drugs. Detective Cray of the Vancouver City Police put it bluntly in his report to the Senate: 'to get drugs out of a man's mouth takes a lot of force.'[92] It was also standard procedure to try to get the offender to regurgitate the drugs by sticking their fingers down the offender's throat.[93] Matthew S. testified that during the arrest of his companion, Ian H., Ian gasped for breath while one detective squeezed his neck and pulled his hair and another tried to pry his mouth open. Ian's throat was left bruised, scratched, and swollen.[94]

Users could be placed in a chokehold by police at almost any time. Matthew S. testified that detectives sometimes 'jump out of doorways and choke you.' He claimed that 'lots of times I have gone down the street in the daytime and they have jumped on me ... when they jump on you they don't know whether you have them [drugs] or not, but they choke you to make sure.'[95] In 1961, a female user told a social worker, 'Every city you get into, as soon as the local police find out you're there, the first thing they do is jump you and choke you because you are a known addict. They don't give you a chance to see if you want to stop.'[96] Not surprisingly, when health professionals doing a study of addiction interviewed drug users at Oakalla Prison Farm, the users expressed anger against the regulations that allowed police to 'search them on sight and to use methods of force.'[97]

Drug users' desperation in the face of police action sometimes led to self-harm. When police apprehended Jerry C. of Regina in 1954, he swallowed his glass hypodermic needle and the rubber bulb of an eyedropper. The RCMP officer reached into his mouth to get the object, but Jerry C. succeeded in swallowing the broken glass and began bleeding profusely. The police took him to hospital where he remained under observation. Fortunately, X-rays showed that his internal organs were not damaged.[98]

Much to the initial discomfort of police, drug users also hid drugs in their vaginas. In 1941, the Division of Narcotic Control became quite alarmed about a Vancouver case. The police believed that there were 'at least 10 decks of opium in a small hotel occupied by a well-known trafficker and his equally well-known female confederate.' When the police broke into the room, they saw the woman grab something from the bedside table and 'place it in her person.' She had no clothes on and told the police that 'she had taken legal advice which was to the effect that, being naked, she was ineligible for search while a search of her actual body would be completely illegal.' The police were hesitant to do anything without consulting with the Special Narcotic Prosecutor in Vancouver, so they wrapped the woman in a few blankets and brought her to the police station. She obtained bail and the police had no alternative but to let her go. Upon consultation, the division concluded that it would be inappropriate for the police to have the power to grab a woman on the street and search her inter-vaginally. They feared that

> we would sooner or later be 'planted' with some highly emotional female, completely capable of producing or simulating a violent attack of hysteria, if not a heart condition. The search of such a person in those circumstances with the subsequent advertisement by the defending lawyer and with also possible headlines in a local paper, rendered it a somewhat difficult matter to determine.

The division decided to appoint a medical man as a justice of the peace in order to do these types of searches. Three matrons were also sworn in as special constables.[99] Soon thereafter, they arrested Anabelle C., a woman they believed was carrying drugs in her vagina for a well-known peddler. The *RCMP Quarterly* reported that 'the prisoner was warned that a compulsory examination would be made if she refused to produce the drugs of her own free will. She not only declined the opportunity to act voluntarily but also resisted angrily when the search was finally made. Two large fingerstalls, each containing twenty decks of opium were found.'[100] Subsequent police reports occasionally mentioned that a matron turned up evidence while searching a woman that the male officers had not found.[101] This was a perfect example of drug users acquiring new techniques and the police being forced to be quite creative in response.

Although women who hid drugs in their vaginas initially embarrassed the police, they had few such hesitations when it came to checking for needle marks. After raiding a room and finding drugs, it was common practice to examine the occupants for needle marks, which were used as evidence at the trial. In 1960 the police entered a room in a residential hotel in the Downtown Eastside. The police found a gelatin capsule and several gees. The police reported that Heather M. had needle marks on the inside of her upper left leg, while the other female in the room had needle marks on her upper right leg. The police must have asked the women to lift up their skirts or take down their trousers.[102]

Men could also be stripped during searches. In 1951 the police surprised John F. and a companion in the very small washroom of a fish and chips shop. The police made the two men take most of their clothing off and searched both them and their clothes for drugs, but found nothing. Police found an eyedropper in the wastepaper basket but decided not to prosecute the case because it was a public washroom, and it would be difficult to determine ownership of the eyedropper.[103]

Drug users regularly fought back against this invasive policing, and police officers as well as users were injured. One day in 1953 police began searching the home of Bob K. in a small town in Manitoba. Bob K. grabbed the constable by the arm and, according to the police report, 'a struggle ensued.' Mrs. K. began 'clawing' at the face of Constable S., and when he attempted to push her away, she crushed a burning cigarette into his face, apparently aiming for his ear. She was pushed away, and Bob K. punched Constable S. in the face. Eventually, Mrs. K. was carried from the home by Constable S. screaming and swearing. Bob K. and Mrs. K. were then lodged in the police cells where Mrs. K. scratched the constable's cheek and throat. The police report failed to mention whether injuries were sustained by Bob K. and his wife in this fight, although the police injuries were carefully noted.[104]

Conclusion

With far more personnel, more information about drug users, better technology, and the development of standard techniques, police grew increasingly successful at arresting drug users. Their control over information and the lack of scandal surrounding narcotics policing in the years after the early 1920s ensured that police were taken very seriously in the courtroom, and they achieved a high rate of convictions. However, as police themselves occasionally bemoaned, enforcement did not stop drug use.[105] Released prisoners continued to use, and new people started.

By the 1950s, the police had developed the necessary resources and techniques to keep extremely close surveillance over drug users. Police knew most of the users and arrested them frequently. In some respects, enforcement was more effective than ever before, or ever since. Does that mean that the 1950s should be regarded as a model of narcotics policing? This chapter has shown that the intensive policing of the post-war period contributed enormously to the anxiety and danger of drug users' lives. While it undoubtedly deterred some users, it may have even led to heavier drug use by some who sought to forget the stresses of their lives. The intensive policing also increased the prestige of drug use among young 'rounders,' or delinquents, especially in Vancouver, and it may have made the idea of becoming a drug user more attractive to young people who wished to visibly defy authority and mainstream norms.

Narcotics policing was regarded as a challenging and difficult area of police work, but it also created many possibilities for corruption and for extremely antagonistic relationships between the police and community members, and it involved lots of tedious work. Police officers in the post-war period were extremely successful at arresting users, but they had relatively little success at catching the higher-ups. Intensive street enforcement kept the price of drugs high, but it did not significantly reduce the supply. Instead, it may have contributed to greater involvement by drug users in other types of crime, as they needed more money to purchase their drugs than they would have needed otherwise.

The police knew quite a lot about drug users and their habits, and they played a vital role in circulating information to a broader public. Journalists, narcotics officials, social workers, and doctors learned much of what they knew about drug use from narcotics officers. However, the police had an extremely antagonistic and often violent relationship with users and were hardly an unbiased source of information. They played a key role in the maintenance of a highly stigmatized image of drug users. They also contributed to a body of knowledge about drug use that curious potential users could access. By publicizing the places where drugs could be sold and the means by which they could be purchased, police officers helped the inquisitive to learn more.

Narcotics policing puts the state in an extremely invasive and often violent relationship with its citizens. 'After a short struggle' was one of the most commonly repeated phrases in RCMP reports describing arrests. The incredible violence and invasiveness of policing what people take into their bodies, and the danger this policing posed to the safety and health of both police officers and drug users, should give us pause.

Proscribing Prescribing: Doctors, Drug Users, and the Division of Narcotic Control

Police officers deliberately sought drug users out, but doctors regarded drug users as troublesome and manipulative patients and were usually happy to stay away from them. And yet, doctors and medical discourses exerted considerable influence over drug users' lives. Individual doctors decided whether to prescribe narcotic drugs to desperate patients, small numbers of psychiatrists 'diagnosed' and treated drug users, and a few influential members of the profession came to play an important role in drug law and policy. At the same time, doctors might have been forgiven if they saw themselves as the ones being regulated.[1] The Opium and Narcotic Drug Act placed strict limits on prescribing narcotic drugs, and doctors were not free to treat patients as they might have wished, especially if that treatment involved maintaining people on opiates. In short, doctors were both regulators and regulated when it came to the control of illicit drugs.

In the early 1920s, the Narcotic Division, which was run by non-doctors, confidently dictated to doctors the manner in which they should prescribe narcotic drugs and treat drug-using patients. Many doctors found themselves in court for violations of the Opium and Narcotic Drug Act (although they were rarely convicted), and the RCMP employed drug users as 'spotters' to make cases against doctors for illegal prescriptions. However, doctors fought back, and over time the division's treatment of doctors became more deferential, a pattern that reflected growing activism by doctors, their greater medical prestige in society at large, and the difficulty the department experienced in making cases against doctors in the courts. After the Second World War, a medical, especially psychiatric, approach to drug use gained wide support, and doctors were put in charge of treatment programs and given a much greater say in drug policy, although the profession as a whole continued to evince little interest in the issue of drug use.[2]

In Canada, the literature on doctors and the state has had two main threads. The first traced the way the 'regulars' organized to exclude homeopaths, midwives, and other 'irregulars' from the practice of medicine in the nineteenth century. Most of these histories end in the late nineteenth century, when doctors gained self-governing institutions and government legislation to protect their interests.[3] The second focuses on the years after the Second World War and examines the introduction of hospital insurance and medicare and the role of doctors in both initiating and protesting state involvement in the provision of medical services.[4] Relatively little has been written on the period in between (from the early twentieth century to the end of the Second World War). In fact, as Barbara Clow's work on cancer treatment in Ontario also shows, the consolidation of professional prestige was far from complete in the first half of the twentieth century.[5]

Canada's control over doctors in the matter of illegal drugs was similar to that of the United States and very different from Britain's. In the United States, the 1914 Harrison Narcotic Act limited a doctor to possessing and dispensing drugs in the 'legitimate practice of his profession.'[6] In 1915 the Treasury Board, which administered the act, declared that 'legitimate practice' did not include prescribing a regular supply for addicts, and the U.S. Supreme Court upheld this decision in 1919. A few narcotic clinics continued to provide maintenance doses into the mid-1920s, but they were eventually forced to close. Between 1914 and 1938, some 3000 doctors went to jail for violations of the Harrison Act.[7]

In Britain, by contrast, the so-called 'British system' allowed doctors to prescribe regular doses of opiates to addicts. In 1924 the Ministry of Health in Britain established a Departmental Committee on Morphine and Heroin Addiction to set guidelines for state policy. The committee, composed entirely of doctors, reported in 1926 and left control of the addict in the hands of the medical profession.[8] The much-celebrated 'British system' partly reflected the better organization and greater political power of the medical profession in Britain, but there were also far fewer users in Great Britain, most of whom had become addicted to opiates through medical use. Britain was spared the worst excesses of the 'drug panics' that played such an important role in motivating drug legislation in the United States and Canada.[9]

Canadian doctors were in no position to fight the Division of Narcotic Control in the early 1920s. Although medicine had been professionalized in the sense that each province had passed licensing legislation, the organizations representing Canadian physicians on the federal stage were not strong. The Canadian Medical Association remained fairly weak until the late 1920s.[10] Annual meetings were poorly attended, the organization was in financial difficulty, and at the 1921 annual meeting there was talk of shutting it down.[11] Canada did not establish its own Royal College of Physicians and Surgeons, which certifies specialists, until 1929. Unlike the United States, where there were several prominent and respectable 'experts' in addiction, no one in Canada could legitimately fill this role. Moreover, doctors saw drug users as extremely bothersome patients. Hospitals refused to take them on the grounds that they required around-the-clock male nurses, and it was difficult for a doctor to gradually cut down the dosages without institutional treatment. By the early 1920s, very few addicts were being created through medical practice, and addicts who bought their drugs on the illicit market were seen as a disreputable, not to mention ill-paying, class of patients.[12]

More importantly, there was no agreement amongst physicians themselves about what constituted appropriate treatment for drug addicts, which made it difficult for doctors to launch a concerted attack against the policies and practices of the Narcotic Division. Some doctors regarded addiction as a simple 'vice,' others believed it was a symptom of an underlying mental disorder, while a number held the view that addiction created physical problems that required medical treatment.[13] There were doctors who favoured maintaining users on steady doses of opiates, but they seem to have been a minority.[14] Most doctors agreed that institutional treatment was ideal for withdrawal, but there were few places that would take addicts, and few addicts could afford hospital care. Some doctors continued to treat patients using the 'gradual reduction' method, meaning that they would slowly cut down the dose over time, in order to avoid the worst of the withdrawal symptoms, while others preferred the sudden withdrawal of all narcotics. In 1923, and again in 1930, the *Canadian Medical Association Journal* condemned the 'so called ambulatory or slow reduction method of cure,' and called for institutions to treat convicted addicts 'not so much as prisoners, but as people diseased.'[15] But debates in the House of Commons and letters to the journal showed that not all doctors agreed.[16] In 1926 the Conservative member of Parliament from Oshawa, Dr. Kaiser, asserted that 'medical men of the highest standing say it is utterly wrong to abruptly cut off drugs from the addict: they are of opinion [*sic*] that the better course is to wean him off gradually. In fact this is the only method of effecting a cure.'[17]

The disagreement among doctors was obvious at the 1924 trial of Dr. Fortune Lachance of St. Boniface, Manitoba, whom the Department of Health dubbed 'the worst offender in the Dominion of Canada.'[18] In a three-month period, Dr. Lachance issued prescriptions for more than seventeen ounces of narcotics, an amount greater than all of the other doctors in Manitoba combined. At the trial, the Crown expert, Dr. E.C. Barnes, superintendent of the Selkirk Mental Hospital, criticized Lachance's 'treatment' and said that he would have 'nothing to do with an addict who was not under proper surveillance.' He claimed that slow withdrawal treatment was 'useless and unsparingly condemned.'

In his defence, Lachance testified that he had been treating addicts for two years, and many of his patients had been treated for free. 'Slow withdrawal' was not ideal, from his point of view, but he felt that he had had some success with it. One patient testified that since Dr. Lachance had treated him, his health had improved and he could now 'much better resist the craving for "dope."'[19] The patient was now working and supporting his wife and three children. Four 'prominent medical practitioners' also testified that sudden withdrawal was dangerous and that they had used the 'slow withdrawal.' Dr. P.H. McNutty, a member of the Advisory Board of the St. Boniface hospital, declared that any physician using the quick withdrawal method 'should be arrested for inhuman treatment.'[20]

As a result of their testimony, Dr. Lachance was acquitted. The Department of Health would have appealed, but Dr. Lachance died soon after the trial. The Lachance trial clearly demonstrated the lack of consensus among prominent medical professionals as to the correct approach to treating and withdrawing addicts. With so little agreement in the field, and with few doctors interested in treating addicts, doctors paid relatively little attention to the drug legislation of the early 1920s, unless it affected their care of non-addicts.

Doctors, Legislation, and the Courts

In both the United States and Britain, doctors played an important role in securing drug legislation.[21] In the United States, Dr. Hamilton Wright became known as the 'father of American narcotic laws.' By contrast, in Canada, this title appropriately belongs to a series of moral reformers without any medical credentials. William Lyon Mackenzie King, who introduced Canada's first anti-drug legislation in 1908 and 1911, did so as a moral reformer concerned about opium use on the West Coast. Before introducing the 1911 legislation, he consulted not with doctors but with the chiefs of police in Vancouver and Montreal. It was not until 1920 that the responsibility of enforcing the act fell to the newly created Ministry of Health, where presumably there would be more of a medical focus. However, the Opium and Drug Branch (later renamed the Narcotic Division and later the Division of Narcotic Control) did not employ anyone with medical credentials between 1920 and 1961 and, as was discussed in chapter 1, the drug legislation of the 1920s was inspired primarily by West Coast anti-drug crusaders, officials within the Narcotic Division, and the RCMP. Few doctors in the House of Commons took an active interest in drug legislation, apart from provisions of the Opium and Narcotic Drug Act that directly affected the manner in which they could prescribe narcotic drugs, which were part of any medical practice of the day, and were primarily prescribed to people who were not addicts.

In 1911 the Opium and Drug Act made it an offence for a physician to prescribe opium, cocaine, and morphine unless the drug was prescribed for medicinal purposes. (Medicinal purposes were not defined, so this could potentially include prescribing drugs to addicts.) There was no minimum penalty. This mild legislation was followed by 1920 legislation that required physicians, veterinary surgeons, and dentists to provide the minister with information, upon request, regarding drugs 'received, dispensed, supplied, given away, or distributed.'[22] If doctors failed to provide this information, they could be punished with a jail term of up to one year, but would normally be given a fine. The government tried to assure doctors in the House of Commons that these new drug laws would have little effect on medical practice. In these early debates, a few doctors complained that the record keeping was too onerous, but other physicians supported the act. Most controversial was the provision of the bills, introduced in 1920 and 1921, which prohibited patients from refilling narcotic prescriptions without the consent of their doctor. Many participants in the debate did not seem to understand that this only applied to drugs that were controlled under the Opium and Narcotic Drug Act and that certain preparations containing only small amounts of these drugs were exempt.

Following complaints by the Division of Narcotic Control about the difficulties of making cases against doctors, the government passed legislation in 1925 making it illegal for a doctor to prescribe for a drug user unless he or she was suffering from a condition other than addiction. The legislation also made it illegal for doctors to give narcotics to drug users for self-administration. In the House of Commons, the politicians responsible for introducing the legislation were either unaware of the influence it would have on medical practice, or they deliberately obscured the possible effects. When Health Minister Henri Beland was asked whether the 1925 amendments regulated the amount that a doctor might prescribe for his patient, he told the House that a doctor would not be allowed to give a man a prescription for a large amount of cocaine.[23] In response, Dr. Ross, a Liberal-Conservative from Kingston, innocently revealed that he probably violated the intention of the act on a regular basis. He admitted that while the Department of Health might look askance at the amount of his narcotic prescriptions, he felt that 'to prohibit a patient who has for years been using a certain amount of a drug would be just as hard as to say even to some members of parliament that you cannot have a chew of tobacco when you want it.' Amazingly, Health Minister Henri Beland replied,

> if an addict comes to me to be treated, and I feel that I should prescribe something for him in the way of morphine or cocaine, and I do prescribe, I do not think that I should be brought before the court for that, or for prescribing as often as I think the man requires the drugs, because he is a diseased man that I am prescribing for.[24]

If Dr. Beland had prescribed in the way that he outlined, he might well have received a sharp letter from the Narcotic Division and faced possible prosecution for his actions. The division interpreted the act (legitimately enough, given the wording) to mean that a doctor could relieve a suffering addict with a shot in his office, but that to prescribe for that addict was against the law.[25]

In the early 1920s, doctors regularly appeared in court for violations of the Opium and Narcotic Drug Act, but doctors were regularly acquitted. The Department of Health was criticized for persecuting doctors, and eventually it backed off, complaining that it was difficult to achieve success in cases against doctors. The department was disheartened by its failure to convict doctors such as Lachance, and alarmed by the support doctors sometimes received from their communities. In a 1920 case against a Dr. R., the Department of Health noted that he had 'been in the habit of issuing prescriptions of morphine and cocaine' for as much as sixty grains at a time (a normal dose would be a half or quarter grain).

The department was particularly outraged that he had accepted a ladies' hat and a new $25 pair of shoes from a prostitute as security for the payment of his fees. Nonetheless, he was strongly supported by members of his community, several of whom made the trip to Calgary for his trial. The judge found him not guilty.[26]

By far the most contested aspect of drug policy in the 1920s was the RCMP practice of employing 'spotters' to make cases against doctors. 'Spotters' were drug users or former drug users who made purchases from doctors on behalf of the RCMP and then testified in court against the physicians. In the 1920s, medical societies and journals, parliamentarians, and even the Social Service Council of Ontario complained about the Narcotic Division's use of spotters.[27] In response to a complaint from the Social Service Council of Ontario, F.W. Cowan, chief of the division, responded that the agent in question had been fairly successful in making cases against doctors and admonished that 'all of these boot-leggers and drug traffickers of course strongly resent our methods of obtaining evidence against them, but they seem to lose sight of the fact that in catering to the addiction of these poor unfortunates, and perpetuating their habit, they are responsible for the continuance of this traffic, and the perpetuation of this vice.'[28] Cowan explained that spotters were carefully watched – they were searched before they entered the doctor's office, they were given marked money, and the drugs were taken from them immediately after they left the office. Cowan further asserted that 'every physician charged with an offence under the Act gets a fair trial, has the right of appeal and gets the benefit of the doubt, should there be any, under the criminal laws of the land. We do not like using addicts as agents any more than the public do, but we have no alternative in many cases.'[29] He further claimed that the Narcotic Division only investigated doctors after they had received complaints from fellow practitioners or druggists, or from the relatives of a drug user.

Despite Cowan's assertions, the unease of the Narcotic Division about these techniques can be seen in a 1925 case against Dr. V. in Ottawa. After RCMP informant Len R. had made several successful purchases from Dr. V., the Narcotic Division told the RCMP that it was prepared to institute proceedings against Dr. V., but asked them to first obtain corroborating evidence from another agent. The Narcotic Division explained that doctors objected to Len R. because he moaned and groaned and behaved so much like an addict that 'a great many honest and conscientious doctors' might prescribe out of sympathy. The Narcotic

Division advised that it would be much better to discontinue using Len R. in cases against doctors, as they suspected that he might still be using drugs.[30] The RCMP employed another agent against Dr. V. before taking the case to court.

By the late 1920s, the division retreated from taking doctors to court, using this only as a last resort. Instead, the division maintained control over doctors through the licensing system and the threat of the Confidential Restricted List, a list of doctors who were prohibited from prescribing drugs controlled under the Opium and Narcotic Drug Act.[31] The licensing system introduced in 1920 allowed the Narcotic Division/ Division of Narcotic Control to carefully scrutinize the narcotic purchases of doctors across the country. Wholesalers and retail druggists sent regular sales reports to the division,[32] and the division entered each transaction on the personal cards of doctors, dentists, and drugstores.[33] Based on these records, the division carried out a vast correspondence with doctors. Physicians received letters asking them to account for their narcotic use when their purchases rose, and the division delivered sharp missives when doctors prescribed for a known 'criminal' addict.

For example, in 1942 Narcotic Chief C.H.L. Sharman wrote to a Vancouver doctor to complain that he had written a series of prescriptions over a six-week period, including thirty tablets of Dilaudid (a synthetic opiate) and ninety-two tablets of morphine sulphate to a drug user who had previously been convicted under the Opium and Narcotic Drug Act.[34] Perhaps to avoid such correspondence, some doctors proactively contacted the Narcotic Division whenever they encountered a transient drug user. In 1931, for example, a doctor in small-town Ontario, Dr. L., reported that Sidney C. called on him claiming to be a drug addict. Dr. L. reported that he gave him a hypodermic and instructed him to seek institutional treatment.[35]

In the late 1920s, the Narcotic Division developed the Confidential Restricted List of doctors. The list may have been based on the Restricted List of druggists, which began in 1920; druggists on the list were prohibited from dispensing narcotic drugs.[36] The Confidential Restricted List was circulated to druggists and wholesalers around the country on a regular basis, and they were instructed not to honour the signature of any physician who appeared on the list. It had no legal basis, although the division used it successfully for at least a quarter century.[37]

The list included doctors who were prescribing inappropriately, or were themselves addicts. For example, in 1938 the Narcotic Division put a doctor from Edmonton on the Confidential Restricted List for having provided large amounts of Dilaudid to drug users in Edmonton. The RCMP believed that at least one of the users he was supplying was peddling some of the drugs he received to other users. Sharman scolded the doctor for not knowing that Dilaudid was on the narcotic list and for being unaware that Dilaudid was even stronger than morphine.[38] Quite a few of the physicians on the list were addicts, and some even requested their inclusion on the list. In 1933 Dr. P. requested that he be put on the Confidential Restricted List because he had once again started to use narcotics. In 1936 he entered treatment, and in early 1937 his name was removed from the Confidential Restricted List. He soon started using again, and his name was placed on the list for a second time.[39] The names of drug-using physicians were usually removed from the list after several years of abstention.

In reality, the Division of Narcotic Control used the Confidential Restricted List as a threat. They threatened to put a doctor on the list well before they actually did so, and in 1954 only sixty-nine physicians were on the list, almost certainly less than the number of drug-using physicians in the country, and considerably less than 1 per cent of all practising physicians.[40] The Vancouver doctor who was reprimanded for providing Dilaudid and morphine sulphate to a 'criminal addict' in 1942 had already received correspondence from the Narcotic Division on two occasions in 1941 as a result of prescriptions to other 'criminal addicts.' Even so, Sharman did not put him on the list, although he told him that it was impossible for the situation to continue.[41]

The Narcotic Division also criticized doctors for carelessness in storing narcotics, or for having them stolen, especially during wartime short-ages. In 1943 a drug user took drugs from a Welland, Ontario, doctor who had left him alone in his office while he went to mix a sleeping powder. Sharman scolded the doctor for leaving the addict alone and complained that the doctor would need to purchase more narcotics to replace the stolen ones: this was a 'drain upon the already depleted stocks in the Country' and took drugs away from 'the sick people in this country who actually need them.'[42] Doctors faced with Sharman's wrath might feel foolish, and might think more carefully about storing narcot-ics and prescribing them, but in reality after the 1920s, doctors faced little threat.

The Opium and Narcotic Drug Act had been widely circulated, and medical journals made doctors aware of the possible penalties. By 1932 the division reassured doctors that it did not prosecute doctors for 'slight divergences' from the requirements of the act, and took action only in cases of gross abuse.[43] They also exerted strict control over the RCMP in their prosecution of doctors, insisting that the RCMP consult with them in cases involving members of the medical profession, and in some cases reprimanding them for their tactics.[44]

Doctors might have resented the big-brother tactics of the Division of Narcotic Control, but in reality, it was the users who suffered. Once doctors became aware of the strict provisions of the act and the possible penalties, they became much less likely to treat addicts, even when drug users wanted to withdraw under medical supervision or were seeking to normalize their lives through some sort of regular supply.

Opening the Window to Maintenance – the 1950s

By the 1950s, doctors were a more powerful and prestigious professional group than they had been in the 1920s. The quality of medical care had improved since the late nineteenth century with the development of germ theory, antisepsis, and improved surgical techniques, but with the introduction of sulpha drugs and antibiotics in the 1930s and '40s, doctors' reputations soared. Their ability to heal was no longer in question; with the growing popularity of psychiatry it seemed that doctors could even cure the mind. Not coincidentally, given the enormous faith placed in the possibilities of modern medical practice, drug addicts were increasingly being defined as 'sick' people who required medical treatment. In 1953 a psychiatrist, George Stevenson, was selected to carry out a federally funded study of drug users at Oakalla Prison Farm.[45] It no longer seemed appropriate for non-doctors at the Division of Narcotic Control to exert so much control over professional practice. The division increasingly consulted with physicians elsewhere in the Department of National Health and Welfare and with medical associations across the country.[46] In 1954 a special committee established within the Department of National Health and Welfare to discuss a new Narcotic Drug Act was composed of nine people, five of whom were doctors employed elsewhere in the department. By the early 1950s the department was discussing the possibility of allowing doctors to provide drugs to addicts on what they described as an 'enlightened treatment basis.' And they allowed a few quiet experiments.[47]

One case involved a young doctor in a mid-sized Ontario city, who maintained two patients on methadone (a synthetic opiate) over several years. Dr. M. began prescribing methadone for Robert N. and Alice M. in January 1953 – ten years before the Narcotic Addiction Foundation of British Columbia began the first methadone maintenance program in

Canada. The Division of Narcotic Control was immediately alarmed by Dr. M.'s prescriptions, since it knew the two patients as 'criminal addicts.' Narcotic Chief K.C. Hossick asked the RCMP to investigate the lifestyle of the two users, as well as M.'s reputation as a doctor. The RCMP confirmed that Robert N. was working as a barber and that he no longer associated with local drug users. Alice M. was living 'quite respectably.' The RCMP reported that Dr. M. was 'not popular with some of the local doctors,' but that this was 'due to racial origin' (he was Eastern European) and that he enjoyed 'a good reputation as a medical practitioner.' The RCMP concluded that the 'treatment given by Dr. M. to Robert N. and Alice M. has probably helped them' and that the two would probably be back on the street without Dr. M.'s treatment.

The behaviour of Dr. M.'s patients, as well as his good reputation, created a difficult situation for the Division of Narcotic Control. In September 1953 the assistant chief, R.C. Hammond, paid Dr. M. a visit in Hamilton and was very impressed with his busy practice, well-equipped office, up-to-date medical literature, and confident manner. Dr. M. agreed to reduce the doses of the two patients, but this proved to be difficult, and he asked the division to advise him as to the maximum amount he could give to each patient. Instead, Hammond was instructed to visit him again and to tell him that his patients should enter the hospital for a complete withdrawal. Dr. M. said that he would cut the patients off if requested to do so by the department, but that both patients were working and Robert N. was supporting his elderly mother. On Dr. M.'s suggestion, Hammond also interviewed Robert N., who told him that he could not work as a barber without methadone and said that if he was denied drugs by Dr. M., he would simply obtain drugs elsewhere at much higher cost and could no longer support his mother. The division eventually agreed that Dr. M. should be allowed to prescribe for his two patients on the basis of their 'existing medical conditions,' and Dr. M. continued prescribing for his two patients for at least the next five years.[48]

At a meeting between top officials of the Department of Health (of which the Narcotic Division was a part) and the Department of Justice, several officials expressed the view that the doctor was doing the right thing by prescribing to the two patients. Dr. R.G. Ratz, the principal medical officer for the Medial Advisory Services, suggested that as long as the dosage did not increase, the situation should be permitted, but that the doctor should submit regular reports. Mr. R.E. Curran of the Department of Justice felt that such a policy would not be legal because the department would be aware that drug users were being supplied with narcotics, which was against the law. Apparently the department decided that ignorance was the best policy, as they stopped their correspondence with Dr. M. until they learned that Robert N. was obtaining drugs from another doctor five years later.[49] The department also allowed other doctors to quietly maintain their patients.[50]

The Division of Narcotic Control increasingly consulted with other doctors in the Department of National Health and Welfare in the 1950s. These discussions revealed that doctors had accused the department of 'unwarranted interference' by laymen in the practice of medicine. For this reason, the division wanted to get out of policing doctors and turn this task over to provincial licensing bodies.[51] The division wanted to remove from the act all sections dealing with physicians who were involved in legitimate medical practice. This did not mean, however, that the division was prepared to completely defer to doctors. On 1 January 1956 the government banned the importation of heroin, although the Canadian Medical Association had twice decided that heroin had a useful place in medical practice.[52]

Nonetheless, the 1961 Narcotic Control Act gave doctors more professional autonomy in that doctors' own organizations, rather than the Division of Narcotic Control, were to henceforth take a greater role in regulating prescribing. Instead of defining specific offences for doctors, the act specified that the governor in council could make regulations concerning licenses, records, and the 'circumstances and conditions under which and the persons by whom narcotics may be sold.' The department could communicate any information obtained under this act to provincial professional licensing bodies, which could discipline doctors accordingly. The law still allowed for a fine not exceeding $500, or a term of imprisonment not exceeding six months, for violating any of the regulations.[53] The minister of national health and welfare announced that the new law was desirable 'in that it leaves to professional interpretation what is or is not a proper use of a narcotic.'[54] The new legislation marked a significant shift in the relationship among doctors, the Division of Narcotic Control, and drug users, and it opened the door to methadone maintenance treatment, which would begin very shortly thereafter.

Treatment Programs

The first methadone program in Canada operated under the auspices of the Narcotic Addiction Foundation of British Columbia (NAF). The provincial government announced the creation of NAF in 1955, but neighbourhood opposition prevented them from opening a site for several years.[55] Finally, in December 1958 the NAF opened a residence (for men only) in central Vancouver and appointed psychiatrist Robert Halliday as director. The NAF quickly realized that most drug users did not want residential treatment, at least not at the NAF, and the residence often operated at less than capacity. As provincial hospital insurance did not cover admittance for withdrawal, there was a pressing need for withdrawal services in BC, so one of NAF's first projects involved providing methadone for withdrawal. Methadone is a long-acting synthetic opiate that is used to prevent withdrawal symptoms in people who want to stop using morphine or heroin. It is taken orally and does not have the same euphoric properties as heroin. The U.S. Public Health Service hospitals began using methadone for withdrawal in 1950, although this was for in-patients. From the late 1950s on, the NAF provided two to three days supply of methadone to out-patients for withdrawal purposes if there was a responsible non–drug-using person who was willing to administer the drug to the user.[56] Users were far more interested in obtaining methadone than in living in the residence and receiving counselling: the number of clients rose when the NAF first started providing methadone and fell when it became clear that methadone was to be used for withdrawal and not for maintenance.[57]

In 1963, with cooperation of the Division of Narcotic Control, the NAF began providing methadone for 'prolonged withdrawal.'[58] This program was directed at older users for whom other sorts of treatment had proven unsuccessful. Thus, before Marie Nyswander and Vincent Dole began their much-heralded methadone maintenance experiments in the United States, methadone maintenance, albeit under a rather deceptive name, was already quietly under way in Canada.[59] In 1964 the Addiction Research Foundation of Ontario followed British Columbia's lead and initiated a methadone treatment program. By the late 1960s, methadone maintenance treatment was widely available across Canada, although new restrictions on doctors in 1972 made it harder for users to obtain methadone in the 1970s and '80s.[60]

Non-Maintenance Treatment Programs

In addition to the maintenance programs, British Columbia and Ontario initiated a number of non-maintenance treatment programs in the 1950s, and doctors, especially psychiatrists, played a role in these programs as well. In 1956, the Ontario government opened a twenty-five-bed facility for male drug addicts at Mimico prison, in Mimico. A part-time psychiatric specialist, two psychologists, and a social worker staffed the clinic, where they provided both individual and group therapy. Patients entered 'voluntarily' for the last four months of their sentence. Administrators were equivocal about the success of the program, commenting that the drug users regarded assistance with suspicion – the drug user felt that it was 'being done "to" him and not "for" him.'[61] A health clinic at the Mercer Reformatory, in Toronto, provided treatment and 'rehabilitation' for female drug users.[62] According to the psychiatrist at the Mercer, Dr. Boothroyd, the intention was to 'try and educate this group that there is a better way of life and they should try to conform to it.'[63]

British Columbia offered penal treatment as well. In 1956, two 'panabode' units were established at Oakalla Prison Farm in Burnaby. George Stevenson was the official head of the program, although he was not in charge of daily operations. The panabode program reflected Stevenson's belief that drug users needed to see themselves as emotionally immature people with multiple problems (this is discussed in more detail in chapter 7). Officials chose the word 'panabode' rather than something with 'drug addiction' in its title 'lest there be inclination among those inmates selected for treatment to feel that drug addiction was their only problem.'[64] Treatment was gendered – during the day, the men did gardening and woodwork, while the women took hairdressing and home-nursing courses and had greater responsibility for the upkeep of their panabode. The program also included educational films, counselling, educational courses, housework, recreational activities, religious services, and outside speakers. According to social worker Lindsay McCormick, the program was designed to 'give the inmate better insight into himself and his manner of functioning and to provide him with a better outlook on and respect for society and his role as one of its members.'[65] The program did not have enough staff to undertake extensive counselling activities, but the set-up itself revealed what was to be learned: women were supposed to be good housekeepers and home-makers, and men were to engage in sports, woodworking, and other 'manly' hobbies.[66] Both male and female drug users were to acknowledge that they had serious personality problems, but that they could be cured through group discussion, self-examination, and interactions with good citizens.

The project had limited success. Since the panabodes were more pleasant than the desperately overcrowded Oakalla facilities, many drug users sought to enter them, but staff felt that this did not indicate a sincere desire for a cure. Director George Stevenson complained that group therapy failed because panabode residents refused to let their 'guard down,' that they chose 'impractical' courses of study and recreation, and refused to participate in planned activities.[67] Critic Mervyn Davis, the executive director of the John Howard Society drew attention to the fundamental contradictions between 'psychotherapeutic' treatment and the restrictive custody of Oakalla Prison Farm. He pointed out that most of the staff's time was spent selecting the inmates who were to live in the 'relatively luxurious accommodation.'[68] In 1958 the male group was briefly disbanded and the women's group fell to three people.[69]

Conclusion

With justification, doctors have been regarded as members of an extremely powerful profession, but in their relationship with Canadian drug users their power lay less in policy making and more in their individual decisions about whether or not to prescribe. Moreover, their influence was not as great in the early part of the century as has been supposed in much of the historiography on professionalization. In the early 1920s, doctors started out in a relatively weak position vis-à-vis the Opium and Narcotic Drug Act. Although users undoubtedly saw them as regulators who refused to prescribe or to relieve the pain of withdrawal, doctors could justifiably regard themselves as the regulated. The Division of Narcotic Control carefully monitored their prescriptions, and some doctors even went to court for violations of the act.

Nonetheless, doctors made significant gains between 1920 and 1961. They stopped the Division of Narcotic Control from employing spotters, they significantly moderated the severity of the provisions of the Opium and Narcotic Drug Act that applied to medical practice, they changed departmental practices in enforcing the act, and a few psychiatrists carved out an important place for themselves in treating drug users. Even so, very few doctors had much interest in providing treatment to addicts. Drug addiction might be seen as a 'disease,' but social workers and police officers would continue to play a greater role in the lives of users.

Chapter 6

Turning Rounders into Square Johns: Drug Users and the John Howard Society

While police officers saw their job as arresting and incarcerating drug users, social workers at the John Howard Society of British Columbia (JHS), a prison-visiting society, aimed to help those who used drugs. This chapter will examine the JHS's work with its drug-using clients from 1931, when the agency first began operation, to 1961, when the new Narcotic Control Act passed. At the JHS, middle-class social workers encouraged drug users to give up their 'rounder ways' and to find employment and friends outside of the drug-using world. They also provided drug users with comfort, occasional financial support, and advocacy. Most users only used the agency sporadically, but a few leaned on it heavily, and some appear to have sincerely appreciated what it offered.

The John Howard Society of British Columbia was the brainchild of the Right Rev. A.H. Sovereign, who, as the minister for St. Mark's church in Vancouver, frequently visited the BC Penitentiary and Oakalla Prison Farm. The society aimed to improve prison conditions, help prisoners and their families, and help former inmates re-establish themselves. The society adopted the name of the English prison-reformer, John Howard, who had fought for cleaner and healthier state-run prisons in the eighteenth century.[1]

The society appointed the Rev. Joshua (J.D.) Hobden, a successful Methodist minister in East End Vancouver as executive director, a position he retained until 1955. At their small offices in the Dominion Bank Building, Hobden and his office assistant (later known as the women's worker) provided short-term material aid – they gave out meal and bed tickets, supplied clothing, found employment, and provided counselling to both inmates and their families.[2] Hobden also visited inmates in jail, giving them comfort and helping them make plans for release. The society thought that by treating prisoners with what social workers regarded as 'respect,' and by providing them with occasional offers of food, clothing, shelter, and employment, they could transform them into law-abiding citizens.

In the early 1950s, the organization expanded and came to be dominated by professionally trained social workers, many of whom were politically active and left of centre. The society increased in size, employing six full-time social workers by the early 1960s,[3] many of whom had extensive experience in the corrections field. At least one of their workers was aboriginal. Unlike many other agencies at the time, the JHS made limited use of volunteers.[4]

Although the society became more secular and increasingly sympathetic to the troubles of drug users, its methods changed very little. In the 1950s, JHS workers spent much of their time visiting people in prison, listening to their problems, encouraging them to make plans for release, and occasionally helping out with employment and housing. It also operated on a drop-in basis, with former prisoners coming by for help as required. With the expansion of the welfare state after the Second World War, the government increasingly provided for material needs of former prisoners, and the society diminished its role in this area; casework became more oriented towards counselling. In keeping with the growing popularity of psychology in the 1950s, and the concurrent belief that self-understanding was the key to change, the society wanted prisoners to engage in a long process of self-examination and reflection to find the roots of their legal problems in their family problems and emotional difficulties, and to work out solutions to these problems in long discussions with their social workers.[5] It saw material aid as the responsibility of the state, delivered through services such as the National Employment Service and the Community Social Services Department.

Social work, as a profession, emerged out of several conflicting traditions, including Christian charity work, the moral reform movements of the nineteenth century, and the more radical settlement house movement.[6] In the 1910s and '20s, social workers began to adopt the 'casework approach' as a way of buttressing their claims to expertise and professionalism. Casework involved extensive investigation, diagnosis, and treatment of individual 'cases,' and in the 1950s it became increasingly psychological in orientation. Many North American scholars have noted that the social work profession became more conservative as professional casework came to dominate over community organizing and social action.[7] By the middle of the twentieth century, most social workers in Canada were employees of the state, engaged in the conservative task of monitoring the distribution of welfare allowances and other state disbursements.

As a prison reform organization, the JHS maintained, at least to a limited degree, the tradition of social action, although the society's cooperation with the criminal justice system, which was necessary to do its work, impeded its efforts at encouraging social change. Also, the left-wing social workers who dominated the JHS in the 1950s never fully adopted the psychological casework approach. There were no sophisticated diagnoses or treatment plans. Social work at the JHS did become more psychological in orientation, but the ultimate aim of forging a close and trusting relationship remained the same throughout. In not fully adopting the casework approach, and in maintaining a small focus on social change, the JHS was more progressive than many other social agencies in Canada at the time.

Part of the conservative turn in social work practice in Canada in the 1950s had to do with the social norms of the era, including the glorification of the nuclear family, limited opportunities for women, pervasive racism, and homophobia. Social workers at the JHS were not immune from the patriarchy, racism, and homophobia of the day, but perhaps because they were dealing with a particular 'deviant' group of clients, they were more focused on keeping their drug-using clients out of prison than they were in forcing them to live their lives according to middle-class norms. JHS workers hoped that their clients would stop using drugs, find employment, and settle into a 'square john' life, but they rarely preached these norms to their clients. Instead, they spent most of their time helping with concrete tasks – finding employment, helping with withdrawal, contacting family members, and acting as advocates with other social welfare and correctional institutions.

JHS workers genuinely cared about the welfare and well being of drug users; they came to the users' aid at all times of the day and night and were among the few sympathetic advocates for drug users in post-war society. Even so, encounters at the JHS took place between two people with vastly different levels of power. Social workers at the JHS were middle class and well educated. Most were white. Their clients were working class (91 per cent) and poorly educated, and a few were Aboriginal (4 per cent), black (0.7 per cent), and Asian (2.5 per cent).[8] These differences must have made some of the clients uncomfortable. That said, drug users were not forced to use the services of the JHS, and most did not. Some drug users used the society sporadically to meet specific needs, and only a few engaged in the therapeutic project that was dear to the hearts of social workers.

The power relationships between the JHS, its clients, the state, and social norms were enormously complex. The JHS was a private agency, but it relied on the Community Chest and Council, composed primarily of prominent Vancouver business people, for its funding. The JHS had to cooperate with the state-run criminal justice system, including prisons and the remission service, to gain access to its clients. The workers of the JHS were constrained by finances, the state, and their need for support from the broader community. Thus, these 'professional' social workers were regulated as well as being regulators. At the same time, social norms and culture coloured how the JHS workers regarded and treated their clients.

The John Howard Society in the 1930s and '40s

In the 1930s and '40s, the JHS was a small organization. The only employees were Hobden and a female caseworker or an office worker. Case notes included cursory impressions of clients, along with notes about material aid rendered and immediate plans, but little else. Hobden spent much of his time at court, or at the prisons, and he kept much of his information about clients in his head. In her laudatory biography of Hobden, Jean Wilton, an employee of the society in the 1950s, describes the extensive relationships Hobden had with his clients, but the case files show little evidence of this.[9]

Research about the drug-using clients of the JHS in the 1930s and '40s is particularly difficult, because the society either did not know, or did not record, whether their clients were drug users or not. It may be that drugs were simply too scarce on the streets of Vancouver in the 1930s and early '40s for workers at the JHS to definitively label certain clients as 'addicts.' Nonetheless, the JHS took an interest in drug use, actively taking part in a mid-1930s Vancouver campaign against codeine use, on account of the 'devastating moral results we have witnessed on the part of our own clientele.'[10] In 1945 the society bemoaned the lack of treatment for drug users, but concluded that they should be segregated in and out of prison.[11]

Drug users or not, Hobden encouraged his clients to develop self-respect. JHS offices were deliberately established in a good business section of town, away from other relief organizations and charities. Former prisoners were challenged to make something of themselves and thereby to 'recover what their social lapse has forfeited ... We refuse to let them think that a discharged prisoner can never become a good citizen.'[12] As a minister, Hobden believed that religion could help his clients, and he encouraged them to sanctify their common-law unions and to turn to God for guidance with their problems. The language of muscular Christianity sometimes informed his counsel, as when he wrote twenty-five-year-old Robert P., 'you have nothing to be ashamed of or to be afraid of. Keep your chin up and play the game always; your freedom depends on this.' In general, Hobden prided himself on plain speaking. A year later, Robert P.'s file indicated that Hobden wanted to know '1) Why he left his brother's business at Kimberly and 2) Why he hasn't got more sense than to go around with Matt when he got in trouble with Matt before.'[13] Some clients apparently responded to this frankness. When Robert P. was on a ticket of leave (parole) in the late 1940s, he sent Hobden snapshots and newspaper clippings about his brother's business, in addition to the letters required by law. John B., a long-time client of the society, told a YMCA worker that he had denounced his Roman Catholic faith on the strength of Hobden's 'sound sense' in his Oakalla sessions. In 1949 he wrote Hobden, 'I want you to have faith in me Mr. Hobden as I think that I owe you very much.'[14]

Like other social workers and agencies in the 1930s, Hobden, and by extension the JHS, was radicalized by harsh economic conditions. Hobden expressed great sympathy for his clients in the 1930s, especially those driven to crime by economic need, and he was highly critical of prison conditions.[15] He was particularly outraged when clients were fined for riding the rails, which many were doing in order to find work. When the war broke out and the employment situation improved, Hobden's tenor changed; he prided himself on the number of clients who had enlisted and told many clients coming to the society for help that their country needed 'good men.'[16]

Hobden also moved away from an emphasis on material relief, and by war's end he announced that relief was never an effective method of rehabilitation. 'Though some good was done,' he admitted, 'it was pauperizing in the extreme as it relieved a man of any initiative he might have to strike out for himself, and become self-reliant and independent.'[17] As a result, the agency began to focus more on direct counselling.

Social Work in the 1950s

While some social workers in the 1950s continued to be involved in social reform, the profession as a whole had moved towards emphasizing individual personality problems, rather than social and economic conditions, as the reasons for 'social problems' such as delinquency, early pregnancy, and drug use. The JHS, deeply embedded within and reliant upon a network of state and privately funded institutions, did not depart in radical ways from this norm. However, beginning in the early 1950s, the JHS of Vancouver increasingly attracted an unusual group of politically active social workers who recognized the many structural constraints faced by their clients, and who were more interested in discussing their clients' problems and providing them with some concrete aid, than in transforming their clients' personalities. In the case of female clients, social workers were much less concerned with their same-sex sexual practices than was the norm within the profession as a whole. Drug use was treated as a problem because it was almost impossible to stay out of jail while using drugs, but there was relatively little moral condemnation of drug use. The next section of this chapter, 'Casework with Female Clients,' shows how social workers at the more radical end of their profession tried to negotiate the financial and political constraints of 1950s Canada while their professional practice simultaneously reflected and reinforced many of the social and cultural injustices of the day.

The change of focus at the JHS began when Hobden began an extended leave to the Western Remission Service in 1951 and then officially retired in 1955. A new group of professionally trained social workers began to work extensively with drug users. They all felt that drug users were 'worthy' of 'help,' and they focused on counselling as a way to assist them. No doubt, their progressive politics help to explain the shift, as well as many of their later careers. Dave Barrett went on to serve as the NDP premier of British Columbia, and Norm Levi served in his cabinet. Ben Maartman wrote an interesting book on social work practice, and others moved into leadership positions in other John Howard Societies across the country. These workers were frustrated by the lack of treatment facilities for drug users, and some of them would have liked to take a more activist role with regard to prison conditions, but they were hampered by the fact that the JHS was fully embedded in the corrections' network.[18] The John Howard Society's board of directors feared that criticizing other players in the corrections field would mean losing some of the privileges that allowed them to carry out their counselling work.[19] Also, many of the workers had previously held positions in corrections and thus had little desire to alienate former and possibly future colleagues and employers. This might explain why the JHS tempered its complaints – about overcrowding, the need for research, the need for more staff, and the difficult employment situation faced by inmates when they were released – with a great deal of praise for the many improvements in prison conditions that took place in British Columbia in the 1950s.[20]

In the 1950s case notes changed from brief handwritten notes to more detailed typed descriptions. The expansion and high turnover rate of JHS staff, along with their more professional training, caused them to take more care in recording the substance of conversations between themselves and their clients, rather than relying on individual memory.[21] By the 1950s, files often included a report on the client by a prison classification officer, or by the National Parole Board, but unlike the 1930s and '40s they rarely included information that the social worker had obtained from other social agencies or from police officers. Instead, workers relied more heavily on what clients themselves said about their lives, their experiences, and their motivation for change.

With the shift from short-term material aid to counselling-oriented casework, the JHS workers were only supposed to distribute funds to clients as part of a longer-term rehabilitation strategy. In theory, larger sums of money were to go to smaller numbers of people who had strong plans for rehabilitation, and the supervisor instructed staff to no longer give handouts.[22] This rule was often broken, as workers found it hard to deny people who arrived at the society in immediate need. In 1960 a former inmate showed up at the JHS and reported that he was looking for work. The worker noted that 'his feet were soaking' and gave him a Woodward's Order for $9.22 to get a pair of shoes so that he could continue his job search.[23]

Often a client's most pressing need was withdrawal, though the society could do very little about this, as there were no facilities for withdrawal in the Vancouver area until the Narcotic Addiction Foundation of British Columbia (NAF) opened its doors in 1958. When seventeen-year-old Irene J. showed up at the JHS, seven months pregnant and undergoing withdrawal, a social worker tried in vain to place her in care, and spent the next two weeks visiting her every day to make sure that she kept medical appointments and interviews with welfare officers. She also corresponded with Irene's mother. But at the end of the two weeks, Irene was still on drugs.[24] In another case, the society tried to find Robert R. a doctor or psychiatrist to help him, but no one would take him. When Robert R. was arrested by police a year later, the assistant executive director of the JHS wrote Robert's lawyer a letter that was read on his behalf in court. It described Robert's unsuccessful efforts to

obtain help and complained about 'the total lack of community resources for dealing with the serious problem of drug addiction.'[25]

With the opening of the NAF, drug users ostensibly had a place to go
for withdrawal, but this did not always work as planned. When Cyril S.
went to the foundation a few days before Christmas in 1960, they told
him that they could not do anything for him until after Christmas. His
JHS worker, after learning of the situation, contacted a few doctors to see
if they would give him withdrawal medication, but no one was willing.
On New Year's Day, Cyril S. called his social worker at home, who picked
him up at his mother's home and took him down to an outpatient clinic.
Two days later, they went down to NAF again, where social workers said
that it would take another week to get him on withdrawal. Finally, on 4
January Cyril met a doctor who thought the situation was ridiculous and
started his medication.[26]

Other concrete tasks performed by JHS social workers included making appointments for clients with other social service agencies (and
occasionally acting as advocates for clients with those agencies), helping
clients with parole papers, and helping them to find jobs. In a few cases,
they supervised parole. The predecessor to the National Parole Board,
the Remission Service, had an unofficial policy of not giving parole to
drug users.[27] The JHS believed that prisoners needed to be rehabilitated
in the community, and the social workers were anxious to secure parole
for their clients.[28] After the National Parole Board was established in
1959, JHS workers supervised parole for a number of clients.

In supervising parole, the JHS felt that the most important thing was
to develop a close and intensive relationship with the parolee. According
to the supervisor of counselling, 'the only truly rehabilitative work comes
about when there is a strong relationship developed between the thera-
pist and the parolee.'[29] Another experienced worker concluded, 'I feel
that I cannot carry on successful casework with an addict unless a satisfactory relationship has been established before release. This usually takes
weeks or months to accomplish.'[30] That this worker placed enormous
confidence in this relationship is evident in her assessment of Barbara
E.: she claimed that even though they had not arranged an apartment or
a job for Barbara, their relationship was strong enough that Barbara
would make a successful parolee.[31]

Casework with Female Clients

Reflecting the strict gender divisions of 1950s Canada, female caseworkers generally dealt with female clients and male caseworkers dealt with

male clients, although there were occasional exceptions. Although there were fewer female than male social workers, female social workers tended to deal far more intensely with drug-using clients, since drug users were a much greater proportion of the female incarcerated population. In keeping with gendered expectations about women's skills in this sort of emotional work, it was the female caseworkers of the JHS who pioneered intensive counselling-oriented casework.

The first task in this type of casework was for the social workers to form intimate relationships with their clients. Social workers wanted to believe that their clients cared for them and that counselling could make a difference to their clients' lives. The expression of what social workers thought were 'real' feelings, especially if they involved warm feelings towards the social worker, was hailed as a significant breakthrough. (Not surprisingly, feelings that were considered 'real' generally involved a desire to stay away from drug use and criminal activity.) So-called 'self-awareness' was a major goal of the counselling process. One female worker proudly wrote that one client stated 'she had never talked about her real feelings to anybody.' By discussing her 'many problems, and her background and family relationships,' the client felt that 'she was growing in self-awareness and could face her problems a great deal better when she was released.'[32] Another worker reported that her client was 'evidencing a little self-awareness' and that 'I feel that I got closer to her than I ever have in the past.'[33] Social workers believed that such honesty, or confessions, on the part of a client was a step towards rehabilitation, as well as a sign of faith in the social worker. The incitement to reveal another self beneath the exterior of the 'rounder' showed how fully psychological discourses had permeated social work practice. It also demonstrated the social workers' need to believe that everyone could change and that they could be an important part of this transformation.

In unsuccessful cases, workers blamed clients who had not sufficiently 'opened up.' Patricia D.'s caseworker was initially sceptical about her potential for rehabilitation, but changed her mind after Patricia made plans for release and submitted parole papers. When her parole was turned down, the worker found her 'flippant' and concluded that she was not 'sufficiently motivated to straighten her life out.' Indeed, Patricia was back in Oakalla just two months after her release. The social worker kept in touch and did small things for her, such as calling Patricia's mother on her birthday, and sending a card to Patricia's daughter. The worker eventually concluded that Patricia 'is very adept at using people for her own end,' and that she had never 'opened up honestly.' Presumably, Patricia would have made better progress in her rehabilitation if she had revealed more of herself.[34]

Once clients had opened up, the second stage was finding them friends and employment away from the drug-using community, which usually meant encouraging them to leave Vancouver. Current research on drug use emphasizes that drug users frequently feel the need to take drugs when they are in places or with people with whom they used to take drugs.[35] This was regarded as common sense in the 1950s, and JHS workers strongly believed that clients needed to stay away from their drug-using companions, often by leaving town, although they appreciated that it was not always easy to do so. One worker suggested that Irene J.'s husband take a job in Kelowna 'to get her out of Vancouver,' but he was reluctant to leave his family, and the social worker did not push the issue.[36] Similarly, Gretchen R. undertook her parole in the interior of the province, but found the weather hot, the pay low, and her parole officer unsympathetic. Her JHS worker indicated that she would rather Gretchen stayed away from the 'influences' in Vancouver after her parole was over, but told her that she would have to make up her own mind on the matter and offered her a place in her home 'any time you want to come.' Gretchen returned to Vancouver at the end of her parole period.[37]

In other cases, clients raised the issue of leaving Vancouver but did not have the resources or social networks to do so. One twenty-two-year-old client told her social worker that she wanted to leave town, but she had no friends or relatives outside of Vancouver, and the worker was reluctant to 'encourage this girl to just go out on her own in an unknown neighbourhood.'[38] Social workers knew that loneliness could be lethal. Others, such as Maureen E., stated that they wanted to leave, but didn't for one reason or another. When Maureen's social worker found a job for her in a cannery in Ladner, she did not show up. Maybe she was insincere about leaving, or perhaps she could not face leaving friends and a plentiful supply of heroin in Vancouver. Notoriously difficult cannery work was probably not too appealing either. She was picked up on a drug charge soon thereafter.[39]

For some users, expressing a desire to leave town may have been a way of currying favour with the social worker. Carol G. told her social worker that 'she realizes she cannot continue to associate with rounders and expect to keep out of trouble.'[40] Mary T. wrote that her main concern was 'to lead a new life devoid of past acquaintances and environments.'[41] Others believed that they could stay away from drugs without abandoning their friends. When her worker suggested that May H. move away from Hastings Street, May told her that 'I feel comfortable down there, if I go too far away and don't see my friends I will get depressed and I would be more likely to take the "stuff."'[42] When the same worker advised Daisy W. to stay away from drug-using friends, Daisy retorted that a 'person could go straight whether they mixed with addicts or not,' and said that a friend of hers had quit even though 'he had stayed downtown with friends.' The worker feared that her outlook on rehabilitation was not 'constructive enough,' but she continued to meet with her.[43] One worker took a more coercive role and contacted the parole officer of one client after discovering that she was living with another drug user.[44]

JHS workers placed more emphasis on finding jobs for men than for women, but they also encouraged female clients to work, usually at traditional female occupations. At Oakalla, female drug users learned hairdressing and power sewing. Although the level of training in the jail was not high, social workers urged clients to find work in these areas. Her JHS worker advised middle-class Rebecca S. to take a course in typing or hairdressing after release, as 'it would be impossible for her to go straight should she replace drugs with a vacuum.'[45] Gretchen R.'s social worker strongly encouraged her to keep working at the Dairy Queen. The same worker recommended that Carol G. take up clerical employment with her flamboyant and somewhat unreliable uncle, since it was better than remaining unemployed.[46]

Female clients were strongly encouraged to have a square-john family member or social worker meet them at the gate after their release from Oakalla, in the hope that these chaperones could stop them from immediately contacting old companions and keep them, at least temporarily, away from trouble. It is not clear why male clients were not subjected to the same pressure. It may be that the much larger ratio of male prisoners to JHS workers' resources made it impossible, or it may have been related to gender norms. Perhaps women were seen as being in greater need of 'protection' and hence required escort from the gates of Oakalla. Another gender difference emerged with respect to clothing: female clients frequently asked social workers to pick up their clothes from downtown hotels, but male clients never did. After picking up clothes for one client three times, a social worker complained that 'clothes play quite a part in her young life – her mind seems to be on them continually.' However, she picked them up, evidently agreeing that clothes were an important item in women's lives.[47]

Caseworkers were very interested in their clients' romantic relationships, and they thought that relationships with non-rounders could be an important step towards rehabilitation. Her social worker regarded Gretchen R.'s dates with neighbourhood boys as a promising start to her parole period.[48] They could take this support to alarming extremes. One worker decided that the square-john husband of thirty-seven-year-old Verna M. would be vital to her rehabilitation, and strongly encouraged them to stay together, even though the relationship was abusive. The social worker did not mention (and perhaps was not aware) that Verna had sexual relationships with women, although this became clear later in the file. She may have known, though, and this may be why she encouraged the relationship so strenuously.[49]

Most drug users were involved with other drug users, and workers discouraged these relationships. When Bea W., eighteen, wanted to visit her boyfriend at the BC Penitentiary, a JHS worker checked and discovered that neither her mother nor her probation officer believed her claim that her current boyfriend was the father of her child. Bea's mother reported that 'the less she hears from him the better we'll all be.' The social worker recommended against giving her visiting privileges.[50] In the case of older clients, however, workers often kept quiet about their relationships. When May H., thirty-nine, was released from Kingston Penitentiary, her JHS worker took her to see her common-law husband at the BC Penitentiary. Within a week she was living in a downtown hotel with another man. After a brief period in hospital with pneumonia, she visited the JHS in the company of a third man and announced that they were considering marriage. The social worker paid little attention to the various men in May's life. She was more concerned that May was hanging out in skid row, using drugs, and not making use of her artificial limb.[51]

Social workers were influenced by post-war discourse on companionate marriages, which emphasized that marriage was a 'partnership' between a man and a woman, and that both needed to assume responsibility in separate spheres of activity.[52] As part of achieving 'maturity,' female social workers often encouraged their female clients to avoid relying too heavily on their male spouses and companions. A JHS worker advised one nineteen-year-old client who was considering marriage that 'this was unlikely to be the solution to problem.'[53] When Irene J. told her social worker that 'their future success is up to her husband,' the social worker wrote that 'she is trying to place a little too much of the responsibility on his shoulders.'[54] Female drug users, like other women, were expected to be mature partners to their husbands and to play a vital role in making the relationship work.

Many female drug users had romantic relationships with other women. Several American books and the National Film Board documentary *Forbidden Love* have described the vibrant working-class lesbian culture of the 1950s. At least 13 per cent of female JHS clients, and probably more, had romantic relationships with other women.[55] Social workers at the JHS, with their experience in jails and prison, where there were many lesbians, were well aware of the strength of this community and were accustomed to dealing with gay women. They almost certainly disapproved of lesbianism, and sometimes tried to protect young clients from it, but most often they ignored it. This approach was not unheard of in the world of corrections. An excellent thesis on the Women's Unit at Oakalla by Dorothy Coutts, who later worked for the JHS, noted that there is a 'belief by some matrons that prison makes too much of lesbianism.' 'The rules against touching and affection,' she added, were 'enforced very unevenly' depending on the attitude of the individual matrons.[56]

Soon after Louise D. arrived in Vancouver, the JHS worker noted that her clothing had become 'very mannish,' and thought that she might be a lesbian. Although the worker and Louise maintained an intensive relationship, including a lengthy correspondence, there was no mention of Louise's sexuality after that initial conjecture.[57] By comparison to Toronto's Street Haven in the late 1960s, where executive director Peggy Walpole measured her success by the number of lesbians she converted to heterosexuality, JHS workers made little effort to counsel their clients about their sexuality.[58] One social worker wrote that Nancy M. wanted to apply for parole, probably because her female partner had been released. The rest of the file concerned her job prospects.[59] Her partner's file dealt primarily with her grief over the death of her son and her unsuccessful efforts to stay away from drugs.[60] In another case, the worker reported that the prison matrons had been having a lot of trouble with a very young and troubled client of the society and that she might be involved in a prison relationship. The rest of the file dealt with the client's ongoing family difficulties and mental illness.[61]

By asserting that several JHS workers took little interest in the same-sex relationships of their clients, I do not wish to underplay the severity of cultural proscriptions against homosexuality in the 1950s, or overlook the brutality of the state in enforcing these proscriptions. Inexperienced social workers, for example, were often much less tolerant. Reflecting the views of contemporary experts, one student caseworker who learned that a client was a lesbian hypothesized that 'her whole attitude and

present outlook and conduct is but the expression of a reaction forma-
tion which had its roots in her childhood,' and declared that 'channel-
ling this client's drives and energies into more socially desirable
alternatives would appear to be a long term assignment.'[62] His response
was very atypical for the JHS, but not for society at large, where gays and
lesbians faced enormous hostility and repression. Medical professionals,
especially those from the 'psy' disciplines, defined homosexuality as a
disease and recommended draconian cures. The federal government
launched a security campaign against gays and lesbians in the public
service, and passed an amendment to the Immigration Act to keep gays
and lesbians out.[63] The John Howard Society's unusual reticence around
their clients' sexual orientation may have made the society a more
welcoming place for a few drug users.

On racial issues, the JHS workers were liberal-minded and acknowledged the special problems encountered by their minority clients, but
they were not immune to stereotyping. A much greater percentage of
female drug-using clients (11 per cent) belonged to racial minority
groups than did male drug-using clients (5 per cent). Female drug-using
clients were often Aboriginal (9 per cent), which reflected the large
involvement of Aboriginal women in prostitution, which often led to
drug use.

Caseworkers wanted to be culturally sensitive. One worker had a
volunteer research Sikhism when she had a young Sikh client, Harpreet
J. Still, when the worker visited her client's home, she found, 'as expected,' that her mother 'is apparently completely dominated by her
very rigid husband.' Her assumption may have been based on what
Harpreet told her about her family or may have been based on her own
assumptions about what a Sikh family might be like. A week later her
stereotypes were challenged when she visited the head of the Sikh
temple to ask if he could help. His 'very attractive' daughter 'took an
intelligent and understanding part in the conversation,' and the caseworker decided that the head of the temple was 'most humane.'[64] Even
her positive pronouncements smacked of white paternalism. This trend
confirms Franca Iacovetta's work, which also found that white social
workers felt that they were entitled to comment on the oppression, or
lack of oppression, of minority women in their own families.[65] When this
same worker went to visit the home of her white client, Irene J., who was
married to a Chinese man, she noted that a 'toothless Chinese uncle'
greeted them with 'a warm smile.' She had previously noted that Irene's
mother-in-law was a 'very nice looking Chinese lady.'[66] Comments re-

garding the appearance of client's parents were unusual and thus suggest that she was somewhat surprised by the attractive Chinese women.
Her comments reflect what Iacovetta has described as the 'folklorization'
of hyphenated Canadians by many liberals in the post-war period.[67]

JHS workers realized that clients of colour faced additional barriers to
finding employment and obtaining aid. In the JHS's annual report of
1951, for example, the society told the story of 'Trudy,' a nineteen-year-
old Aboriginal drug user who was facing a charge of retaining stolen
property. The report read,

> Trudy need not go to jail – this is only her first offense. But what else can she
> do? Any job that she can get on her own, and even these jobs are limited will
> take her right back to the part of town and the people where and with whom
> she will get into trouble again. We thought it would be a good idea to get
> her a job doing housework in a nice home, living in. Have you ever tried to
> get an Indian girl a job, especially one who has been on drugs? We spent
> many days phoning up advertisements in the newspapers for housekeepers.
> We received many explanations, with only one meaning – no.[68]

Yet, JHS workers themselves participated in the oppression of minority
women by finding them job placements in the least attractive occupation – domestic service – which many white women shunned. The JHS
rarely found domestic placements for white women, but Trudy and the
Sikh client described earlier were encouraged to work in the homes of
white Canadian families. It is not clear whether minority women were
encouraged to find work with white families as part of an unstated
'Canadianization' campaign, or whether workers simply accepted the
limitations placed on minority women by a racially discriminatory labour
market.

Like Irene J., many of the female clients of the JHS dated interracially,
but the files contain no overt disapproval of this practice, although it is
hard to know how caseworkers acted in interviews. White female drug
users delighted in telling social workers about dating black men, clearly
hoping to shock them. This usually fit with a larger pattern of resistance
to the social work relationship. Eugenia C., a twenty-six-year-old white
client, told different tales about her life and men every time she saw her
worker in Oakalla, but she was also quite effective at getting her worker
to conduct various tasks on her behalf, including investigating the possibility of changing her name to 'Lucky Martin' and her chances of joining
the army. She told her worker that 'white men make her sick, their skins

are too pale.' The worker concluded that her 'co-operative attitude' was 'an act' and that it would 'be interesting to discover the motivation of her attachment to Negroes.' The worker assumed that there was some 'psychological' reason for her sexual preference.[69] At the same time, reflecting the liberal approach that dominated within the agency, at least one white social worker was furious when the mother of one client refused to allow the client's African-Canadian boyfriend into their home.[70]

Casework with Male Clients

Male caseworkers also wanted to achieve close relationships with their clients based around self-analysis, although female drug-using clients appear to have engaged in this type of relationship with their female caseworkers much more readily than male clients did with their male caseworkers. There were exceptions, such as Will M., who approached the JHS for clothing but soon began a fairly intensive relationship with his worker. Like many of the male clients who formed a close bond with caseworkers, Will M. was left-wing, interested in the NDP, and well-educated, having taken university-level courses at Kingston Penitentiary. His worker arranged for Will to take a welding course and receive social assistance. His worker concluded that Will M. had 'many positive aspects,' despite 'a certain degree of hostility under a conforming shell.' The worker recommended that contact be maintained at Will M.'s request.[71]

Other social workers also wanted their relationships with male clients to be based around growing self-awareness and self-analysis. For example, one worker noted that a client 'has a great deal on the ball extremely acute around the self conscious level.' Like female caseworkers, male caseworkers often assumed that self-understanding was the key to a client 'ultimately straightening himself out.'[72] It was the best-educated men, like Richard T. who had several years of university education and experience as a union activist, or articulate union activist Charles T., who were the most interested in this type of discussion, and they subsequently received the most attention.[73] Social workers encouraged male clients like these to speak out on behalf of drug users, urging Charles T., for example, to make a presentation to a committee from Toronto about plans for a treatment centre there, and inviting him to attend corrections institute meetings.

Male caseworkers could be far more patronizing in the case of less-educated clients. One worker formed a close relationship with Garry H.

and wrote him warm encouraging letters, despite his condescending assessment of Garry as 'very co-operative, easily impressed and led, person of limited intelligence.' He particularly enjoyed Garry's bumbling efforts to make good, such as the time Garry came into the office 'all dressed up and with sales pamphlets protruding.' Asked about his sales pitch, 'he went into a tense spasm and started spouting chapter and verse of the SHP [Stanley Home Products] manual.' On another occasion the worker reported, 'Garry was in with 'big problem.' He owed $10 for having bumped a car but could not afford to pay the debt until he was paid the following day. The worker suggested he ask for a one-day grace; 'This he did successfully. Amazed that worker could think of such a bright thing.' When the worker left the JHS, he wrote: 'SOMEONE PLEASE KEEP IN TOUCH WITH Garry!'

Before he left the JHS, this worker kept in contact with Garry's parents (Garry being nineteen years old and unmarried). His mother was keen to maintain the connection, calling the JHS several times to complain that Garry was not working, and on another occasion to gripe that a girl had left a suitcase of clothing at the house.[74] It was not at all unusual for family members to be drawn into male social work, particularly if the man had a non-using wife. Director Merv Davis felt that for the rehabilitation of a drug user to be successful, there had to be another interested party, such as a mother, a wife, or some other person, who could provide supervision.[75] The JHS operated a 'wives' group,' which brought the female partners of male inmates together to talk about their problems[76] – this group reflected the gendered expectations of male social workers that women would help in the rehabilitation of their partners. As Elaine Tyler May and others have pointed out, in post–Second World War culture, women were responsible for the bulk of emotional work involved in maintaining relationships. Not surprisingly, there was no 'husbands' group' for the male partners of female offenders.[77]

Wives without criminal records could also be appropriate recipients of casework at the JHS, although the reverse pattern did not occur. John M., for example, approached the JHS in 1957 regarding a ticket-of-leave (parole). After his daughter's school called the JHS, the entire family began receiving social work. One of the workers involved with the family decided that the mother and daughter were 'such a fine looking pair' that the mother must be jealous of her daughter's good looks. After several weeks of counselling, Mrs. M. admitted that she felt some rivalry with her daughter and 'resentment of her ability to share interests with father.' During the summer, the daughter was put on probation after being picked up drunk by the police. The family decided not to tell John, who was still in prison, although the worker wrote that 'I have continually emphasized the right of a father to know about the important things that are happening to his family members' and stressed that he should be allowed to participate in family affairs as much as possible. The families of female drug users were never given such instructions about the importance of recognizing the drug user's place within the family. After his release from prison, John successfully completed a three-month parole. He and his family continued to contact the JHS, but within six months John was using again, and he was arrested on another charge.[78] Although the family continued to make contact with the JHS, there was no clear indication that they found all of this counselling useful or helpful.

These contacts show how workers established their own ideas about the nature of clients' problems and then began an elaborate counselling process, which not surprisingly resulted in a confirmation of their initial diagnosis. Was Mrs. M. really jealous of her daughter, Sylvia, or did her contacts with an 'expert' like the JHS social worker lead her to believe that this was a problem? Perhaps she agreed to please the caseworker. The worker's construction of the 'problem' relied heavily on stereotypical ideas about female rivalry over beauty and men. While it is not impossible that this was a problem for Sylvia and her mother, it seems more likely that their conflicts derived from the many difficulties inherent in their living situation and economic circumstances. Like Gretchen R., who was diagnosed by her social worker as having deep feelings of rejection, other clients of the JHS were also forced to negotiate through the assumptions that social workers made about their 'problems' and their lives.

Like female caseworkers, male caseworkers were quite supportive about the difficulties of quitting and were understanding when clients lapsed. Chris M. was released from BC Penitentiary in mid-September 1957 and stayed away from drugs for nearly a year until he was reduced to part-time work and began using again. He wanted to go work on a ranch outside of Williams Lake where a relative had offered him room and board, but there was no place for his wife. He asked the JHS to arrange for a welfare check to his wife. Chris was given a ticket to Williams Lake and dropped off at the doctor's. The worker reported that 'Chris had done so well for so long without any help that his plan merited support from somewhere.' Unfortunately, he was convicted again on a drug charge within six weeks.[79] The willingness of JHS social workers to give drug users a second (or third or fourth) chance was fairly unique. Magistrates, police officers, and prison officials tended to assume that once a drug user, always a drug user. That someone believed they could make it and was willing to put resources behind them might have made a difference to at least a few of the people who used the society's services.

Male users, like female users, were encouraged to leave Vancouver and go into the interior, or to Vancouver Island where drugs were less available. In the early 1960s, one worker proposed a more radical solution for a few long-term male drug users, encouraging them to leave Vancouver and go to England, where doctors were allowed to prescribe maintenance medication. George F., thirty, had come to Canada as a boy under the Fairbridge boys scheme and started using drugs at seventeen; he spent most of the 1950s incarcerated. His mother advertised for him in several Canadian papers, and they began corresponding. George decided to return to England to make a fresh start. The JHS contacted the Fairbridge Home Alumni Association for funds and provided a fair amount of cash itself, and in the spring of 1961 George returned to England. He wrote his worker to say 'thank you for making this happen. I am very happy. Lovely home and people, all beyond my wildest hopes and dreams. New life, new chance, want to take big strides in new direction.'[80] This relationship involved no psychological analysis. George was very determined to return home, and the worker thought it was a good plan and helped him put it into action.

The JHS helped at least two others go to England in the early 1960s. These users joined a stream of Canadian users who went to England in the late 1950s and early '60s.[81] Many of these Canadian users were treated by Lady Frankau. Her extensive narcotic prescriptions spawned a new debate over maintenance in Great Britain, and some British analysts blamed the Canadians for the development of a heroin problem in Britain in the mid-1960s.[82]

Close Relationships between Social Workers and Clients?

The vast majority of the JHS's drug-using clients had fairly limited contact with the society. They used the society to find employment, to arrange for welfare, or for other small tasks. Only a few clients actively engaged in the therapeutic project that was dear to the hearts of the JHS workers, but in some of these cases a very close relationship developed between social worker and client.

Some users appreciated the active interest and affection of their social workers. Gretchen R. signed her letters to her worker with 'love,' and she pleaded with her worker to write again soon. After arriving at Kingston Penitentiary, Louise D. wrote her worker to say,

> I wonder if you could possibly know how much I've appreciated all that you have endeavoured to do for me. I did so want to confide in you when the problem began to get too big for me, but I explained my reasons for not doing so, so we shall not dwell on that ... I have found you to be a wonderful friend, and aside from your work, what I would term 'a good Joe.' You must accustom yourself to our language and this last quote is the highest compliment I can give you ... In closing, I once again express my deepest gratitude for all you've been to me: friend, counsellor, and above all human.

It is possible that these words were a 'con' of sorts. Louise planned to apply for parole and hoped that her worker would supervise it for her.[83] Nonetheless, it is just as possible that there was affection and gratitude behind these words.

Men also expressed affection for their workers. Will M. wrote, 'And what of Will M. and his latest foray into narcotics? I don't know ... I really don't. Excuses were never my forte. Nor explanations. But I feel you above all deserve to know what motivated this.' He added that 'I never tried to shove and con you (and couldn't even if I wanted) and you always levelled with me.'[84] Letters like this were unusual, but they demonstrate that at least a few clients found the JHS a helpful and supportive place.

Conclusion

Social workers wanted clients to stay out of prison and to stop using drugs. They thought that the best way to do this was for their clients to leave Vancouver, make new 'square-john' friends, find employment, and engage in an extensive process of self-examination. Clients sometimes shared their social workers' view of the rehabilitative process and tried to do these things, but more often they made their own decisions about their lives. Clients engaged in the therapeutic relationship insofar as it met some purpose of their own. Some clients wanted to understand the psychological reasons behind their drug use, and others simply wanted to convince the worker to supervise parole or hoped to get some money out of the society. Others were less sure of what they wanted out of the relationship.

Social workers are not a unified group – some have been more interested in achieving community development and social change, while others have sought to change their individual clients. The JHS focused more on changing their clients than changing the economic and social inequalities that often led their clients to use drugs. The institutional constraints within which the JHS operated, including the need to cooperate with various facets of the criminal justice system, and the reliance on funding from the Community Chest and Council, meant that JHS workers were unlikely to propose radical solutions. Their power was limited by forces larger than themselves. Nonetheless, workers at the JHS believed in social justice and recognized the very serious barriers faced by their clients. They established close and meaningful relationships with at least some of their clients, and they advocated for drug users within the criminal justice system and beyond. If they sometimes also imposed their own judgements and values on drug users' lives, they at least tried to be of assistance. Few others in the harsh legal climate of the classic period of narcotic control did as much.

Chapter 7

Free Drugs or Prison for Life?
Changing Approaches to Treatment

Even in the 1920s, journalists and social reformers demanded treatment for the unfortunate drug user, but their pleas fell on deaf ears. The Narcotic Division insisted that treatment was a provincial matter. They encouraged the provinces to pass legislation to provide for the treatment of addicts, but only Alberta and Nova Scotia passed such legislation, and only Alberta put it into effect.[1] When the drug panic of the early 1920s faded, and the 'nefarious' Asian trafficker disappeared from the drug discourse, the idea that addicts were 'sick' people who required treatment grew in strength. In part, the Great Depression increased sympathy for the disadvantaged, including drug users.[2] But also, from the 1930s on, an increasing number of the drug offenders in Canada were white. Exclusionary legislation meant that the Chinese population in Canada began to shrink, and many of the Chinese who had been involved in the drug trade were deported. The number of Chinese appearing in the courts for drug offences plummeted; as a result, foreigners could no longer be blamed for the drug problem in Canada. Instead, drug use was conceived of as an internal problem, and this led to a more serious effort to understand the causes of addiction.

In the 1930s there was considerable public support for the idea that addiction was an illness requiring medical treatment. An article in the *Winnipeg Free Press* claimed, for example, that authorities had long since regarded drug addiction as a disease, not a crime, and it argued that prison was not the place for curing disease.[3] In the United States, the addiction specialist Dr. Lawrence Kolb authored an extraordinarily influential series of papers in the 1920s arguing that addiction stemmed from underlying character defects. Kolb called for the creation of specialized psychiatric hospitals to treat addiction.[4] As psychiatry grew more influential in the 1930s and '40s, problems like addiction were increasingly regarded as a matter of individual psychopathology.[5] Slowly, a psychiatric version of the disease model of addiction displaced older ideas about addiction as a moral failure. While these views stigmatized addicts, they also held out the possibility that they could be cured through expert treatment. The U.S. Public Health Service opened a prison hospital in Lexington, Kentucky, to provide psychiatric care for narcotic addicts in 1935. A second, in Fort Worth, Texas, followed in 1938.

Officials in Ottawa were less optimistic. In the period before the Second World War, the Division of Narcotic Control's communication with the few institutions across the country that were attempting to treat drug users, and with officials in the United States, gave them little reason to believe that cures were easily obtained. The doctor in charge of curing drug users at Ponoka Mental Hospital in Alberta in the 1930s complained that the same patients entered repeatedly, and while it was easy to withdraw the drug user, they quickly became troublesome around the hospital, demanding their release and interesting other patients in using drugs.[6] The privately run Homewood Sanatorium in Guelph accepted drug users occasionally, but the Narcotic Division was very sceptical about the treatment provided there and complained that patients received drugs from visiting friends and relatives.[7] By the 1930s, the Narcotic Division had concluded that treatment was hopeless.[8] The Royal Commission to Investigate the Penal System of Canada (1938) agreed, reporting that 'we can find no evidence that they are ever cured.'[9]

Public demands for treatment escalated with the expansion of the welfare state after the Second World War. Beginning in the late 1940s, a CCF member of the British Columbian legislature, E.E. Winch, roundly criticized Canada's approach to addiction, arguing that addicts should be treated as people with an illness, and recommended that Canada implement the British system of registering addicts and giving them their required dosages of drugs. As proof of the British system's effectiveness, he and his supporters, including his son Harold Winch, pointed to the small number of users in Great Britain.[10] In reality, however, the few hundred people who obtained opiates on prescription in Great Britain were people who had become addicted as a result of illness, and were a quite different population from the users in Canada.[11]

In the spring of 1952, the police arrested a small number of juvenile addicts in Vancouver, raising alarm about teenage drug use and feeding into the juvenile delinquency panics of the era.[12] The media highlighted the case of a seventeen-year-old waitress who told the court that she had been using drugs since she was fifteen.[13] Another headline declared, 'Teen-Age Girls Tell of Dope Orgies.'[14] At the same time, there was growing concern about the links between addiction and crime, especially shoplifting. A 1952 editorial in the *Vancouver Sun* accused drug addicts of all manners of 'vicious crimes,' including 'shooting people in holdups,' and 'knocking them over the head on the streets.'[15] Vancouver newspapers regularly detailed how much addiction was costing the city of Vancouver, usually providing estimates in the millions of dollars. At the same time, drug use was frequently portrayed in the media as being contagious. T.E.E. Greenfield, a former RCMP Drug Squad member warned that 'drug addiction is catching. We segregate smallpox victims to prevent them from contaminating others. Yet we lock up dope addicts and non-addicts in the same prison.'[16] *Saturday Night* claimed 'addicts breed more addicts,' explaining, 'misery likes company and the addict likes to introduce new members to his circle. It gives him companionship and perhaps the clubman's sense of belonging.'[17]

In response, the Vancouver Community Chest and Council, the forerunner of the United Way, established a committee to study the problem of drug addiction. With considerable fanfare, the Vancouver Committee, led by Dr. Lawrence Ranta, released its report in the summer of 1952. The committee recommended that the provincial and federal governments provide a pilot medical treatment centre, that the Community Chest and Council and other organizations carry out an educational campaign on the dangers of addiction, and, most radically, that the federal government establish narcotic clinics where registered narcotic users could receive their minimum required dosages of drugs.[18]

The controversial clinic proposal generated the greatest publicity. The leading dailies in Vancouver endorsed the proposal: the *Vancouver Sun* urged that it be put in place as quickly as possible and the *Province* declared that 'all the intelligent persons' who had given any serious thought to the problem supported it.[19] By contrast, the Division of Narcotic Control was horrified. K.C. Hossick, the chief of the division, went out to Vancouver to meet with the Community Chest and Council, and the federal government subsequently agreed to fund a study into drug addiction in British Columbia.[20] Not surprisingly, given the trend towards seeing drug use as a psychiatric disorder, they appointed a psychiatrist, George H. Stevenson, a professor of psychiatry at the University of Western Ontario and a past president of the American Psychiatric Association, to head the project, which was conducted under the auspices of the University of British Columbia. The research team consisted of a psychiatric social worker, a physician, and a psychologist. The Stevenson report, released three years later, would have an important influence on legislation and treatment programs in Canada.

The Stevenson report comprised a number of different studies. The team initially planned to compare two groups of one hundred prisoners (one group who used drugs and one who did not) but they ended up studying seventy-four drug-using prisoners and forty-one non-using prisoners. The non-users were initially regarded as a 'control group,' but the researchers quickly realized that non-using prisoners were quite different from the general population, and that the non-drug-using prisoners were likely to start using drugs in the future. At the end of the first year, they abandoned this study to undertake others. A Consecutive Conviction Study recorded statistical data on every drug user admitted to Oakalla Prison Farm; a Sibling Study compared twenty-five drug-using siblings to twenty-five non-drug-using siblings, but it was not completed; there were detailed psychological studies of sixty-four drug-using prisoners and sixty-four non-drug-using prisoners; and there was a study of people who had stopped using heroin (also not completed). Despite the ad-hoc research design, the Stevenson report painted a vivid picture of the Vancouver drug-use scene. It also firmly refuted the idea that the drug problem could be solved by providing addicts with a regular supply of drugs.

Stevenson regarded drug users as immature, selfish, undisciplined, and immoral. He wrote:

> in our interviews with adult addicts we have been constantly impressed with their close resemblance to children, in their restlessness, hedonism, selfishness, ingratitude, parasitism, cruelty, resentment of discipline and lack of concern for the future ... they live only for immediate needs; their moral principles are immature or weak; they have low frustration tolerance, are easily depressed or discouraged, they are adventuresome and reckless, often generously foolhardy; they are emotionally immature generally, although intellectually they have average adult intelligence.[21]

He lambasted them for refusing to fulfil what he regarded as adult responsibilities, citing their lack of interest in the democratic process, their failure to pay income tax and to carry life insurance, and their refusal to pay hospital insurance premiums under the British Columbia Hospital Insurance Plan.[22] He condemned their unwillingness to take personal responsibility for their drug use, their criminal activity, and their regular prison sentences.

Stevenson opposed the compulsory treatment of addicts, arguing that the will to be treated was an important aspect of achieving a cure.[23] He argued that a prison hospital, similar to those established in the United States in the 1930s, would not be worth the expense. He advised that drug users sentenced to jail for drug or other offences should be provided with treatment and that addicts outside of the criminal justice system should receive help with withdrawal in hospitals or mental hospitals. He argued that that the six-month penalty for possession was too severe and should be removed, and he advised that rehabilitative treatment be provided through the Narcotic Addiction Foundation, which had been established in British Columbia with grants from the provincial government in 1955.

Stevenson became an influential opponent of the narcotic clinics proposed by the Vancouver Community Chest and Council. In 1955 he published his widely circulated 'Arguments For and Against the Legal Sale of Narcotics,' which concluded that the legal sale of narcotics would fail to solve addiction problems and would, in fact, make them worse. Drawing on historical examples, including the brief experience with narcotic clinics in the United States in the early 1920s, and the legal availability of opium in China in the nineteenth century, Stevenson argued that permitting addicts to receive legal drugs would not reduce crime or lead addicts to find employment. Since drug use was part of the drug user's 'general personality disorder,' he argued that there was no reason to think that 'supplying him with all the drugs he wants at minimum prices will solve his problem.'[24] Stevenson was not alone in his opposition to clinics. The Senate of Canada conducted its own detailed study on the traffic in narcotic drugs in 1955 and unanimously rejected narcotic clinics. Instead, it recommended severe penalties for traffickers and called on provincial governments to establish treatment facilities.[25] As a result, the Community Chest and Council stopped pushing the clinic proposal and the *Vancouver Sun* rescinded its support.[26]

In the meantime, the Division of Narcotic Control, located in the now activist Department of National Health and Welfare and led by a more treatment-oriented chief, K.C. Hossick, was making its own plans for a treatment centre. In 1951 the chief of the Mental Health Division of the Department of Health suggested that the former quarantine station at William's Head British Columbia could be used as a narcotic treatment centre, but this proposal was abandoned.[27] In 1954 Health Minister Paul Martin Sr. and C.M. Roberts (chief of the Mental Health Division) visited the large U.S. prison treatment facility for addicts in Lexington, Kentucky. The department envisaged building a similar 500-bed institution in central Canada close to a university.[28] Pressure from British Columbia, and the obvious fact that there were more drug users in Vancouver than anywhere else in the country, however, caused the department to eventually shift the site to British Columbia.

In developing its own plan, the federal government paid careful attention to the Stevenson report, but it rejected the idea of voluntary treatment.[29] First, in keeping with the post-war penchant for large-scale social engineering, the government was under pressure to develop a comprehensive program that would permanently rid Canada of the problem of drug addiction – a voluntary treatment program would only reach a small portion of addicts. Second, despite the cultural shifts that had given greater legitimacy to a medical approach to the problem, the Division of Narcotic Control continued to have strong ties with enforcement officials, and leading police officers wanted drug users to be incarcerated for long periods. R.S.S. Wilson, a former RCMP superintendent who sat on the Department of National Health and Welfare's Technical Advisory Committee on Drug Addiction, argued that drug addicts should be committed for a period of at least ten years to a 'narcotic hospital operated by the Federal government,' where the addict would receive psychotherapy. After a year in hospital, the addict could be released on parole, but if he or she was recommitted more than twice, the addict would be classed as 'incurable' and sent to an institution for life.[30] RCMP Commissioner L.H. Nicholson also favoured compulsory isolation or quarantine for an unspecified period of time. He argued that 'forced detention' would actually improve addicts' quality of life.[31]

At the federal level, the views of enforcement officials won out over Stevenson's program of voluntary treatment and the clinic proposal. Under Part II of the 1961 Narcotic Control Act, anyone convicted of possession, trafficking, or importation could be sentenced to an indefinite period of custody for 'treatment.' If this was a first offence, the custody would expire at the end of ten years. Otherwise, it could be indefinite, although the act anticipated that people would be released after they had been 'cured' and would then be paroled for ongoing supervision.[32] The government also announced that a new prison 'treatment centre' would be built for addicts in British Columbia. All members who spoke to the bill saw it as a progressive step forward, although Harold Winch, the CCF member from Burnaby, the son of E.E. Winch, and an outspoken advocate of narcotic clinics, argued that addicts should also be allowed to commit themselves voluntarily. No one expressed concern that it meant that people would serve indefinitely long terms for simple possession. Even Winch argued that 'Some might take the view and, indeed, they would be right, that in legislation of this kind we are moving into the realm of civil rights.' But, he elaborated, 'there is no infringing of the civil rights of an individual when it is being done not only for his own benefit but for the protection of the majority.'[33] There was some opposition, both in the House of Commons and in British Columbia, to the establishment of the first 'treatment centre' in Matsqui, located forty-five minutes outside of Vancouver, but this was based on practical concerns that the institution was too far away and that it was premature to invest $5 million in a new institution when the effectiveness of institutional treatment was unknown.[34] The most strenuous debate over the act came from members of the House of Commons who wanted to see the death penalty imposed on traffickers.

The 1961 act would have unintended consequences in that it also removed the minimum penalties for possession, with the idea that people would be sentenced to treatment instead. The Minister of National Health and Welfare, J. Waldo Monteith, asserted that the minimum penalties were removed at the suggestion of the Senate committee of 1955, but in fact, that report did not make this recommendation.[35] The Stevenson report, on the other hand, did advise ending the minimum penalties on the grounds that sending relatively new users to jail for six months, where they would only become further enmeshed in a network of drug-using friends, made little sense. Stevenson argued that if the minimum penalty was discontinued, these young addicts could be rehabilitated and treated apart from 'older and more criminal types.'[36] Given the growing concern about juvenile addiction in the 1950s, it is far more likely that the minimum penalties were removed for this reason. In the end, the removal of the minimum penalties would be more important than the government's elaborate plans for treatment, since Part II of the Narcotic Control Act was never signed into effect.

That said, the minimum penalties were not really removed, at least not right away. Because the Canadian Criminal Code did not permit judges to sentence people to a fine for an indictable offence that carried a maximum sentence of more than five years in prison, prison sentences remained mandatory.[37] For the first several years after the passage of the 1961 act, sentences of six months or a year remained common. Moreover, in the early 1960s, the Division of Narcotic Control encouraged prosecutors to proceed against drug users under the Habitual Criminal Act, a piece of 1948 legislation that allowed for the indefinite detention of repeat offenders. In 1966, after some delays, the treatment centre at Matsqui prison was finally opened, but it only operated for three years as an institution exclusively devoted to the treatment of drug users.[38]

In the meantime, the drug scene in Canada changed dramatically. Marijuana, with its promise of peacefulness and consciousness expansion wafted its way across university campuses and into the high schools. The hallucinogen LSD opened a door into breathtaking (and sometimes frightening) new worlds. Later, injection amphetamine use ('speed') took the bloom off flower-power with the threat of violence and addiction. Arrests skyrocketed – in 1960, 21 people were convicted for possession of marijuana. Ten years later, 5,399 people were convicted for the same offence.[39] When middle-class young people began flooding the courts, alarm grew about the long sentences being handed down for narcotic offences. Amendments to the Narcotic Drug Act in 1969 made it possible to proceed either by summary or indictment, enabling judges to give a simple fine in the case of possession. By 1971, fines were given out in 77 per cent of all cases involving the possession of cannabis.[40] Even heroin users were treated more leniently – in 1971, 15 per cent received a fine, 29 per cent received probation or a suspended sentence, and 18 per cent were given a sentence of less than six months for simple possession.[41] In 1972, changes to the criminal code made it easier to obtain a pardon for drug offences. Drugs remained illegal, but the classic period had come to a decisive end.

In the middle years of the twentieth century, police officers, government bureaucrats, and parliamentarians all held the hope that with proper psychiatric care, drug users might be cured. Fearful that drug use was contagious and that drug users were responsible for a large amount of crime, they decided to isolate drug users in penal institutions rather than carry out the 'cure' in the community. In reality, the treatment project never got off the ground. By the time the first treatment prison was built, growing scepticism about the value of prisons, asylums, and other total institutions, and the rise of middle-class marijuana use meant that the compulsory segregation and treatment of addicts would lose the appeal it had had in 1961. The 1961 Narcotic Control Act was a product of the 1950s, arising from a faith in experts, especially psychiatric experts, from conservative social norms, and from a willingness to experiment with new social programs to address Canada's perceived ills. But in 1961, Canada was at the dawn of a new age, and the solutions of 1961 were quickly abandoned.

Conclusion

The world of drug use has changed dramatically since 1961. There is a much broader range of drugs in use, there is far more polydrug use, and there are dramatically more users from a much greater diversity of backgrounds. The increased volume and velocity of international trade, the growth of global inequalities, the intensification of consumerism, and the technological changes allowing for many small underground laboratories have made controlling the drug market even less feasible than it was in the years 1920–61. The large number of users makes it impossible for the police to even contemplate the type of comprehensive surveillance that characterized the 1950s. There is also a much broader array of treatment options for users, including therapeutic communities and methadone programs. Since the 1980s, harm-reduction measures, such as needle exchanges, have been established in urban centres across the country. And in the first years of the twenty-first century, there is considerable support by the public and parliamentarians for changes to Canada's drug laws, especially for the decriminalization of marijuana.

Notwithstanding all these changes, the story of drug use and regulation between 1920 and 1961 still has a few lessons for today. First, it alerts us to the fact that drug enforcement can have unforeseen negative consequences. In the 1920s, the need to avoid police led drug users to switch from smoking opium to using less bulky drugs, such as heroin, usually by injection, with serious consequences for their health. We should be wary of the detrimental effects of strict drug enforcement, especially the danger of the substitution of more harmful drugs and drug-using practices when less-harmful drugs become unavailable. Second, the harsh enforcement of the classic period may have made drug use more attractive to young people who wished to visibly defy the authorities and social norms. The intensive policing of narcotics users and the prestige that this granted those in 'delinquent' subcultures made the idea of becoming a drug user more attractive to young 'round-ers.' The illegality of drug use continues to make it attractive to many young people today. Third, intensive policing contributed to the high cost of drugs and the difficulty of scoring them. The expensive and time-consuming life of a drug user made it hard for drug users to find and keep regular employment, and it significantly disrupted their family lives and living situations. Users may have found it difficult to maintain jobs and relationships in any case, but the intensive policing and high cost of drugs made it almost impossible. Fourth, while policing was effective in the sense that the police made many arrests and secured many convic-tions, the violence of policing in the post-war period, especially the throat holds, made police operations dangerous for both police officers and users. Finally, because of the nature of narcotic policing, the possi-bilities for corruption are great. Police officers are sometimes forced to use drugs themselves, or to participate in drug deals to try and capture traffickers. All this said, the intensive policing of the classic years did play a role in reducing drug use in the 1920s and '30s, and perhaps in keeping it low in the 1940s and '50s, and enforcement has to be consid-ered as at least part of a multi-pronged approach when it comes to dealing with drug problems today. Vancouver has included enforcement as part of its innovative Four Pillars approach to dealing with addiction in that city.[1]

This study also suggests that we need a broader array of treatment options for drug users. In the classic period, few doctors wanted drug users as patients, and they took relatively little interest in drug policy. And yet, patients lucky enough to find treatment, such as the drug users treated by Dr. M. (mentioned in chapter 5), often did quite well. By the 1950s, psychiatrists were looked to as experts in the field, but few had much interest in assuming this role. One of the few who did, George H. Stevenson, who headed the Oakalla study, had little sympathy for users, but he produced valuable research and made some important recom-mendations, including the removal of six-month minimum sentences for possession and the establishment of voluntary treatment programs. Since the AIDS epidemic began in the 1980s, doctors have taken a greater interest in the problems of drug users, but even today patients can find it difficult to locate a doctor willing to prescribe methadone, especially in the rural areas, and we need a greater variety of treatment options. Doctors must do more to look after the health of drug users.

We also need to listen to the users when it comes to treatment. Throughout the classic period, many users insisted that a legal supply of drugs would enable them to get their lives back on track. The first such program – methadone maintenance – although it is not without its problems, continues to be the most successful treatment available. A preliminary heroin trial is finally scheduled to begin in Canada in 2005 – if we had listened to users, it might have been scheduled for 1952.[2]

The work of the John Howard Society, especially in the 1950s, provides a more positive example of what can be done. Drug users today often encounter judgmental attitudes even among people who are supposed to be helping them.[3] Social workers who understand the many difficulties of addicts and who are equipped to provide concrete aid can be very helpful. Not everyone will use their services, and many who do will probably continue using drugs; however, social workers, nurses, and community development workers who provide counselling, needle exchanges, and safe-injection sites, who link users with other social and health services, and who promote community development do very valuable work. These workers may do little to attack the root causes of drug use (which, in my view, lie in social inequalities and a consumer-driven society), but they can do much to ease the daily pain of users.

Ideas about the causes of addiction have been in flux throughout the twentieth century. There is no reason to believe that we have the answer today, any more than we have had in the past, and lawmakers should be suspicious of simplistic solutions. Drug use is usually part of a total life experience. Female users in the 1950s, for example, frequently complained that in order to make money, they needed to engage in sex work, but in order to engage in sex work, they needed to take drugs. Not much has changed for many female sex workers today. In the early twenty-first century, as in the years 1920–61, heavy drug use is often a way of coping with the difficulties posed by life for the most disadvantaged members of our society – people with mental health problems or who have relatively few opportunities due to lack of education, racial discrimination, and poverty. The solution to drug 'problems' cannot be examined in isolation from the multiple difficulties, especially poverty, faced by most addicts.

Appendix

Notes on Confidential Case Files

I consulted a wide range of sources in writing this book, including newspapers, magazines, Hansard, medical journals, the administrative records of the Division of Narcotic Control, reports by doctors and social workers, court records, coroner's inquests, social welfare and police records, as well as the annual reports of the RCMP, the Department of Health, and the Remission Service/National Parole Board. I also used two sets of confidential case files, and this appendix outlines the procedures I used to collect, organize, and analyze this material.

Case files provide one of the few windows into the life experiences of marginalized people, but as many historians have cautioned, case files often tell us more about the people who generated the files than they do about the subjects of the files. This appendix describes these files in more detail and explains why they were preserved and what can be learned from them.

The Division of Narcotic Control Files

The Division of Narcotic Control, part of the Federal Department of Health, was created in 1920 to enforce the Opium and Narcotic Drug Act. Beginning sometime in the 1920s, the division kept case files on every person that it identified as being a drug user across the country. The Department of Health deposited a selection of these files at the National Archives of Canada in the early 1990s. The collection includes eighteen boxes of case files on 'Addicts and Traffickers.' The earliest of these files began in 1928, and the last began in 1959; the vast majority end in the early 1970s. The collection was culled before reaching the National Archives, and the archivist responsible for the collection does not know why these particular files were preserved.[1] According to researchers who worked with these files (or ones like them) in the 1970s, the standard procedure was to remove the case files if the Bureau of Dangerous Drugs (which replaced the Division of Narcotic Control) received reports of death or deportation, or if they had received no report about the person in ten years (for illicit users) or five years (for 'professional users,' i.e., doctors.) However, there were a few files in which the user was noted as 'deceased' but the file was still in the box. This may have been a clerical error.

The files contained mug shots, police reports, criminal records, and departmental correspondence with doctors, prosecutors, police officers, and the parole board. Each time a drug user was arrested by the RCMP, a police report would be placed in the file. These were usually two or three pages of single-spaced text that described every aspect of the arrest. The reports were later used by police when they testified in court, so they were extremely detailed and were written up to make the best possible case against the user. The police also wrote a two to three page report on the trials of drug users. These reports described the testimony, the verdict, the sentence, and the judge's reasoning. The Division of Narcotic Control used these reports to inform the RCMP and the special prosecutors about standards of evidence and procedures for achieving successful cases. The files also contained correspondence with the specially appointed narcotic prosecutors on the case, again with the purpose of sharing information to make successful cases. A full criminal record was placed in the file every time someone was convicted. When the department noticed that a drug user had been obtaining drugs from a doctor, they often asked the police to investigate, and these reports were also placed in the drug user's file, along with departmental correspondence with doctors.

Many of the earliest files are missing individual documents, such as police reports or trial reports from convictions that were recorded in the file, but for the period after the Second World War, the files are remarkably complete. Moreover, while it is impossible to know the absolute number of users in post-war Canada, the division seems to have been remarkably successful at creating and maintaining files on a large proportion of so-called 'criminal' users. In contrast to today, when the majority of drug users go unrecorded, police officers, doctors, and drug researchers in early post-war Canada all agreed that it would be difficult to use drugs for very long without coming to the attention of authorities.[2]

The database I created for these files included approximately half of the available files. In selecting files, I only included people who used themselves, although there were a number of files on non-using traffickers. Second, since there were fewer files for the earlier part of the time period, all of the files that started in the 1920s and '30s were included in my database. Third, several files that began in each year from 1940 to 1961 were included. The primary goal was to ensure that there were files that began in every year. No other criteria were used in selecting files.

This resulted in a total of 159 files: 35 from the 1920s and '30s, and 124 from the 1940s and '50s. For the period after 1945, the case files are fairly representative, by gender and race, of the people who were arrested for narcotic offences (see tables 1–3 at the end of the appendix). For the period before 1945, the case file subjects were disproportionately female and white, compared to arrest statistics. This is because many of the Chinese drug users, who were virtually all male, were older and would have died before the early 1970s, when the division stopped keeping these records. Their files subsequently would have been discarded long before they were turned over to the National Archives.

Most people in the Division of Narcotic Control files were what the division described as 'criminal addicts'; doctors were not included in these files. The division apparently had a separate filing system for doctors, but to the best of my knowledge, these files are not available. Significantly, nurses (2.5 per cent of the cases examined) were included in this set of files, as were men and women who obtained drugs almost exclusively from doctors.

Under the terms of the research agreement, I photocopied the files (excluding the mug shots), and then blacked out the names of all of the users. I worked in the access division of the archives, rather than in the regular reading room, to protect the identities of the users and to give me access to the photocopier. The photocopies were then reviewed by an access officer to ensure that all of the names had been blacked out. Someone else photocopied the materials a second time to ensure that the names were fully blocked.

I created a database, coding the gender, race, ethnicity, class, and date of birth of the drug user. I also included place of residence, occupation, dates when the case file opened and closed, the number of times the person had been convicted of a narcotic offence, the number of times they had been convicted of other offences, the types of crimes they were convicted of (theft, vagrancy, break and enter, forgery, etc.), age of first drug use, drugs used, whether they ever quit, and whether they ever obtained drugs from doctors.

Not every case file contained all of the information. For example, only 19 of the 159 files mentioned the age at which the person first started using drugs. In other cases, the information was undoubtedly incomplete. Many users, for example, probably obtained drugs from doctors without ever getting caught. Similarly, other evidence indicates that most users quit at one time or another, but this information was rarely recorded in their file. Finally, I took notes on every case, including a brief description of each arrest and how it happened, and of every encounter with a doctor and its result. These notes were keyword-searchable. The users who appeared in these files came from across the country, and I was able to determine regional and urban/rural differences in drug users' occupations, ways of life, and methods of drug procurement.

These case files were particularly useful in assessing drug users' encounters with police officers and with doctors. There were hundreds of police reports in the files, containing full details of how arrests were made. There was extensive correspondence with doctors and many police reports explaining how drug users obtained drugs from doctors. The files also gave critical information about the Division of Narcotic Control's power over drug users' lives and over the lives of their regulators. The Division of Narcotic Control, for example, was one of the agencies contacted by the parole board when a drug user was under consideration for parole, and the division almost always counselled against giving parole. Although the division was not the only body involved in parole decisions, it played a role in ensuring that very few drug users were granted parole. Similarly, it was the Division of Narcotic Control that tracked down doctors who prescribed to drug users, reprimanded them, and threatened them with being placed on the confidential restricted list. Above all, the Division of Narcotic Control used this information to keep abreast of drug-using practices, to keep other relevant players informed, and to enforce the law in the most effective way.

John Howard Society of British Columbia Case Files

The John Howard Society of British Columbia created its own set of case files, which are located at the Simon Fraser University Archives. Since Vancouver was the largest centre of drug use over the time period studied in this book, it made sense to focus on a social work agency in

Vancouver. I obtained a research agreement to look at these files, and I agreed to protect the identities of the subjects involved. These papers consist of several thousand case files in thirty-three boxes. Every single file was reviewed, although I only closely examined files in which the client was noted as being a drug user, or had been convicted of a narcotic offence. Not every drug user was identified as such, and undoubtedly more than a few clients who were drug users were missed. Moreover, many of the records were extremely brief. In total, my database included 390 files ranging from single index cards to inch-thick file folders. This represented every single file I found in which the person was identified as a drug user. The files consisted of social workers' notes and sometimes included prison classification reports, correspondence with clients, and newspaper clippings.

I created a separate database for these files. Again, I recorded the client's race/ethnicity, class, gender, and date of birth, as well as the name of their social worker, whether or not they had been noted to have had same-sex relationships, whether or not they had children and how many, their place of birth, the age at which they started using drugs, the date (approximate) when they started using drugs, their age and the date when they first approached the John Howard Society, and the date that the file ended. Complete information was not available for most of the clients. In the notes section of this database, which was also keyword searchable, I recorded information on the particularities of the relationship between the social worker and client. This set of case files was particularly valuable in examining the interactions between drug users and their social workers, and for learning more about drug users' experiences in prison, their childhoods, and their home lives.

Naming

The identities of all people in the two sets of case files have been fully protected. I chose to fully alter the names because the drug-using community in Canada in my time period was quite small. There are historians, such as Geoffrey Reaume, who have taken the view that changing names is a way of further dehumanizing the people who appeared in the case files.[3] However, the information in the files is highly personal, the people involved never gave permission for this information to be released, and I felt that it was only respectful to protect their identities to the fullest extent possible. In changing the names, an attempt was made to be true to the ethnicity of the people studied and to the styles of naming in practice at the time. The names of police officers, doctors, and social workers that appeared in the confidential case files have also been concealed, on the request of the two archives involved. On the other hand, if the names of police officers, doctors, or social workers came up in records that are openly available, or in newspaper reports that were unconnected to the confidential case files, their real names have been used. For the National Archive case files, the actual case numbers have been used in the footnotes, as anyone else wanting to gain access to these files would have to go through the same process of obtaining a research agreement that I did and would also be obliged to protect the identities of the people involved. In the case of the John Howard Society case files, new case numbers have been assigned in accordance with my research agreement with Simon Fraser University Archives.

Using the Databases

The two databases allowed me to determine trends, such as age of first drug use, place of residence, types of drugs used, and occupation, and to contrast this with information contained in the media, government documents, studies by social workers and doctors, medical journals, and annual reports. Quantitative information from the databases was compared with criminal statistics from the Dominion Bureau of Statistics, as well as with information from the Stevenson report that examined drug users in British Columbia. This comparison made it clear that these case files were fairly representative of drug users who came to the attention of regulatory authorities in Canada between 1920 and 1961. In most cases in the book, I used the data from the Dominion Bureau of Statistics or the Stevenson study, rather than the data from the case files because they were dealing with larger numbers of users.

More important than the quantitative information, however, was the rich qualitative material in these case files. Throughout, I drew representative qualitative material from the confidential case files to illustrate the details of drug users' lives. Additionally, the qualitative sections of the two databases enabled me to determine trends, such as theft of drugs from doctors, and changes in police tactics and social work techniques.

The research methodology for case files does not greatly differ from other types of historical research, but this field has attracted fierce debate between poststructuralists and more traditional social historians.[4] Carolyn Strange, for example, argues that the capital case files she examined should be seen as a 'textual artifact of competing truths –

multiple, discordant interpretations of condemned person's lives.'[5] By contrast, social historians have argued that these files can be read 'against the grain' to reveal the stories of regulated others.[6] My own approach was closer to that of social historians. From the John Howard Society files, it is evident that the majority of drug users grew up in economically disadvantaged homes and that many experienced foster care or abusive family situations. I do not pretend that the case files revealed the 'truth' of their subjects, and I have used the insights of the poststructuralists to be aware of how knowledge was constructed in the case file. I have tried to convey to the reader why the information in the file may have appeared in the form and manner in which it did, but in the end I spent less time deconstructing the files and more time using them to tell something of drug users' daily lives.

Tables

The following tables show how quantitative data from the case files helped me construct the details of drug users' lives, including their gender, race, class, where they were born, the age at which they started using drugs, the number of times they were convicted of narcotic and other offences, and finally, whether or not they obtained drugs from doctors. These data also helped me construct how drug users' lives changed after the Second World War, so some of the data here are broken down into two time periods.

TABLE 1
Gender, race, and class for the case files

	% of John Howard Society case files	% of Division of Narcotic Control case files
Gender		
Male	72	71
Female	28	29
Class		
Working class	93	92
Middle class	7	8
Race		
Aboriginal	4	1.2
African Canadian	0.7	1.9
Asian Canadian	2.5	0.6
Euro Canadian	91	96

TABLE 2
Gender by date in Division of Narcotic Control case files

	Male (%)	Female (%)
Files, 1922–45 (n=62)	77	23
Files, 1946–61 (n=98)	66	34

TABLE 3
Gender by date in conviction statistics kept by the Dominion Bureau of Statistics

	Male (%)	Female (%)
Convictions, 1922–45	94	6
Convictions, 1946–61	71	29

TABLE 4
Place of birth in John Howard Society case files

Place	Percentage (n=281)
British Columbia	40
Alberta	13
Saskatchewan	15
Manitoba	7
Ontario	9
Quebec	3
Atlantic provinces	3
Born outside of Canada	10

TABLE 5
Average age of first drug use in John Howard Society case files

Female	19.1
Male	22.4
Overall average	21.1

TABLE 6
Average number of convictions in Division of Narcotic Control case files

	Average number of drug convictions	Average number of other convictions
Female	3	6.5
Male	3.4	10.8
Overall average	3.3	9.5

TABLE 7

Drug users obtaining drugs from doctors (Division of Narcotic Control case files)

	All users	Male users	Female users
Case files, 1928–46	34 (49%)	22 (42%)	12 (79%)
Case files, 1947–61	10 (11%)	6 (10%)	4 (13%)

Notes

Introduction

1 Schaler, *Drugs*. This book contains many classic articles in the debate. Also see MacCoun and Reuter, *Drug War Heresies*. Ethan Nadelmann's Drug Policy Alliance (http://www.drugpolicy.org) is one of the most active and critical voices against the war on drugs. Also see Nadelmann, 'Commonsense Drug Policy.'

2 Courtwright, *Dark Paradise*; Musto, *The American Disease*; Berridge, *Opium and the People*; Acker, *Creating the American Junkie*; Trocki, *Opium, Empire and the Global Political Economy*; McAllister, *Drug Diplomacy*; Bewley-Taylor, *The United States and International Drug Control*; Spillane, *Cocaine*; Zhou, *Anti-Drug Crusades in Twentieth-Century China*; Dikotter, Laamann, and Xun, *Narcotic Culture*; Massing, *The Fix*; Booth, *Opium*; Jonnes, *Hep-Cats, Narcs, and Pipe Dreams*; Valverde, *Diseases of the Will*; White, *Slaying the Dragon*.

3 Terry and Pellens, *The Opium Problem*, 807–48, 969–81.

4 Courtwright, Joseph, and Des Jarlais, *Addicts Who Survived*, 1. Acker, *Creating the American Junkie*.

5 Simon Fraser University Archives (hereafter SFUA), John Howard Society Case File (hereafter JHSF) #1.

6 The Aboriginal community breakdown caused by residential schools, displacement from their land, and missionization is well known. Miller, *Skyscrapers Hide the Heavens*.

7 SFUA, JHSF #2.

8 Noel, *Canada Dry*; Cook, 'Through Sunshine and Shadow'; Heron, *Booze*.

9 Roy, *The Oriental Question*; Ward, *White Canada Forever*.

10 For a critique of 'social control,' see Gordon, 'Family Violence, Feminism and Social Control.' For an excellent discussion of the differences between

social control and moral regulation, see McLaren, Menzies, and Chunn, 'Introduction' in *Regulating Lives*.

11 Foucault, *The History of Sexuality*, 90.

12 Nancy Fraser stresses that not all forms of power are 'normatively equivalent' in her article 'Foucault on Modern Power.'

13 See Canada, Dominion Bureau of Statistics, *Annual Report of Statistics of Criminal and Other Offences* for the years 1922–61. In this same time period, less than 10 per cent of all Canadians lived in British Columbia, with approximately 30 per cent of the population being in Ontario, 30 per cent in Quebec, 10 per cent in the Maritimes, and 20 per cent on the prairies. Statistics Canada, Historical Statistics of Canada, Series A2, Population of Canada, by province, census dates, 1851 to 1976, http://www.statcan.ca/english/freepub/11-516–XIE/sectiona/toc.htm.

14 Akers, 'Addiction: The Troublesome Concept.'

15 Erickson and Alexander, 'Cocaine and Addictive Liability,' reprinted in Schaler, *Drugs*.

16 An interesting discussion of withdrawal can be found in Keane, *What's Wrong with Addiction?* 45–54.

17 Alan Leshner, 'When the Question Is Drug Abuse and Addiction, the Answer Is "All of the Above",' *NIDA Notes* 16, no. 2 (May 2001) http://www.nida.nih.gov/nida_notes/nnvol16n2/dirrepvol16n2.html (accessed 20 June 2005); DrugScope, 'Heroin Misconceptions,' http://www.drugscope.org.uk/DS%20Media%20Project/media_heroin.htm (accessed 3 November 2004). National Institute on Drug Abuse, 'Heroin: Abuse and Addiction,' http://www.drugabuse.gov/PDF/RRHeroin.pdf (accessed 3 November 2004).

18 Courtwright, *Dark Paradise*, 123–37; Acker, *Creating the American Junkie*.

19 Levine, 'The Discovery of Addiction.'

20 Becker, *The Outsiders*; Preble and Casey, 'Taking Care of Business'; Agar, *Ripping and Running*; Faupel, *Shooting Dope*; Bourgois, *In Search of Respect*; Rosenbaum, *Women on Heroin*; Adler, *Wheeling and Dealing*.

21 Parr, *Labouring Children*; Strange, *Toronto's Girl Problem*; Dubinsky, *Improper Advances*; Iacovetta, 'Gossip, Contest and Power' and 'Making "New Canadians."'

22 Backhouse, *Colour-Coded*; Roy, *A White Man's Province*; Roy, *The Oriental Question*; Ward, *White Canada Forever*; Palmer, *Patterns of Prejudice*.

23 Iacovetta and Valverde, *Gender Conflicts*; McPherson, Morgan, and Forestell, *Gendered Pasts*; Strong-Boag et al., *Painting the Maple*; Parr and Rosenfeld, *Gender and History*; Parr, *A Diversity of Women*; and, of course, the many titles

in the Studies in Gender and History series published by University of
Toronto Press.

24 Palmer, *Working-Class Experience*; Heron and Storey, *On the Job*.

Chapter 1

1 Hathaway, 'Marijuana and Lifestyle,' extensively details people's different
experiences with the use of marijuana.

2 Brock, *Making Work, Making Trouble*; Pearson, *Hooligan*; Hall, Critcher, Jefferson, Clarke, and Roberts, *Policing the Crisis*; Gusfield, *Contested Meanings*.

3 Ward, *White Canada Forever*, 3–78.

4 Lai, 'Chinese Opium Trade.'

5 Canada, House of Commons, 'Report on the Need for the Suppression of
the Opium Traffic in Canada,' *Sessional Papers of the Dominion of Canada*,
3 July 1908, paper 36b. The international opium movement was spear-
headed by missionaries, and Canadian churches had already forwarded a
variety of resolutions demanding government action against the drug trade.
For these letters, see National Archives of Canada (hereafter NAC), RG 6,
vol. 119, file 1724; Lodwick, *Crusaders against Opium*.

6 An Act to Prohibit the Importation, Manufacture and Sale of Opium for
Other than Medicinal Purposes, Statutes of Canada 1908, c. 50.

7 An Act Respecting Proprietary or Patent Medicines, Statutes of Canada
1908, c.56; Malleck, '"Its Baneful Influences Are Too Well Known"'; Murray,
'The Road to Regulation.'

8 Canada, Parliament, *House of Commons Debates*, 26 January 1911, 2518–54.

9 Murray, 'Cocaine Use in the Era of Social Reform.'

10 Courtwright, *Dark Paradise*, 110–44.

11 Warsh, *Moments of Unreason*, 155–71.

12 Stanley Cohen provided the classic definition of a moral panic: 'Societies
appear to be subject, every now and then, to periods of moral panic. A
condition, episode, person or group of persons emerges to become defined
as a threat to societal values and interests; its nature is presented in a stylized
and stereotypical fashion by the mass media: the moral barricades are
manned by editors, bishops, politicians and other right thinking people;
socially accredited experts pronounce their diagnoses and solutions; ways of
coping are evolved or (more often) resorted to; the condition then disap-
pears, submerges or deteriorates and becomes more visible.' Cohen, *Folk
Devils and Moral Panics*, 9. Also see Hall et al., *Policing the Crisis*; Goode and
Ben-Yehuda, *Moral Panics*; Ben-Yehuda, *The Politics and Morality of Deviance*.

13 An Act to Amend the Opium and Narcotic Drug Act, Statutes of Canada 1921, c. 42; An Act to Amend the Opium and Narcotic Drug Act, Statutes of Canada 1922, c. 36; An Act to Prohibit the Improper Use of Opium and Other Drugs, Statutes of Canada 1923, c. 22.

14 Malleck, 'Its Baneful Influences Are Too Well Known'; Malleck, 'Refining Poison, Defining Power'; Warsh, *Moments of Unreason*, 155–71.

15 Trasov, 'History of Opium and Narcotic Drug Legislation'; Small, 'Canadian Narcotics Legislation'; Green, 'A History of Canadian Narcotics Control'; Solomon and Green, 'The First Century'; Boyd, 'The Origins of Canadian Narcotics Legislation'; Comack, 'The Origins of Canadian Drug Legislation'; Chapman, 'The Anti-Drug Crusade'; Chapman, 'Drug Usage and the Victoria Daily Colonist'; and Chapman, 'The Drug Problem.'

16 Mosher, *Discrimination and Denial*, 139.

17 Giffen, Endicott, and Lambert, *Panic and Indifference*, 534.

18 Letter from F.W. Cowan to W.J. Egan, 11 January 1924, NAC, RG 76, vol. 591, file 831,196, Part 2.

19 In another article, I more fully explored the 'narratives of narcoticism.' Carstairs, 'Innocent Addicts, Dope Fiends and Nefarious Traffickers.'

20 The literature on anti-Asian racism on the West Coast includes Ward, *White Canada Forever*; Roy, *A White Man's Province*; Roy, *The Oriental Question*; and Creese, 'Exclusion or Solidarity?'

21 Strange, *Toronto's Girl Problem*.

22 Sanders, *Emily Murphy*, 186; Mander, *Emily Murphy*, 117.

23 Bliss, *The Discovery of Insulin*, 225. Thanks to Michael Bliss for pointing this out to me.

24 The Department of Health was pleased with Murphy's first article and furnished her with considerable information. See NAC, RG 29, vol. 602, file 325-1-3. However, by 1923 the department was obviously disillusioned. In a 25 January 1923 letter, F.W. Cowan wrote to D.M. Donald, the medical health officer in Saskatoon, that 'Had I known Mrs. Murphy, as well, at the time, I furnished her with considerable information as I do now, I can assure you that I would have been more cautious in my dealings with her.' In NAC, RG 29, vol. 551, file 320-6-5.

25 Murphy's dedication read, 'To the members of the Rotary, Kiwanis and Gyros Clubs and to the White Cross Associations who are rendering valiant service in impeding the spread of drug addiction, this volume is respectfully dedicated.'

26 Murphy, 'The Grave Drug Menace,' 9.

27 Ibid.

28 For an excellent account of the association of the Chinese with hidden passages, see Pon, 'Like a Chinese Puzzle.'

29 Murphy, 'The Underground System,' 55; Murphy, 'Fighting the Drug Menace,' 11.

30 Murphy, *The Black Candle*, 187–8.

31 In the introduction to Murphy's second article, the editors of *Maclean's* wrote that newspapers across the country commented on the first article and that *Maclean's* had received a large number of letters as a result. A collage of some of the newspaper clippings was featured in the second article. Murphy, 'The Underground System,' 12.

32 'Chinatown – or Drug Traffic?' *Vancouver Daily Sun*, 22 March 1920, 6. See also 'Chinatown and the Drug Traffic,' *Vancouver Daily Sun*, 31 March 1920, 6.

33 'Drug Habit Is Rampant: Chief of Police Says,' *Vancouver Daily Sun*, 18 March 1920, 1; 'Kiwanis Club to Aid Helpless,' *Vancouver Daily Sun*, 2 April 1920, 7.

34 According to McKim's newspaper guide, the *Vancouver Daily Sun* was the fastest growing newspaper in Western Canada. McKim, *The Canadian Newspaper Directory*, 418. The circulation for the year ended 30 September 1923 was 22,666 daily.

35 'War Veteran to Be Given Lashes,' *Vancouver Sun*, 18 March 1921, 1. In a subsequent interview, Kehoe admitted that he had used drugs before he went overseas. 'Kehoe, Now in Prison, Whipped the Germans at Every Turn But He Couldn't Beat His Old-Time Enemy "The Dope,"' *Vancouver Sun*, 27 March 1921, 1.

36 'May Reduce War Hero's Sentence,' *Vancouver Sun*, 19 March 1921, 1.

37 'Kehoe, Now in Prison,' *Vancouver Sun*, 1.

38 'Dope Peddler King Is Taken,' *Vancouver Sun*, 12 April 1921, 1.

39 Ward, *White Canada Forever*, 124–8; Anderson, *Vancouver's Chinatown*, 110–13.

40 'War Opens on Drug Traffickers: Mass Meeting of Citizens Demand Federal Action,' *Vancouver Sun*, 21 April 1921, 1.

41 'Death of Dope,' *Vancouver Sun*, 28 April 1921, 1.

42 'Ex-Crook and Reformed Drug Fiend Aids City Police in Fight on Dope Ring,' *Vancouver Sun*, 3 May 1921, 1.

43 'Drug Exposure Causes Mass Meeting to Be Called to Fight Evil,' *Vancouver Sun*, 12 May 1921, 1.

44 Canada, Parliament, *House of Commons Debates*, 3 May 1921, 2897.

45 Ibid., 19 April 1921, 2268.

46 Ibid., 3 May 1921, 2904.

47 Ibid., 19 April 1921, 2264.

48 Ibid., 3 May 1921, 2905.

49 Ibid., 2903.

50 Ibid.

51 'Clubs to Report on "Dope" Probe,' *Vancouver Sun*, 28 January 1922, 3.

52 The circulation of the *Vancouver Daily World* averaged 16,182 in 1921. *The Canadian Newspaper Directory*, 463. The directory referred to the *World* as the 'oldest and most influential newspaper.'

53 In an advertisement in the newspaper directory, the newspaper claimed that its circulation for February 1922 was 21,353, much higher than it had been for the year ending 30 September 1921. The population of Vancouver was 116,700, indicating that the *World* campaign reached a broad Vancouver audience. The *Vancouver Province* had a much wider circulation than either the *Vancouver Sun* or the *Vancouver Daily World*, but it was distributed throughout British Columbia.

54 'Drug Soaked Addicts Pass on Way to Jail,' *Vancouver Daily World*, 16 January 1922, 1.

55 'Three Thousand Addicts in City, Inquiry Shows,' *Vancouver Daily World*, 6 February 1922, 1.

56 'All Boats from Asia Bring in Illicit Drugs,' *Vancouver Daily World*, 16 January 1922, 1.

57 'Dying Lad Tells How Boys and Girls Are Made Drug Addicts,' *Vancouver Daily World*, 17 January 1922, 1.

58 In the year ending 30 September 1922, 519 Chinese were convicted of drug offences in British Columbia. For the year ending 30 September 1921, 656 Chinese were convicted of drug offences in British Columbia, meaning that the newspapers' statistics were far off. Canada, Dominion Bureau of Statistics, *Annual Report of Criminal Statistics for the Year Ended September 30, 1921* (Ottawa: F.A. Acland, 1922), 334–5; ibid., *Annual Report of Criminal Statistics for the Year Ended September 30, 1922* (Ottawa: F.A. Acland, 1922), 312–13.

59 'Deport the Drug Traffickers,' *Vancouver Daily World*, 18 January 1922, 1.

60 'Call on Liberal Executive to Take Action on Drugs,' *Vancouver Daily World*, 7 March 1922, 9. The *Vancouver Daily World* claimed that over 300 of these resolutions were generated and sent to Ottawa by various organizations. It is hard to know what happened to all of these resolutions or whether they all passed. Giffen, Endicott, and Lambert, who did their research at the Division of Narcotic Control before these papers were turned over to the National Archives, indicate that the division received 57 copies of this resolution (see Giffen, Endicott, and Lambert, *Panic and Indifference*, 206). At least 19 copies of the resolution were sent to H.H. Stevens by various groups, including churches, the Vancouver Board of Trade, the Vancouver

YMCA, the British Columbia Woman's Christian Temperance Union, and the Parent Teacher Federation. H.H. Stevens Papers, *Drug Abuse Vancouver 1922*, Vancouver City Archives, MSS 69.

61 'Waterfront Open Gate for Drugs; Child Welfare Society Joins Fight,' *Vancouver Daily World*, 18 January 1922, 1.

62 'Urges People to Help Vancouver World in Its Campaign Against Drugs,' *Vancouver Daily World*, 23 January 1922, 1.

63 'Dragged Down by Drugs from Post Giving Big Pay,' *Vancouver Daily World*, 21 January 1922, 1, 28.

64 'Ten Years for Drug Sellers Demanded by 2000 Citizens,' *Vancouver Daily World*, 30 January 1922, 1. The *Vancouver Sun* said that 1800 people attended the meeting. 'Prison and Lashes Is Urged as Punishment for the Drug Peddlers,' *Vancouver Sun*, 30 January 1922, 13.

65 'Ten Years for Drug Sellers,' *Vancouver Sun*, 1.

66 'Mayor and Council Endorse World's Anti-Drug Campaign,' *Vancouver Daily World*, 31 January 1922, 1; and 'City to Join in the Drug Crusade,' *Vancouver Sun*, 31 January 1922, 2.

67 'Women Ask for Special Hospital for Care of Local Drug Addicts,' *Vancouver Daily World*, 3 February 1922, 3.

68 Ibid., 3.

69 'Drug Fight Joined by Board of Trade and Labor Council,' *Vancouver Daily World*, 8 February 1922, 1.

70 English translation of the *Chinese Times*, 11 February 1922, 3, in the University of British Columbia Archives, Chinese Canadian Research Collection, Box 4. Also see 'Chinese Plan to Join Fight against Drugs,' *Vancouver Daily World*, 10 February 1922, 1.

71 'Call on Liberal Executive to Take Action on Drugs,' *Vancouver Daily World*, 7 March 1923, 9.

72 Letter from L.J. Ladner to H.S. Beland, Minister of Health, 3 April 1922, cited in Giffen, Endicott, and Lambert, *Panic and Indifference*, 207.

73 Canada, Parliament, *House of Commons Debates*, 8 May 1922, 1509.

74 Ibid., 1529–31.

75 Ibid., 15 June 1922, 3014.

76 Ibid., 12 June 1922, 2824.

77 Ibid..

78 Ibid., 15 June 1922, 3015.

79 Ibid., 3016. Neither Manion's biography nor autobiography provide any further information about his change of mind. Manion, *Life Is an Adventure*; Piovesana, *Robert J. Manion*.

80 Canada, Parliament, *House of Commons Debates*, 15 June 1922, 3017.

81 Ibid., 12 June 1922, 2824.

82 Letter from F.W. Cowan to Elizabeth MacCallum, 9 April 1923, NAC, RG 29, vol. 605, file 325-4-7.

83 Canada, Parliament, *House of Commons Debates*, 23 April 1923, 2132.

84 Ibid., 2117.

85 In his work on hobos in Canada during the Great Depression, Todd MacCallum turned up one example of them using Jamaican ganja, which was presumably marijuana. However, this appears to be an isolated example. Todd MacCallum, conversation with the author, 28 May 2002.

86 Green, 'A History of Canadian Narcotics Control,' 54; Small, 'Canadian Narcotics Legislation,' 40; Solomon and Green, 'The First Century,' 321–3.

87 Murphy, *The Black Candle*, 331–7.

88 Taylor, *American Diplomacy*, 98–108.

89 Musto, *The American Disease*, 203.

90 NAC, R29, vol. 602, file 325-2-5.

91 Morrison, 'Regulatory Control of the Canadian Government.'

92 'Should Pot Be Legalized,' 5 January 1998, http://www.cannabisculture.com/whatsnew/jan7/index.html (accessed 4 February 2001). A Google search for 'Emily Murphy' and 'marijuana prohibition' returns hundreds of hits, most blaming Murphy for the 1923 ban.

93 Canada, Parliament, *House of Commons Debates*, 12 February 1929, 62.

94 Ibid., 65.

95 Ibid., 29 May 1929, 2971.

96 Canada, Dominion Bureau of Statistics, *Annual Report of Statistics of Criminal and Other Offences for the Year Ended September 30, 1929* (Ottawa: F.A. Acland, 1930), 148–9.

97 Perry, 'The Dope Traffic in Canada,' *Western Home Monthly* (August 1929); and Warling, 'Canada's Greatest Menace,' *Canadian Home Journal* (August 1930).

98 Clayton Mosher's thesis shows that 85.9 percent of people convicted of drug offences in five Ontario cities between 1921–8 were working class or had no occupation. Mosher, 'The Legal Response to Narcotic Drugs,' 123.

99 Murphy, 'The Grave Drug Menace,' 9.

Chapter 2

1 In reaching these conclusions, I have been influenced by the growing literature on harm reduction. Erickson et al., *Harm Reduction*. See Zimring

and Hawkins, *The Search for Rational Drug Control* for a good description of different approaches to drug policy.

2 Memo to His Excellency The Governor General in Council from the Minister of Trade and Commerce, 15 August 1919, National Archives of Canada (hereafter NAC), RG 13, series A-2, vol. 329, file 1805-1824/191.

3 Berridge, *Opium and the People*, 250.

4 Morton and Wright, *Winning the Second Battle*, 118, 131.

5 Heron, *Booze*, 231, 272; Cook, 'More a Medicine than a Beverage'; Cook, 'Wet Canteens and Worrying Mothers.'

6 *Annual Report of Canada to the United Nations 1943*, NAC, RG 29, vol. 592, file 322-5-3, vol. 3.

7 Canada, Department of Health, *Annual Report of the Department of Health for the Year Ended March 31, 1925* (Ottawa: F.A. Acland, 1925), 24.

8 May, 'The International Control of Narcotic Drugs.' For more information about the international control of narcotic drugs, see Bruun, Pan, and Rexed, *The Gentlemen's Club*; Taylor, *American Diplomacy*; Walker, *Drug Control in the Americas*; and McAllister, *Drug Diplomacy*.

9 Meyer and Parssinen, *Webs of Smoke*, 31.

10 Canada, Department of Health, *Annual Report of the Department of Health for the Year Ended March 31, 1924* (Ottawa: F.A. Acland, 1924), 36.

11 Throughout the early 1920s, many more people were arrested in British Columbia than in Quebec for drug offences, giving support to the idea that the numbers for BC were too low and did not include Chinese opium smokers. However, this might also reflect differences in policing practices between the two provinces.

12 Canada, Department of Pensions and National Health, *Annual Report of the Department of Pensions and National Health for the Year Ended March 31, 1939* (Ottawa: J.O. Patenaude, 1939), 109.

13 An excellent discussion of the problems associated with criminal statistics can be found in Pearson, *Hooligan*, 213–8.

14 By 1935, seizures of opium were less than a third of what they had been twelve years earlier, and seizures of morphine and cocaine were less than a seventh of what they had been. Canada, Department of Health, *Annual Report of the Department of Health for the Year Ended March 31, 1923* (Ottawa: F.A. Acland, 1923), 40; Canada, Department of Pensions and National Health, *Annual Report of the Department of Pensions and National Health for the Year Ended March 31, 1936* (Ottawa: J.O. Patenaude, 1936), 118.

15 Dikotter, Laamann, and Xun, *Narcotic Culture*, 46–92.

16 Chan asserts that there were eleven opium factories in Victoria in 1883. By

1901, three Victoria firms with eighteen partners had a monopoly on opium manufacture. Chan, *Gold Mountain*, 76–7. Mackenzie King reported in 1908 that there were at least seven factories in Vancouver, Victoria, and New Westminster, and that their annual gross receipts were between $600,000 and $650,000. The factories were all owned by Chinese. Canáda, House of Commons, 'Report on the Need for the Suppression of the Opium Traffic in Canada,' *Sessional Papers of the Dominion of Canada*, 3 July 1908, paper 36b. Much of the opium produced in these factories was probably exported to the United States, where it was illegal to produce or sell opium. Chan, *Gold Mountain*, 75. See Lai, 'Chinese Opium Trade.'

17 Wickberg, et al., *From China to Canada*, 87.
18 Harvison, *The Horsemen*, 40–2.
19 Chan, *Gold Mountain*, 76.
20 Newman, 'Opium Smoking in Late Imperial China,' 775.
21 Ibid., 787.
22 Zinberg, *Drug, Set and Setting*.
23 Works on the Chinese-Canadian experience include Chan, *Gold Mountain*; Wickberg, et al., *From China to Canada*; Li, *The Chinese in Canada*; and Yee, *Saltwater City*.
24 Mosher, 'The Legal Response to Narcotic Drugs'; Mosher and Hagan, 'Constituting Class and Crime,' 626–9; Mosher, *Discrimination and Denial*, 252–319.
25 Canada, Dominion Bureau of Statistics, *Annual Report of Criminal Statistics for the Year Ended September 30, 1919* (Ottawa: Thomas Mulvery, Printer to His Most Excellent Majesty, 1920).
26 Wages for Chinese men in 1902 ranged from $40 to $50 per month for a cannery worker and from $20 to $25 for an agricultural worker. Li, *The Chinese in Canada*, 44, cited from Canada, *Report of the Royal Commission on Chinese and Japanese Immigration 1902* (Ottawa: Dawson, 1902), 44–197.
27 For example, on 19 January 1918, the owner of a smoking den was sent to prison for three months. A resident of the den at the time of the arrest was given a $50 fine or two months in jail. English translation of the *Chinese Times*, 19 January 1918, 3; 22 July 1918, 3; 8 August 1918, 3, in the University of British Columbia Archives, Chinese Canadian Research Collection, Box 4.
28 Letter from J.A. Amyot to Deputy Minister, Department of Justice, 5 September 1922, NAC, RG 13, Series A-2, vol. 2174, file 1625/1922.
29 Police Department Investigation Report, 1928, Vancouver City Archives, Boxes 37 D6 to 37 D8, pp. 121–2.

30 RCMP Report, 15 July 1924, NAC, RG 29, vol. 234, file 324-1-1, Part 3. The name has been changed to protect privacy.

31 Craig Heron has drawn attention to elite opposition to temperance and prohibition. 'Approaches to Alcohol and Drug History: A Roundtable,' Canadian Historical Association Annual Meeting, Toronto, 27 May 2002.

32 Tom MacInnes, 'The Futile Fight against Dope,' 3, 5.

33 RCMP Report, 6 April 1932, NAC, RG 29, vol. 601, file 324-6-2.

34 Letter from the Acting Deputy Minister of Health to the Deputy Minister of Justice, 15 December 1924, NAC, RG 29, vol. 234, file 324-1-1. The name has been changed to protect privacy.

35 Letter from Acting Deputy Minister of Health to the Deputy Minister, Department of Justice, 14 September 1925, NAC, RG 29, vol. 234, file 324-1-1, Part 3.

36 Giffen, Endicott, and Lambert, *Panic and Indifference*, 136–8.

37 An Act to Amend the Opium and Narcotic Drug Act, Statutes of Canada 1922, c. 36, sec. 5.

38 'Chinese Will Be Deported,' *Vancouver Sun*, 16 April 1924. The name has been changed to protect privacy.

39 Canada, Department of Pensions and National Health, *Annual Report of the Department of Pensions and National Health for the Year Ended March 31, 1933* (Ottawa: J.O. Patenaude, 1933), 70.

40 Answer to a question in the House of Commons asking about the average length of time deported aliens had been in Canada. Canada, Parliament, *House of Commons Debates*, 27 February 1929, 508–9.

41 RCMP Report, 23 September 1922, NAC, RG 18, vol. 3291, file HQ-189-Q-1; Harvison, *The Horsemen*, 40.

42 John Fry to F.W. Cowan, 4 January 1923, NAC, RG 29, vol. 551, file 320-6-5.

43 See *Annual Reports* of the RCMP for lists of seizures. The RCMP were inconsistent in their labelling, so charting these statistics is not worthwhile. In the 1920s, they seized hundreds of opium pipes, bowls, and stems every year. In the 1930s, this fell to tens, and after 1937 it fell to almost none.

44 Letter from C.H.L. Sharman to Deputy Minister, 13 October 1927, NAC, RG 29, vol. 231, file 323-13-5, Part 1.

45 Letter from Sharman to Deputy Minister, 11 November 1927, NAC, RG 29, vol. 223, file 323-9-25.

46 Archives of Alberta, Acc. 72.26, box 54, file 3570.

47 A fascinating discussion of 'red pills' can be found in Dikotter, Laamann, and Xun, *Narcotic Culture*, 156–60. The pills were coloured with red cinna-

bar, which they described as 'a time honoured ingredient of Daoist al-
chemy.' Dikotter, Laamann, and Xun argue that the cinnabar gave the pills
an 'imperial cachet.'

48 NAC, RG 29, vol. 556, file 321-3-11, Part 1.

49 RCMP Report, 18 June 1937, NAC, RG 29, vol. 556, file 321-3-11, vol. 2.

50 NAC, RG 29, vol. 556, file 321-3-11, Parts 2 and 3.

51 Chinese Benevolent Association, 'Proclamation of the Chinese Benevolent
    Association,' Vancouver, BC, 30 April 1938, NAC, RG 29, vol. 556, file
    321-3-11, Part 3.

52 Wickberg et al., *From China to Canada*, 182.

53 RCMP Report, St. John, 25 June 1936, NAC, RG 29, vol. 228, file 323-12-6,
    Part 2.

54 H.F. Price, 'The Criminal Addict,' in RCMP, *Annual Report for the Year Ended
    March 31, 1946* (Ottawa: Edmond Cloutier, 1946), 73–82.

55 Canada, Department of Pensions and National Health, *Annual Report of the
    Department of Pensions and National Health for the Year Ended March 31, 1940*
    (Ottawa: Edmond Cloutier, 1940), 111; Campbell, *Sit Down and Drink Your
    Beer*, 19.

56 Canada, Department of Pensions and National Health, *Annual Report of the
    Department of Pensions and National Health for the Year Ended March 31, 1934*
    (Ottawa: J.O. Patenaude, 1934), 82.

57 RCMP Report, 22 December 1939, NAC, RG 29, vol. 3331, file 327-S-57.

58 Morton, *At Odds*, 108–34; Anderson, *Vancouver's Chinatown*, 106–43.

59 Report by C.E. Wilcox, Officer Commanding Quebec District, 18 February
    1922, NAC, RG 29, vol. 226, file 232-12-2, Part 1; RCMP Report, Montreal,
    25 January 1922, NAC, RG 29, vol. 226, file 232-12-2, Part 1.

60 British Columbia Archives, GR-0602, Vancouver Lock-Up Charge Books,
    vol. 5. The Vancouver lock-up charge books show that it was quite common
    for Chinese men to be charged with possession of both morphine and
    cocaine. They often received longer sentences when both drugs were
    involved. A similar pattern can be seen in Alberta court cases: Archives of
    Alberta, Acc. 72.26.

61 RCMP Report, 10 February 1923, NAC, RG 18, vol. 3308, file HQ-189-4-C-5.
    The names have been changed to protect privacy.

62 Commissioner J.P. Smith, *Report* (Duplicate Copy), Commission of Inquiry,
    NAC, RG 18, vol. 3170, file G494-7: 167–75. The name has been changed to
    protect privacy.

63 NAC, RG 18, vol. 3291, file 1922 H.Q. 189-O-1; 'Twenty Year Old Girl on
    Trial for Death from Drug,' *Montreal Star*, 21 September 1922, 1.

64 RCMP Report, 20 May 1922, NAC, RG 18, vol. 3291, file 1922 HQ-189-Q-1.

Robert Campbell reported that a hotel in Vancouver was selling beer for twenty or twenty-five cents a bottle in 1922; Campbell, *Sit Down and Drink Your Beer*, 19.

65 RCMP Report, 18 March 1922, NAC, RG 18, vol. 3291, file 1922 HQ-189-Q-1.

66 Estimates on wages come from the *Labour Gazette* 21 (1921): 1230.

67 RCMP Report, 8 March 1922, NAC, RG 18, vol. 3291, file 1922 HQ-189-O-1.

68 RCMP Report, 23 May 1923, NAC, RG 18, vol. 3296, file 1923 HQ-189-C-1.

69 I draw this idea from Norman Zinberg, who hypothesized that 'current social policy is discouraging primarily those who use drugs only moderately, while heavy users, to whom the substance is more vital, are flouting the law in order to make their "buys." Thus, since it is the moderate, occasional users who develop controlling sanctions and rituals, the policy whose goal it is to minimize the number of dysfunctional users may actually be leading to a relative increase in the number of such users.' Zinberg, *Drug Set and Setting*, 195; See also Becker, *The Outsiders*; and Blackwell, 'Drifting, Controlling and Overcoming.'

70 NAC, RG 29, vol. 3330, file 327-C-51.

71 Richards, 'Medical and Legal Aspects of Drug Addiction,' 70.

72 Statistics Canada, Historical Statistics of Canada, Series A125–63, Origins of the population, census dates, 1871 to 1971, http://www.statcan.ca/english/freepub/11-516–XIE/sectiona/sectiona.htm#Population.

73 Richards, 'Medical and Legal Aspects of Drug Addiction,' 66–74.

74 There is a growing literature on the recovery from opiate addiction, including Waldorf, 'Natural Recovery from Opiate Addiction: Some Preliminary Findings'; Waldorf, 'Natural Recovery from Opiate Addiction: Some Social-Psychological Processes of Untreated Recovery'; and Biernacki, *Pathways from Heroin Addiction*.

75 Biernacki, *Pathways from Heroin Addiction*.

76 There were four coroner's inquests into deaths caused by narcotic drugs in 1921. British Columbia Archives, GR-1327. Unfortunately, the Dominion Bureau of Statistics did not keep statistics on deaths resulting from overdoses of illicit drugs.

77 Haywood, 'Vice and Drugs in Montreal.'

78 NAC, RG 18, vol. 3291, file 1922, HQ-189-O-1; 'Germany Blamed for Growth Here in Sale of Drugs,' *Montreal Star*, 21 September 1922, 1.

79 Richards, 'Medical and Legal Aspects of Drug Addiction,' 71–2.

80 Ibid., 72.

81 RCMP Report, 2 February 1943, file 43 D 189-3-E-1, NAC, RG 29, vol. 543, file 320-4-9.

82 Canada, Department of Pensions and National Health, *Annual Report of the*

Department of Pensions and National Health for the Year Ended March 31, 1930 (Ottawa: F.A. Acland, 1930), 69–70.

83 NAC, RG 29, vol. 541, file 320-3-4, Part 5.

84 'Specialist Report' (Prince Rupert, BC) 9 December 1942, NAC, RG 29, vol. 541, file 320-3-4. The name has been changed to protect privacy.

85 Brasset, *Doctor's Pilgrimage*, 85–6. Thanks to Sasha Mullally for drawing my attention to this biography.

86 NAC, RG 29, vol. 3331, file 327-S-77.

87 NAC, RG 29, vol. 3331, file 327-S-68. For more on the working conditions of private nurses, see McPherson, *Bedside Matters*.

88 NAC, RG 29, vol. 3331, file 327-S-68.

89 Letter from C.H.L. Sharman to Dr. Kelly, 4 December 1937, NAC, RG 29, vol. 552, file 320-7-3.

90 NAC, RG 29, vol. 3331, file 327-N-7.

91 Canada, Department of Pensions and National Health, *Annual Report of the Department of Pensions and National Health for the Year Ended March 31, 1931* (Ottawa: F.A. Acland, 1931), 85.

92 NAC, RG 29, vol. 3331, file 327-W-52.

93 Letter from F.W. Cowan to Mr. Brown, 28 November 1925, NAC, RG 29, vol. 610, file 325-5-4. This letter from Cowan to Brown said that codeine was removed from the schedule 'in view of the fact that there is no evidence available, in so far as can be ascertained, showing that codeine is of a habit-forming nature and also in view of the further fact that shipments of codeine were continually coming forward from other countries without the necessary license required for the importation of all narcotic drugs into the country, because of the fact that many countries do not include codeine in their narcotic laws.'

94 Canada, Department of Pensions and National Health, *Annual Report, 1933*, 82.

95 *Annual Report of Canada to the League of Nations 1934*, NAC, RG 29, vol. 592, file 325-5-3.

96 Canada, Department of Pensions and National Health, *Annual Report, 1936*, 121.

97 Ibid., 124.

98 Canada, Department of Pensions and National Health, *Annual Report of the Department of Pensions and National Health for the Year Ended March 31, 1937* (Ottawa: J.O. Patenaude, 1937), 101.

99 Gordon Root, 'Codeine Fiends Seldom Seen by Normal People,' *Vancouver News Herald*, 28 July 1936, in Simon Fraser University Archives, John Howard Society of British Columbia Papers, box 11, file 1-1-6-52.

100 Letter from C.H.L. Sharman to Gilbert Agar, 29 April 1933, NAC, RG 29, vol. 605, file 325-4-7, Part 2.

101 NAC, RG 29, vol. 3330, file 327-W-132.

102 NAC, RG 29, vol. 3330, file 327-C-51.

103 Government of Canada, *Report by the Government of Canada for the Calendar Year 1936 on the Traffic in Opium and Other Dangerous Drugs*, NAC, RG 29, vol. 592, file 325-5-3, Part 3, p. 1.

104 NAC, RG 29, vol. 3330, file 327-N-4.

105 Government of Canada, *Report by the Government of Canada for the Calendar Year 1939 on the Traffic in Opium and Other Dangerous Drugs*, NAC, RG 29, vol. 592, file 325-5-3, Part 3.

106 Letter from C.H.L Sharman to A.W. Haydock, 25 April 1944, NAC, RG 29, vol. 544, file 320-4-9, Part 5.

107 Similar patterns were observed for the United States. See McCoy, *The Politics of Heroin*, 24–5.

108 Chief Constables Association of Canada, *Journal of Proceedings of Annual Conference* (1941), 38.

109 Canada, Department of Pensions and National Health, *Annual Report of the Department of Pensions and National Health for the Year Ended March 31, 1942* (Ottawa: Edmond Cloutier, 1942), 119; Canada, Department of Pensions and National Health, *Annual Report of the Department of Pensions and National Health for the Year Ended March 31, 1943* (Ottawa: Edmond Cloutier, 1943), 35; Canada, Department of Pensions and National Health, *Annual Report of the Department of Pensions and National Health for the Year Ended March 31, 1944* (Ottawa: Edmond Cloutier, 1944), 37.

110 Canada, Department of Pensions and National Health, *Annual Report, 1943*, 32.

111 NAC, RG 29, vol. 3332, file 327-C-100.

112 NAC, RG 29, vol. 3336, file 327-G-11.

113 NAC, RG 29, vol. 242, file 336-2-14, Parts 1–4. For the American version of this story, see Jackson, 'The Amphetamine Inhaler.'

114 Letter from K.C. Hossick to Dr. Morrell, 2 December 1946, NAC, RG 29, vol. 242, file 336-2-14, Part 4.

115 These case files are open and available at the National Archives of Canada, and they mark the beginning of the intensive psychiatric examination of drug users. NAC, RG 29, vols. 540–2. For information on Canadian psychiatry and World War II, see Copp and McAndrew, *Battle Exhaustion*.

116 RG 29, vols. 540–2.

117 Price, 'The Criminal Addict,' 73–82.

Chapter 3

1 In 1949 the Department of National Health and Welfare estimated that
there were approximately 3500 known addicts. Yearly departmental estimates for the years from 1954 to 1961 ranged between 3000 and 3500.
Canada, Department of National Health and Welfare, *Annual Report for the
Year Ended March 31, 1949* (Ottawa: Edmond Cloutier, 1950), 53; ibid.,
Annual Report for the Year Ended March 31, 1962 (Ottawa: Queen's Printer,
1963), 20. In 1959, for example, the Department of National Health and
Welfare estimated that there were 3412 addicts in Canada, including 320
people who were taking narcotics because of a medical condition, and 134
'professional' addicts. 'Professional' addicts were usually doctors, although
they sometimes included pharmacists, veterinarians, and other professionals. Canada, Department of National Health and Welfare, *Annual Report for
the Year Ended March 31, 1959* (Ottawa: Queen's Printer, 1960), 94. By contrast, in the year 2000, researchers estimated that there were between 50,000
and 100,000 injection drug users in Canada. Eric Single, *Canadian Community Epidemiological Network on Drug Use: Overview Report 2000* (Ottawa: Canadian Centre on Substance Abuse, 2000). Vancouver City Police estimates
were always higher than those provided by the Division of Narcotic Control
because the Division of Narcotic Control derived their numbers from the
case files of people who had been convicted of a narcotic offence, while the
Vancouver City Police were aware of users who had not yet been arrested.
In 1955 the former reported that there were 1500 'criminal addicts' in
Vancouver, while the latter estimated that there were 1101 'criminal addicts'
in all of British Columbia. Stevenson, 'Drug Addiction,' 412–3.
2 Courtwright, *Dark Paradise*, 151.
3 Canada, Dominion Bureau of Statistics, *Annual Report of Statistics of Criminal
and Other Offences* for the years 1946–61.
4 In Canada in 1961, 0.2 per cent of the population was African Canadian, 0.7
per cent was Asian, and 1 per cent was Aboriginal. In British Columbia in
1961, African Canadians accounted for 0.06 per cent of the population,
Asians accounted for 2.5 per cent, and Aboriginals accounted for 2 per cent.
Canada, Dominion Bureau of Statistics, *Census of Canada 1961: Population
General Characteristics* (Ottawa: Dominion Bureau of Statistics, 1965).
5 There were seven robberies at Vancouver drugstores in one month in 1945.
National Archives of Canada (hereafter NAC), RG 29, vol. 544, file 320-4-9,
Part 6. In 1946 the RCMP reported that a break-in at the Anglo-Canadian
drug company in Oshawa netted more than $500,000 worth of drugs. One
man in Winnipeg was arrested with 10,000 tablets in his possession. RCMP,

Annual Report for the Year Ended March 31, 1947 (Ottawa: Edmond Cloutier, 1948), 25.

6 Stevenson reported that very few of the subjects he studied 'have ever seen marihuana and fewer still have used it.' Stevenson, *Drug Addiction*, 128. Canada, Dominion Bureau of Statistics, *Annual Report of Statistics of Criminal and Other Offences* for the years 1946–61.

7 The police and the Department of Health regularly claimed that there was no problem with marijuana in Canada, and there were few seizures of the drug during this time period. There were 120 drug offences involving marijuana in Canada from 1920 to 1961. Canada, Dominion Bureau of Statistics, *Annual Report of Statistics of Criminal and Other Offences* for the years 1920–61.

8 In 1959, for example, three people were charged with illegal possession of marijuana, including a professional football player and an airline hostess. NAC, RG 29, vol. 3345, file 327-D-220. The other three case files that indicate marijuana use also concerned heroin users and were more representative of my case files in general. See NAC, RG 29, vol. 3340, file 327-S0144; ibid., vol. 3345, file 327-B-400; and ibid., vol. 3345, file 327-G-243.

9 Coleclough and Hanley, 'Marijuana Users in Toronto.'

10 Simon Fraser University Archives (hereafter SFUA), John Howard Society Case File (hereafter JHSF) #3.

11 NAC, RG 29, vol. 3334, file 327-W-82.

12 NAC, RG 29, vol. 3348, file 327-M-391.

13 *Maclean's*, 'Hastings Street,' 1 March 1958, 38.

14 Beaudoin and Stanké, *La Rage Des 'Goof-Balls,'* 37–8.

15 The reasons for the low rate of drug use in Montreal in the post-war period are unclear. For information on the lack of drug use among prostitutes in Montreal at this time, see Lacasse, *La Prostitution féminine à Montréal*, 58.

16 NAC, RG 29, vol. 3342, file 327-J-154.

17 In the case files from the Division of Narcotic Control, 61 per cent of people who came to the attention of the division before 1945 obtained drugs from doctors. The numbers were undoubtedly higher, as it was fairly easy to obtain drugs from doctors without getting caught. Of the people who came to the attention of the division after 1945, the records show only 10 per cent of them obtaining drugs from doctors.

18 Three out of 159 files in the National Archives of Canada showed evidence of use of Demerol.

19 NAC, RG 29, vol. 3342, file 327-B-499.

20 See Canada, Dominion Bureau of Statistics, *Annual Report of Statistics of Criminal and Other Offences* for the years 1946–61.

21 SFUA, JHSF #4 and JHSF #5.

22 Stevenson, *Drug Addiction*, 41–2.

23 SFUA, JHSF #6 and JHSF #7.

24 Drug users were disproportionately Catholic, especially considering that very few drug users were French Canadian. See Canada, *Census of Canada*, 1951, compared to Canada, Dominion Bureau of Statistics, *Annual Report of Statistics of Criminal and Other Offences* for the years 1945–61.

25 Stevenson, *Drug Addiction*, 39.

26 Ibid., 171.

27 These problems may have been caused, at least in part, by poverty. Hagan and McCarthy argue, on the basis of a large body of evidence, that 'parental economic problems can lead to mistreatment of children and youth.' Hagan and McCarthy, *Mean Streets*, 56.

28 Stevenson, *Drug Addiction*, 42.

29 Ibid., 32.

30 SFUA, JHSF #5.

31 SFUA, JHSF #8.

32 SFUA, JHSF #9.

33 SFUA, JHSF #10.

34 Stevenson, *Drug Addiction*, 385.

35 Ibid., 131.

36 SFUA, JHSF #11.

37 Becker, *The Outsiders*, 41–58; Zinberg, *Drug, Set and Setting*, 82–134.

38 SFUA, JHSF #12. According to Barron H. Lerner, 'rounders' in early twentieth century Seattle were people 'who made the rounds of a particular community, living in lodging houses but frequently requiring admission to hospitals or jail.' Lerner, *Contagion and Confinement*, 29. By the mid-twentieth century in Vancouver and Toronto, rounders were people who were involved in criminal activity.

39 Stevenson, *Drug Addiction*, 135.

40 Thornton, *Club Cultures*.

41 Stevenson estimated that capsules contained a tenth of a grain. Stevenson, *Drug Addiction*, 534. RCMP annual reports indicated that caps contained between a quarter grain and a full grain. RCMP, *Annual Report for the Year Ended March 31, 1955* (Ottawa: Edmond Cloutier, 1955), 19. In February 1963, R.C. Hammond, the chief of the Division of Narcotic Control wrote that 'it is doubtful if the average heroin addict in Canada is able to obtain a dosage of 1 to 1¼ grains per day. In fact we are inclined to believe it is much less than this.' Alcoholism and Drug Addiction Research Foundation, 'Proceedings of the Conference on Narcotic Addiction,' Niagara Falls, ON,

21–4 February 1963. A 1959–60 study of heroin capsules seized in Canada determined that 95 per cent of the 229 seizures contained 24–68 mg of heroin per capsule, with a mean of 46 mg. Quoted in Canada, Commission of Enquiry into the Non-Medical Use of Drugs, *Final Report of the Commission of Inquiry into the Non-Medical Use of Drugs* (Ottawa: Information Canada, 1973), 303. One grain is 64.78 milligrams. RxDesktop Weights and Measures, http://www.rxdesktop.com/weights_measures.htm.

42 RCMP, *Annual Report for the Year Ended March 31, 1952* (Ottawa: Edmond Cloutier, 1952); RCMP, *Annual Report for the Year Ended March 31, 1955* (Ottawa: Edmond Cloutier, 1955); RCMP, *Annual Report for the Year Ended March 31, 1957* (Ottawa: Edmond Cloutier, 1957).

43 Stevenson, *Drug Addiction*, 139–40.

44 Larner, ed., *The Addict in the Street.*

45 Claude Brown describes young people being attracted to heroin in 1950s Harlem in his autobiography, *Manchild in the Promised Land*, in similar ways.

46 SFUA, JHSF #11.

47 Coutts, 'Social Structure of the Women's Unit at Oakalla,' 58. The physician at Oakalla in the 1950s, Guy Richmond, agreed that 'heroin seemed to be a status symbol.' Guy Richmond, *Prison Doctor*, 54.

48 Willis, *Learning to Labor.*

49 Stevenson, *Drug Addiction*, 113.

50 Ibid., 181.

51 'John Turvey,' in Canning-Dew, *Hastings and Main*, 151.

52 NAC, RG 29, vol. 3345, file 329-M-391.

53 SFUA, JHSF #13.

54 NAC, RG 29, vol. 3348, file 327-T-182.

55 Coutts, 'Social Structure of the Women's Unit at Oakalla,' 68.

56 Canada, Senate, *Proceedings and Report of the Special Senate Committee on the Traffic in Narcotic Drugs in Canada*, 414.

57 Hanley, 'Functions of Argot among Heroin Addicts,' 294–307.

58 This was true of Louis S., who first used narcotics in 1950, but six years later a British Columbia Penitentiary Classification Assistant wrote, 'I doubt whether he ever has really been addicted.' SFUA, JHSF #14.

59 SFUA, JHSF #15.

60 NAC, RG 29, vol. 3334, file 327-F-60.

61 From 1947 through 1961, 56 percent of narcotic offenders were married or had been married, which is quite high considering that many offenders were in their late teens or early twenties. Canada, Dominion Bureau of Statistics, *Annual Report of Statistics of Criminal and Other Offences* for the years 1947–61.

62 Stevenson, *Drug Addiction*, 92.
63 Ibid., 97.
64 SFUA, JHSF #16.
65 SFUA, JHSF #17.
66 SFUA, JHSF #11.
67 SFUA, JHSF #18.
68 SFUA, JHSF #19.
69 SFUA, JHSF #20.
70 SFUA, JHSF #21.
71 National Film Board of Canada, *Forbidden Love*; and 'John Turvey,' in Canning-Dew, *Hastings and Main*, 154.
72 Chenier, 'Tough Ladies and Troublemakers.'
73 SFUA, JHSF #22.
74 SFUA, JHSF #23.
75 SFUA, JHSF #24, JHSF #25, and JHSF #26.
76 SFUA, JHSF #27.
77 SFUA, JHSF #28, JHSF #28, JHSF #18, and JHSF #30.
78 NAC, RG 29, vol. 3336, file 327-F-6.
79 Stevenson reported that of fifty-three male addicts at Oakalla, seven were labourers, eight were loggers, and six were truck drivers. Three were cooks, three salesmen, and three seamen. The other twenty-three had a diverse array of working-class occupations. Stevenson, *Drug Addiction*, 54. In the National Archives of Canada case files, 38 per cent of the men were reported to be labourers, 9 per cent were loggers, and 6 per cent were truck drivers. Some had more than one occupation listed, so there is some overlap here.
80 Stevenson, *Drug Addiction*, 59.
81 SFUA, JHSF #31.
82 SFUA, JHSF #16.
83 SFUA, JHSF #32.
84 SFUA, JHSF #33.
85 NAC, RG 29, vol. 3334, file 3327-F-60.
86 NAC, RG 29, vol. 3336, file 327-D-60.
87 Canada, Dominion Bureau of Statistics, *Advance Statement on Employment and Average Weekly Wages and Salaries* for the years 1957–71.
88 Stevenson, *Drug Addiction*, 96.
89 SFUA, JHSF #5.
90 SFUA, JHSF #34.
91 The $10 per trick price was regularly repeated in *Hush* magazine. See, for example, 'Call Girls Inflate "High Cost of Loving,"' *Hush*, 22 February 1958, 6.

92 Coutts, 'Social Structure of the Women's Unit at Oakalla,' 184.

93 SFUA, JHSF #35.

94 Coutts, 'Social Structure of the Women's Unit at Oakalla,' 172.

95 SFUA, JHSF #36.

96 SFUA, JHSF #16.

97 'John Turvey,' in Canning-Dew, *Hastings and Main*, 154–5.

98 Faupel, *Shooting Dope*. James M. Walters found that approximately half of all black heroin users he studied had a 'main hustle' – usually thefts, robberies, or con games. '"Taking Care of Business" Updated: A Fresh Look at the Daily Routine of the Heroin User,' in Hanson et al., *Life with Heroin*, 36.

99 SFUA, JHSF #37.

100 SFUA, JHSF #38.

101 SFUA, JHSF #39.

102 Preble and Casey, 'Taking Care of Business.'

103 Sutter, 'Worlds of Drug Use on the Street Scene'; Hanson et al., *Life with Heroin*; Johnson et al., *Taking Care of Business*; Faupel, *Shooting Dope*; Stevens, *The Street Addict Role*.

104 SFUA, JHSF #40.

105 SFUA, JHSF #41.

106 SFUA, JHSF #42.

107 Stevenson, *Drug Addiction*, 187. Kathleen C.'s half-sister died of an overdose in 1960. See SFUA, JHSF #43.

108 SFUA, JHSF #44.

109 SFUA, JHSF #45.

110 Stevenson, *Drug Addiction*, 186–92.

111 Death dates are not given for most files at the National Archives. The policy was to discard files on drug users about whom a death report had been received. However, clerical errors meant that some files remained. D-121 and M-119 both died in their mid-fifties. C-310 died in his late forties, and M-391 died of an overdose in his mid-forties. NAC, RG 29, vol. 3336, file 327-D-121; vol. 3342, file 327-M-119; and vol. 3345, files 327-C-310 and 327-M-391.

112 NAC, RG 29, vol. 3330, file 3327-F-4.

113 SFUA, JHSF #46.

114 SFUA, JHSF #47.

115 SFUA, JHSF #48.

116 SFUA, JHSF #49.

117 Stevenson, *Drug Addiction*, 144.

118 Ibid.

119 Drugs certainly did enter Canadian jails and penitentiaries. See Anderson,

Hard Place to Do Time, 64. However, this certainly did not mean that all
prisoners had access to drugs at all times. Courtwright, Joseph, and Des
Jarlais, in *Addicts Who Survived,* concur that while drugs were occasionally
available in prison in the United States at this time, it was unlikely that
anyone could keep up a 'habit' while incarcerated (p. 249).

120 Stevenson, *Drug Addiction,* 145.
121 British Columbia, Sessional Papers, *Annual Report of Inspector of Gaols for the
    Year Ended March 31, 1957* (Victoria, BC: Queen's Printer, 1958), BB39.
122 SFUA, JHSF #32.
123 SFUA, JHSF #50.
124 SFUA, JHSF #51
125 SFUA, JHSF #52.
126 Interesting discussions of quitting can be found in Waldorf, Reinarman,
    and Murphy, *Cocaine Changes;* and Biernacki, *Pathways from Heroin Addiction.*
    Both books found that users do quit permanently without treatment, and
    that they have a variety of methods for doing so.
127 Beaudoin and Stanké, *La Rage des 'Goof-Balls,'* 85–8.
128 Stevenson, *Drug Addiction,* 145. Subjects sometimes combined more than
    one of these methods at once.
129 Coutts, 'Social Structure of the Women's Unit at Oakalla,' 158.
130 SNAP was initiated in 1962.
131 Maartman, *The Strange Thing about Miracles,* 15. Maartman had previously
    worked at the John Howard Society.
132 SFUA, JHSF #53.
133 SFUA, JHSF #15.
134 NAC, RG 29, vol. 3336, file 327-R-24.
135 Maartman, *The Strange Thing about Miracles,* 28.
136 Bourgeois, *In Search of Respect;* Rosenbaum, *Women on Heroin.*

Chapter 4

1 There is very little literature on the history of twentieth-century policing in
  Canada. Most has been written by Greg Marquis: 'Towards a Canadian
  Police Historiography'; *Policing Canada's Century;* 'Vancouver Vice'; 'The
  Technology of Professionalism'; 'The Police as a Social Service'; 'Police
  Unionism in Early 20th Century Toronto'; and 'Working Men in Uniform.'
  See also Weaver, *Crime, Constables and Courts;* Myers, 'Women Policing
  Women'; and Talbot, Jayewardene, and Juliana, *Canada's Constables.* There
  is also important work on security policing, including Kealey and Whitaker,
  RCMP Security Bulletins; Hewitt, *Spying 101;* Kinsman, Buse, and Steadman,
  Whose National Security.

2 Steve Hewitt argues that narcotic policing helped ensure the survival of the RCMP in the difficult years after the merger. Hewitt, 'While Unpleasant It Is a Service to Humanity.'

3 Manning, *The Narc's Game*, 45.

4 Haggerty and Ericson, 'The Military Technostructures of Policing'; Ericson and Haggerty, *Policing the Risk Society*; Ericson, *Reproducing Order.*

5 The best works include Manning, *The Narc's Game*; Moore, *Buy and Bust*; Kleiman, *Against Excess*; and Tonry and Wilson, *Drugs and Crime.* As Richard Ericson pointed out in *Reproducing Order*, it is not an easy matter to do ethnographic work with police officers, which may help explain the scarcity of literature on this topic (see p. 45). There are a few 'on the beat' accounts in Canada, but these eulogistic renderings have little critical analysis. Malarek, *Merchants of Misery*; Stroud, *The Blue Wall.*

6 Kleiman and Smith, 'State and Local Drug Enforcement'; Moore, 'Supply Reduction and Drug Law Enforcement.' A more optimistic view can be found in Uchida and Forst, 'Controlling Street-Level Drug Trafficking.' An interesting debate can be found in Chaiken, *Street-Level Drug Enforcement.* A nice summary is provided in Sharp, *The Dilemma of Drug Policy*, 109–30.

7 Worden, Bynum, and Frank, 'Police Crackdowns on Drug Abuse and Trafficking,' 101.

8 Mark Moore convincingly makes the argument that demand is not perfectly inelastic, as some have argued. However, he admits that demand does not decrease as rapidly as price increases. Moore, *Buy and Bust*, 6–10.

9 RCMP, *Annual Report for the Year Ended September 30, 1923* (Ottawa: F.A. Acland, 1924), 16.

10 Speech by C.H.L. Sharman, in Chief Constables Association of Canada, *Journal of Proceedings of the Annual Conference* (1941), 37.

11 Both C.H.L. Sharman, who was chief from 1927 to 1946, and K.C. Hossick, who was chief from 1946 to 1959, were former mounted police officers.

12 Giffen, Endicott, and Lambert, *Panic and Indifference*, 251–9; Solomon, 'Drug Enforcement Powers.'

13 In the late 1960s and early '70s, police forces other than the RCMP claimed to the Commission of Inquiry into the non-medical use of drugs that they were at a disadvantage because they lacked the writ of assistance. The commission reported that this was one of the reasons they preferred to act with the RCMP. Canada, *Final Report of the Commission of Inquiry into the Non-Medical Use of Drugs*, 950.

14 Canada, Senate, *Proceedings and Report of Special Senate Committee on the Traffic in Narcotic Drugs in Canada*, 408.

15 Metro Toronto Police, *Annual Report 1957* (Toronto: Ryerson Press, 1958), 33.

16 MacLeod, 'The RCMP and the Evolution of Provincial Policing.'

17 Walden, *Visions of Order*; Dawson, 'That Nice Red Coat Goes to My Head Like Champagne'; Dawson, *The Mountie from Dime Novel to Disney*.

18 RCMP, *Annual Report for the Year Ended September 30, 1922* (Ottawa: F.A. Acland, 1923), 17.

19 National Archives of Canada (hereafter NAC), RG 18, vol. 3162, file G-494-2.

20 J.P. Smith, *Report of Commissioner* (Duplicate Copy), Commission of Inquiry, Vancouver and Victoria, BC, NAC, RG 18, vol. 3170, file G494-7.

21 F.W. Cowan, the chief of the Narcotic Division, believed that 'the whole trouble has been brought to a head through certain jealousies existing in the ranks of the British Columbia Provincial Police, as it is common knowledge that they are anxious to see the Federal Police withdrawn from British Columbia.' Letter from F.W. Cowan to J.G. Shearer, Secretary, The Social Service Council of Canada, 11 December 1923, NAC, RG 29, vol. 605, file 325-4-7.

22 This interesting possibility is raised by Ken Stoddart's work in the 1970s. His interviews with users suggested that in the 1960s, people were able to obtain drugs in the interior of BC without being detected by police. See Stoddart, 'The Enforcement of Narcotics Violations in a Canadian City.'

23 Canada, Senate, *Proceedings and Report of the Special Senate Committee on the Traffic in Narcotic Drugs in Canada*.

24 In 1954–55 there were twenty RCMP officers on the Vancouver Drug Squad and fourteen men on the Vancouver City Police Drug Detail. 'Commissioner's Report,' in RCMP, *Annual Report for the Year Ended March 31, 1955* (Ottawa: Edmond Cloutier, 1955), 19. The Vancouver Drug Detail was expanded from four men to fourteen on 6 November 1954. Tupper, *Interim Report*, 68–9. The Tupper inquiry was the result of a scandal that struck the Vancouver City Police in 1955; it did not involve the narcotic squad or narcotics policing in any way. Macdonald and O'Keefe, *The Mulligan Affair*. In 1961 there were twenty-two RCMP officers and twelve Vancouver City Police officers dedicated to drug work. 'R. v. Dale,' *RCMP Quarterly* 27, no. 1 (July 1961): 43. Vancouver Police Chief Walter Mulligan estimated that there were 1581 addicts or suspected addicts in Vancouver in February 1955. The Division of Narcotic Control estimated that there were 1185 addicts in all of British Columbia. Stevenson, *Drug Addiction*, 413. Stevenson believed that all of these estimates were probably on the high side (p. 416).

25 Canada, Senate, *Proceedings and Report of the Special Senate Committee on the Traffic in Narcotic Drugs in Canada*, 404. Stevenson, *Drug Addiction*, 413. Estimates of the number of addicts come from the Division of Narcotic Control.

26 Marquis, *Policing Canada's Century*, 181.

27 Greenfield, *Drugs (Mostly)*, 8.

28 Wilson, *Undercover for the RCMP*, 12.

29 RCMP, *Annual Report for the Year Ended September 30, 1929* (Ottawa: F.A. Acland, 1930), 25.

30 Wilson, *Undercover for the RCMP*, 12–13.

31 RCMP, *Annual Report for the Year Ended March 31, 1934* (Ottawa: J.O. Patenaude, 1934), 20.

32 Letter from C.H.L. Sharman to S.T. Wood, 24 December 1936, NAC, RG 29, vol. 601, file 324-6-2.

33 RCMP memo, 7 January 1936, NAC, RG 29, vol. 601, file 324-6-2.

34 RCMP, *Annual Report* (Ottawa, 1948), 25. This class was offered for at least the next five years. *Annual Report of Canada under the Convention Limiting the Manufacture and Regulating the Distribution of Narcotic Drugs 13 July 1931, for the Year 1947*, NAC, RG 29, vol. 592, file 3322-5-3, Part 5.

35 Vancouver City Police, 'Annual Report for the Year 1956,' 6.

36 Metro Toronto Police, *Annual Report for the Year Ended December 31, 1960* (Toronto: Ryerson Press, 1961), 20.

37 NAC, RG 29, vol. 3331, file 327-D-32.

38 J.P. Smith, *Report of Commissioner* (Duplicate Copy), Commission of Inquiry, Vancouver and Victoria, BC, p. 143, NAC, RG 18, vol. 3170, file G494-7, Part 1. For evidence of the many raids that were made and that did not net any drugs, see NAC, RG 18, vol. 3297, file 1920-HQ-189-E-1.

39 Harvison, *The Horsemen*, 40–2.

40 He added that a trafficker in Montreal 'bitterly complains that we have knocked the bottom out of his traffic by merely making a point to travel Benoit St. whenever possible, of course he still sells there but only on a very decreased margin and in continual fear of being caught.' RCMP Report, 31 January 1922, NAC, RG 29, vol. 226, file 323-12-2 Part 1.

41 The number of deaths from liver cirrhosis fell dramatically during prohibition in the United States, and liver cirrhosis is positively correlated with per capita consumption of alcohol. Paul Aaron and David Musto conclude that 'there is now little dispute about the fact that the annual per-capita consumption level declined as the result of prohibition. Because of the long war of statistics fought between wet and dry forces, data, no matter how useful, have often been assumed to be little more than disguised polemics. There was, of course, a surfeit of spurious evidence churned out by both sides. But there is a body of credible information suggesting that the 18th Amendment had a substantial impact on drinking patterns.' Aaron and Musto, 'Temperance and Prohibition in America,' 164–5; Canada, *Final Report of the*

Commission of Inquiry into the Non-Medical Use of Drugs, 396; Kleiman, *Against Excess*, 244–5.

42 For an interesting look at single-occupancy hotels, see Groth, *Living Downtown*.

43 NAC, RG 29, vol. 3331, file 327-F-33.

44 RCMP Report, 22 August 1956, NAC, RG 29, vol. 3342, file 327-J-154.

45 RCMP Report, 1 September 1960, NAC, RG 29, vol. 3348, file 327-M-542.

46 NAC, RG 29, vol. 3340, file 327-H-156.

47 *Maclean's*, 'The Streets of Canada: Hastings,' 1 March 1958, 40.

48 'Information bulletins,' Series 201 (1960), Vancouver City Archives.

49 RCMP Report, 20 September 1960, NAC, RG 29, vol. 3340, file 327-A-39.

50 Phillips, *Police Pictures*; Marquis, 'Towards a Canadian Police Historiography,' 489.

51 'R. v. Bancroft and Burke,' *RCMP Quarterly* 8, no. 1 (July 1940): 9–10.

52 Canada, Senate, *Proceedings and Report of the Special Senate Committee on the Traffic in Narcotic Drugs in Canada*, 270.

53 NAC, RG 29, vol. 3331, file 327-W-52.

54 Unfortunately, there is no information in the study about how many addicts were asked about their dreams. The report only stated that over thirty had this dream. G.H. Stevenson, 'Some Medical and Psychological Aspects of Drug Addiction,' p. 17, NAC, RG 29, vol. 604, file 3253-2, Part 2.

55 Maynard, 'Through a Hole in the Lavatory Wall,' 240.

56 Manning's *The Narc's Game* also shows heavy use of informers.

57 Chief Constables Association of Canada, *Journal of Proceedings of the Annual Conference* (Ottawa, 1943), 104.

58 NAC, RG 29, vol. 3330, file 327-W-195.

59 Simon Fraser University Archives, John Howard Society Case File #54.

60 Wilson, *Undercover for the RCMP*, 19.

61 Greenfield, *Drugs (Mostly)*, 52.

62 Steve Hewitt found that in the 1920s, the RCMP paid $50 per tip, which was equivalent to approximately $500 in 1998 dollars. Hewitt, 'The RCMP's War on Drugs.' Thanks to Steve Hewitt for allowing me to look at this paper.

63 NAC, RG 18, vol. 3291, file 1922 HQ-189-C-2.

64 RCMP Report, 15 April 1938, NAC, RG 29, vol. 3331, file 327-B-183.

65 NAC, RG 29, vol. 3331, file 327-D-62.

66 J.P. Smith, *Report of Commissioner* (Duplicate Copy), Commission of Inquiry, Vancouver and Victoria, BC, p. 141, NAC, RG 18, vol. 3170, file G494-7, Part 1.

67 Report by Detective Sergeant Salt, 30 June 1923, NAC, RG 18, vol. 3296, file 1923 HQ-189-C-1. The name of the informant has been changed to protect privacy.

68 RCMP Report, 7 March 1940, NAC, RG 29, vol. 3330, file 327-C-90.

69 NAC, RG 29, vol. 3342, file 327-J-154.

70 NAC, RG 29, vol. 3331, file 327-D-32.

71 NAC, RG 29, vol. 3331, file 327-F-33.

72 NAC RG 29, vol. 3332, file 3327-M-24.

73 'What Else Could I Do? Dad Asks,' *Vancouver Sun*, 16 March 1960, 1.

74 'Drug Group Could Have Aided Girl,' *Vancouver Sun*, 26 January 1961, 2; 'Girl Saved from Slavery of Dope,' ibid., 26 January 1961, 1. The name has been changed to protect privacy.

75 Memo from Cortlandt Starnes to Officer Commanding RCMP (Vancouver), 11 July 1922, NAC, RG 18, vol. 3163, file G494-5.

76 Wilson, *Undercover for the RCMP*, 163.

77 Ibid., 15.

78 Greenfield, *Drugs (Mostly)*, 30.

79 Canada, Senate, *Proceedings and Report of the Special Senate Committee on the Traffic in Narcotic Drugs in Canada*, 269.

80 In 1954, for example, the RCMP instructed a narcotics officer from Edmonton to go undercover in Windsor to make a case against a trafficker, but he was recognized by one of the trafficker's associates, who had spent time in Edmonton. NAC, RG 29, vol. 3345, file 327-D-156.

81 Canada, Senate, *Proceedings and Report of the Special Senate Committee on the Traffic in Narcotic Drugs in Canada*, 62.

82 RCMP, *Annual Report for the Year Ended March 31, 1962* (Ottawa: Roger Duhamel, 1962), 20.

83 'Undercover Men in City Drug Roundup Carefully Trained for Perilous Roles,' *Vancouver Province*, 10 August 1953, 21.

84 See, for example, RCMP Report, 2 August 1955, NAC, RG 29, vol. 3334, file 327-W-139; and RCMP Report, 21 July 1955, NAC, RG 29, vol. 3348, file 327-T-116.

85 Manning and Redlinger, 'Working Bases for Corruption,' 81.

86 Greenfield, 'The Hopheads Are Ahead,' 67.

87 RCMP Report, 21 September 1955, NAC, RG 29, vol. 3345, file 327-L-283.

88 Courtwright, Joseph, and Des Jarlais, *Addicts Who Survived*; Larner and Tefferteller, *The Addict in the Street*.

89 Wilson, *Undercover for the RCMP*, 170.

90 J.P. Smith, *Report of Commissioner* (Duplicate Copy), Commission of Inquiry, Vancouver and Victoria, BC, p. 149, NAC, RG 18, vol. 3170, file G494-7, Part 1.

91 'Statement,' 14 October 1921, NAC, RG 18, vol. 3288, file 1921 HQ-189-E-1. See other items in the file for further allegations of violence against RCMP informants.

92 Canada, Senate, *Proceedings and Report of the Special Senate Committee on the Traffic in Narcotic Drugs in Canada*, 240.
93 Chief Constables Association of Canada, *Journal of Proceedings of the Annual Conference* (1954), 159.
94 The name has been changed to protect privacy. BC Archives, GR 2335, Box 2, file 47/49.
95 BC Archives, GR 2335, Box 2, file 47/49.
96 Coutts, 'Social Structure of the Women's Unit at Oakalla,' 173.
97 Stevenson, *Drug Addiction*, 173.
98 'R. v. C.,' *RCMP Quarterly* 20, no. 1 (July 1954): 54–5. The name has been changed to protect privacy.
99 Letter from C.H.L. Sharman to H.J. Anslinger, 23 August 1941, NAC, RG 29, vol. 225, file 323-9-25.
100 'R. v. Chapman,' *RCMP Quarterly* 9, no. 3 (January 1942): 256. The name has been changed to protect privacy.
101 NAC, RG 29, vol. 3336, file 327-G-113.
102 NAC, RG 29, vol. 3330, file 327-M-95.
103 NAC, RG 29, vol. 3330, file 327-F-4.
104 NAC, RG 29, vol. 3330, file 327-N-4.
105 In 1953 Commissioner Nicholson complained to the Department of National Health and Welfare, 'we are tired of handling addicts and addict peddlers over and over again. We think they should be isolated and quarantined compulsorily.' Letter from L.H. Nicholson to K.C. Hossick, 27 May 1953, NAC, RG 29, vol. 223, file 320-5-9, Part 6.

Chapter 5

1 The interactions between doctors and the state have been explored in Leavitt, *The Healthiest City*; Reagan, *When Abortion Was a Crime*; and Ladd-Taylor, *Mother-Work*, 167–96.
2 P.E. Bryden argues that the Canadian Medical Association had the ear of the government in 1942 when an advisory committee on health insurance was formed. The report of this committee was written 'with considerable input from the medical community,' and it 'incorporated all of the principles' on health insurance that had been 'issued by the CMA in 1937.' Bryden, *Planners and Politicians*, 4.
3 Gidney and Millar, *Professional Gentlemen*; Howell, 'Reform and the Monopolistic Impulse'; Howell, 'Medical Professionalization and the Social Transformation of the Maritimes'; Howell, 'Elite Doctors and the Development of Scientific Medicine'; Shortt, 'Physicians, Science and Status'; Naylor,

'The CMA's First Code of Ethics'; Naylor, 'Rural Protest and Medical Professionalism.' For the United States, see Starr, *The Transformation of American Medicine.*

4 Naylor, *Private Practice, Public Payment;* Duffin, 'The Guru and the Godfather'; Taylor, *Health Insurance and Canadian Public Policy.*

5 Clow, *Negotiating Disease.*

6 'Harrison Narcotics Tax Act, 1914,' in Schaffer Library of Drug Policy, http://www.druglibrary.org/schaffer/history/e1910/harrisonact.htm (accessed 7 July 2004).

7 White, *Slaying the Dragon,* 114; also see Musto, *The American Disease,* 186–9.

8 Berridge, *Opium and the People;* Parssinen, *Secret Passions, Secret Remedies;* Berridge, 'Professionalization and Narcotics'; and Peters, 'The British Response to Opiate Addiction.'

9 There were drug panics in Great Britain, but they were not as severe as those in North America. See Kohn, *Dope Girls.*

10 Coburn, Torrance, and Kaufert, 'Medical Dominance in Canada', 416; Lewis, *The Royal College of Physicians and Surgeons of Canada,* 7–8.

11 Coburn, 'Canadian Medicine,' 99. Coburn says this took place in 1920, but MacDermot says 1921 in *History of the Canadian Medical Association,* 3. Other histories of medical organizations in Canada include Bennett, *History of the Canadian Medical Association 1954–1994;* McNab, *A Legal History of Health Professions in Ontario;* and Kerr, *History of the Medical Council of Canada.*

12 Warsh, *Moments of Unreason,* 167–70; Courtwright, *Dark Paradise,* 114–47.

13 The best summaries of the complex world of addiction research can be found in Courtwright, *Dark Paradise;* Acker, *Creating the American Junkie;* and White, *Slaying the Dragon.*

14 R.D. Rudolph, 'Narcotic Addiction in Canada,' 431–2.

15 'Dangerous Drugs,' *Canadian Medical Association Journal* 13, no. 1 (January 1923): 55.

16 Canada, Parliament, *House of Commons Debates,* 7 June 1926, 4123. Letters to the editor of *Canadian Medical Association Journal:* Rudolph, 'Narcotic Addiction in Canada,' 431–2, and James McCallum, 'Narcotic Addiction in Canada,' *Canadian Medical Association Journal* (April 1930), 575.

17 Canada, Parliament, *House of Commons Debates,* 7 June 1926, 4123.

18 Memo from F.W. Cowan to the Deputy Minister of Justice, 19 September 1924, National Archives of Canada (hereafter NAC), RG 29, vol. 234, file 324-1-1, Part 3.

19 'Drug Charge against Dr. Lachance Continues,' *Manitoba Free Press,* 9 January 1924, 9.

20 'Four Doctors Tell of Treating Drug Addicts,' *Manitoba Free Press,* 23 January 1924, 9.

21 Musto, *The American Disease*; and Berridge 'Professionalization and Narcotics,' 361–72.

22 An Act to Amend the Opium and Narcotic Drug Act, Statutes of Canada 1920, c. 31.

23 Canada, Parliament, *House of Commons Debates*, 27 May 1925, 3603.

24 Ibid., 3605.

25 For a long list of cases against doctors, see Memo from F.W. Cowan to the Deputy Minister of Justice, 19 September 1924, NAC, RG 29, vol. 234, file 324-1-1, Part 3.

26 Provincial Archives of Alberta, Acc. 72.26, box 48, file 3183/C; Letter from F.W. Cowan to Deputy Minister, Minister of Justice, 19 September 1924, NAC, RG 29, vol. 234, file 324-1-1.

27 NAC, RG 29, vol. 236, file 324-1-2, Part 1 (notes on index cards); NAC, RG 29, vol. 605, file 325-4-5; NAC, RG 29, vol. 605, file 325-4-5; 'Medical Men and Narcotics: A Warning,' *Canadian Medical Association Journal* 20, no. 1 (January 1929): 92; 'Medical Men and Narcotics: A Warning,' *Canadian Journal of Public Health* (February 1928): 57–61. Question asked in the House of Commons by Mr. Anderson of Halton, in Canada, Parliament, *House of Commons Debates*, 13 February 1928, 382.

28 Letter from F.W. Cowan to Gilbert Agar, 15 May 1926, NAC, RG 29, vol. 605, file 325-4-7.

29 Ibid.

30 Letter from F.W. Cowan to the Commissioner of the RCMP, 4 June 1925, NAC, RG 18, vol. 3308, file HQ-189-1-A-1.

31 From 1920 to 1923, the courts prosecuted an average of nineteen doctors per year for violations of the Opium and Narcotic Drug Act, but in the 1930s and 1940s, only three doctors per year were convicted of narcotic offences. The Department of Health did not list the number of doctors who were convicted in 1925 and 1926, which is unfortunate, as RCMP files indicate that they were actively investigating doctors. All of these cases were investigated by the RCMP on behalf of the Department of Health. There may have been other cases that were investigated by provincial or municipal police forces. See the table compiled from the annual reports of the Department of Health in Giffen, Endicott, and Lambert, *Panic and Indifference*, 324. There is no data on whether doctors were convicted of offences under the act before 1920.

32 Canada, Department of Health, *Annual Report of the Department of Health for the Year Ended March 31, 1921* (Ottawa: F.A. Acland, 1921), 16.

33 Letter from C.H.L. Sharman to M.D. Perrins, 27 February 1928, NAC, RG 29, vol. 601, file 324-7-3.

34 NAC, RG 29, vol. 3330, file 327-M-95.

35 NAC, RG 29, vol. 3330, file 327-C-51.

36 Letter from F.W. Cowan to B.J. McConnell, 26 March 1920, NAC, RG 29, vol. 236, file 324-1-2, Part 1.

37 *Minutes of the Technical Advisory Committee,* 25 June 1954, NAC, RG 29, vol. 604, file 325-3-3.

38 NAC, RG 29, vol. 3331, file 327-B-183.

39 Letter from C.H.L. Sharman to Colonel Davis, 6 July 1942, NAC, RG 29, vol. 543, file 320-4-9, Part 1.

40 *Minutes of the Technical Advisory Committee Meeting,* 29 July 1954, NAC, RG 29, vol. 604, file 325-3-3. In its annual report for 1961, the Department of National Health and Welfare wrote that there were 3295 addicts in the country, including 2929 'criminal' addicts and 237 'medical addicts.' This would leave 129 'professional' addicts, most of whom were likely doctors. Canada, Department of National Health and Welfare, *Annual Report of the Department of National Health and Welfare for the Year Ended March 31, 1961* (Ottawa: Queen's Printer, 1961).

41 NAC, RG 29, vol. 3330, file 327-M-95.

42 Letter from C.H.L. Sharman to Dr. S., 22 October 1943, NAC, RG 29, vol. 3332, file 327-M-24.

43 Canada, Department of Pensions and National Health, *Annual Report of the Department of Pensions and National Health for the Year Ended March 31, 1932* (Ottawa: F.A. Acland, 1932), 92.

44 NAC, RG 29, vol. 601, file 324-6-2.

45 Stevenson, *Drug Addiction,* 4–5.

46 NAC, RG 29, acc. 1983–84/118, box 36, file 320-2-8.

47 Memo from K.C. Hossick to Dr. C.A. Roberts, 22 June 1954, NAC, RG 29, vol. 604, file 1324-3-2, Part 2.

48 NAC, RG 29, vol. 3331, file 327-N-43.

49 *Minutes of the Technical Advisory Committee,* 29 July 1954, NAC, RG 29, vol. 604, file 325-3-2.

50 NAC, RG 29, vol. 3346, file 327-B-271.

51 NAC, RG 29, acc. 1983–84/118, box 36, file 320-2-8.

52 MacDermot, *History of the Canadian Medical Association,* 2:132.

53 *An Act to Provide for the Control of Narcotic Drugs,* Statutes of Canada 1960–1, c. 35, sec. 12.

54 Canada, Parliament, *House of Commons Debates,* 7 June 1961, 6001.

55 'Addict Clinic Work Starts,' *Vancouver Sun,* 6 May 1958, 17.

56 Narcotic Addiction Foundation, Report of the Director, in 'Annual Report 1959–60' (Vancouver, 1959–60), n.p.

57 Narcotic Addiction Foundation, Report of the Senior Counselor, in 'Annual Report 1959–60' (Vancouver, 1959–60), n.p.; Narcotic Addiction Foundation, Report of the Senior Counsellor, in 'Annual Report 1960–61' (Vancouver, 1960–61), n.p.
58 Paulus and Halliday, 'Rehabilitation and the Narcotic Addicts,' 655–9.
59 Courtwright, 'The Prepared Mind.'
60 Fischer, 'Prescriptions, Power and Politics,' 191.
61 Ontario, Department of Reform Institutions, *Annual Report of the Department of Reform Institutions for the Year Ended March 31, 1956* (Toronto: Baptist Johnston, 1957), 10. 'Report by the Sub-committee of the Welfare and Housing Committee appointed by the Council of the Municipality of Metro Toronto to prepare a study on the use of the "Riverdale Hospital" as a treatment centre for narcotic drug addicts,' and 'Supplement to the Report,' Metro Toronto Archives, 3–4 Series 100, file 2043.
62 'Supplement to the Report by the Sub-committee of the Welfare and Housing Committee.'
63 Ibid.
64 McCormick, 'Group Living for Drug Addicts,' 41.
65 Ibid., 46.
66 Dummitt, 'Finding a Place for Father: Selling the Barbecue in Postwar Canada.'
67 British Columbia, *Annual Report of the Director of Corrections for the Year Ending March 31, 1958* (Victoria, 1958), p. DD23.
68 Letter from Mervyn Davis to Roger S. Beames, 29 May 1956, Simon Fraser University Archive, John Howard Society of British Columbia Papers, Container 17, F1-2-6-4.
69 British Columbia, Department of Correction, *Annual Report of the Department of Correction for the Year Ended March 31, 1958* (Victoria, 1958), p. DD23.

Chapter 6

1 'History,' John Howard Society of Canada, http://www.johnhoward.ca/jhsback.htm; Gordon Hay, 'Biography of John Howard,' The John Howard Society of Canada, http://www.johnhoward.ca/bio.htm; Cooper, 'Ideas and Their Execution.'
2 Wilton, *May I Talk to John Howard.*
3 John Howard Society, 'Annual Report for 1962.'
4 Becki Ross and Franca Iacovetta point out that there were volunteers at Street Haven and at International House. Ross, 'Down at the Whorehouse?'; Ross, 'Destaining the (Tattooed) Delinquent Body'; Iacovetta, 'Making "New Canadians."'

5 Gleason, *Normalizing the Ideal*; Rose, *Inventing Our Selves.*
6 Ehrenreich, *The Altruistic Imagination*; Gordon, *Pitied but not Entitled*; Kunzel, *Fallen Women, Problem Girls*; Walkowitz, *Working with Class*; Wills, *A Marriage of Convenience*; Graham, 'A History of the University of Toronto School of Social Work'; Ross, 'Destaining the (Tattooed) Delinquent Body'; Iacovetta, 'Gossip, Contest and Power'; Iacovetta, 'Making "New Canadians."'
7 Walkowitz, *Working with Class*; Wills, *A Marriage of Convenience.*
8 Race was not identified for every client. However, JHS workers seem to have included race in their introductory file cards whenever the client was not white. These figures are based on clients that were identified as Aboriginal, black, and Asian. Class background was not listed on file cards, but where possible I assumed class based on the occupation of the drug user, and in some cases on the occupation of their parents. Drug-using clients of the JHS very rarely had middle-class occupations, although a few came from middle-class families. I entered these drug users as middle class, because in many of these cases their parents were willing to give them assistance, which meant that they had middle-class privilege. Class background was only identified for 226 of the 397 case files.
9 Wilton, *May I Talk to John Howard.*
10 John Howard Society, 'Annual Report for 1935.'
11 John Howard Society, 'Annual Report for 1945.'
12 'Report of the Executive Secretary,' in John Howard Society, 'Annual Report for 1932,' 2.
13 A good discussion of muscular Christianity can be found in Howell, *Northern Sandlots*, 105–6; Simon Fraser University Archives (hereafter SFUA), John Howard Society Case File (hereafter JHSF) #55.
14 SFUA, JHSF #56.
15 'Report of the Executive Secretary, 14 March 1934,' in John Howard Society, 'Annual Report for 1933.'
16 'Report of the Executive Secretary for the Year 1941,' presented at the Annual Meeting, 10 March 1942, in John Howard Society, 'Annual Report for 1941.' Hobden proudly told the board that 'Our "Honour Roll" of en-listments contains 200 names ... To many it has meant the first real chance ever to pass their way, and they have not failed to measure up to its challenge.'
17 'Report of the Executive Secretary, 20 March 1945,' in John Howard Society, 'Annual Report for 1944,' 3.
18 One worker wrote to another on 31 January 1961 that 'Unfortunately, imprisonment does not seem to be the answer to their [drug users'] problems.' SFUA, JHSF #57. Two workers were very frustrated when they were unable to find any treatment for a couple who came to them for help, and

one wrote a letter to the man's lawyer detailing his effort to stay away from drugs, and the society's inability to help. SFUA, JHSF #58 and JHSF #24. In the 'Annual Report for 1955,' the society recommended that drug users be given a three-year sentence, only three months of which would be spent incarcerated. The remainder would be spent on parole. 'This would give both an opportunity for physical cure within an institution and rehabilitation on the outside, with the unfinished part of the sentence acting as a strong deterrent factor against further criminal behavior.' John Howard Society, 'Annual Report for 1955,' 6. Social worker John Webster wrote a memo to the board of directors detailing a variety of problems with the British Columbia Penitentiary, including overcrowding, meagreness of the vocational training, overemphasis on custodial care, and inadequate gate money in the late 1950s (date unspecified). See 'Some Critical Comments about the British Columbia Penitentiary from an After-Care Point of View,' in SFUA, JHS Administrative Records, Container 12, file F-1-2-1-7.

19 The executive director was rapped on the wrist by the JHS board of directors for failing to maintain good relationships with other organizations, especially the National Parole Board, in 1961. SFUA, JHS Administrative Records, Container 10, file F-1-1-6-44. Interestingly, when the Community Chest and Council of Greater Vancouver reviewed the work of the society in 1952, the society was criticized for failing to be more critical of the penal system. Vancouver City Archives, United Way of the Lower Mainland, Add Mss 849, 617-F-2 file 2.

20 See John Howard Society, annual reports for the years 1950–61 ('Annual Report for 1950,' etc.). There was a great deal of penal reform in British Columbia prisons at this time. See Topping, 'The Rise of the New Penology.'

21 Salaries at the John Howard Society of British Columbia were lower than salaries in other correctional services and were lower than those offered in other provinces. Many staff members left because they were offered higher-paying positions elsewhere. Board of Executive Minutes, 15 September 1959, 20 October 1959, and 20 December 1960, SFUA, JHS Administrative Records, Box 2, F-1-1-1-9.

22 In 1957 the Executive Board minutes indicated, 'we are attempting to make use of the funds we have as part of a plan the individual has.' Board of Executive Minutes, 15 May 1957, SFUA, JHS Administrative Records, Box 2, F-1-1-1-9.

23 SFUA, JHSF #59.

24 SFUA, JHSF #60.

25 SFUA, JHSF #24.

26 SFUA, JHSF #30.

27 In 1959 JHS worker B.K. Stevenson told the Welfare and Housing Committee appointed by the Council of the Municipality of Metro Toronto that
'From the National Parole Board's point of view their experience over the
years has been that the drug addict does not make a good risk for parole so
there is no interference as a general rule. Recently, however, they have
modified this and are willing to experiment in the release of some addicts
under direct supervision.' 'Report by the Sub-committee of the Welfare and
Housing Committee appointed by the Council of the Municipality of Metro
Toronto to prepare a study on the use of the "Riverdale Hospital" as a
treatment centre for narcotic drug addicts,' Metro Toronto Archives, Series
100, file 2043. For more information on parole, see National Parole Board,
'Annual Report of the National Parole Board for the Calendar Year Ended
December 31, 1959'; and Canada, Parliament, Standing Senate Committee
on Legal and Constitutional Affairs, *Parole in Canada* (Ottawa: Information
Canada, 1974).

28 The supervisor of counselling services wrote the National Parole Board in
1961 that no institutional setting, regardless of treatment approach, could
ever deal with the real problems of drug addiction. Letter, 15 July 1961,
SFUA, JHSF 14,171.

29 SFUA, JHSF $61.

30 SFUA, JHSF #62.

31 SFUA, JHSF #63.

32 SFUA, JHSF #35.

33 SFUA, JHSF #64.

34 SFUA, JHSF #65.

35 See, for example, Waldorf, Reinarman, and Murphy, *Cocaine Changes*;
Zinberg, *Drug, Set and Setting*.

36 SFUA, JHSF #60.

37 SFUA, JHSF #12.

38 SFUA, JHSF #66.

39 SFUA, JHSF #4.

40 SFUA, JHSF #67.

41 SFUA, JHSF #68.

42 SFUA, JHSF #69.

43 SFUA, JHSF #70.

44 SFUA, JHSF #26.

45 SFUA, JHSF #11.

46 SFUA, JHSF #67.

47 SFUA, JHSF #18.

48 Adams, *The Trouble with Normal*; and Bailey, *From Front Porch to Back Seat*.

49 SFUA, JHSF #71.

50 SFUA, JHSF #4.

51 SFUA, JHSF #69.

52 Gleason, 'Psychology and the Construction of the "Normal" family'; Iacovetta, 'Making "New Canadians"'; May, *Homeward Bound.*

53 SFUA, JHSF #41.

54 SFUA, JHSF #60.

55 National Film Board of Canada, *Forbidden Love*; Chenier, 'Tough Ladies and Troublemakers;' Kennedy and Davis, *Boots of Leather, Slippers of Gold*; Faderman, *Odd Girls and Twilight Lovers.*

56 Coutts, 'Social Structure of the Women's Unit at Oakalla,' 117.

57 SFUA, JHSF #57.

58 Ross, 'Destaining the (Tattooed) Delinquent Body.'

59 SFUA, JHSF #23.

60 SFUA, JHSF #62.

61 SFUA, JHSF #41.

62 SFUA, JHSF #40.

63 Kinsman, *The Regulation of Desire*; Kinsman, '"Character Weakness" and "Fruit Machines"'; and Robinson and Kimmel, 'The Queer Career of Homosexual Security Vetting.'

64 SFUA, JHSF #72.

65 See Iacovetta, 'Making "New Canadians"' for more information about how social workers judged the gender relations of their ethnic clients.

66 SFUA, JHSF #60.

67 'Folklorization' refers to the way in which white Canadians praised 'new Canadians' for adding interesting 'ethnic' food, costumes, and dancing to Canadian life in the 1950s.

68 John Howard Society, 'Annual Report for 1951,' 10.

69 SFUA, JHSF #73.

70 SFUA, JHSF #64.

71 SFUA, JHSF #74.

72 SFUA, JHSF #51 and #75.

73 SFUA, JHSF #16 and #17.

74 SFUA, JHSF #76.

75 'Report by the Sub-committee of the Welfare and Housing Committee appointed by the Council of the Municipality of Metro Toronto to prepare a study on the use of the "Riverdale Hospital" as a treatment centre for narcotic drug addicts.'

76 SFUA, John Howard Society of British Columbia Papers, Container 13, file F-1-2-1-28.

77 May, *Homeward Bound.*

78 SFUA, JHSF #77.

79 SFUA, JHSF #78.

80 SFUA, JHSF #79.

81 SFUA, JHSF #80 and #81.

82 Frankau, 'Experience with Canadian Addicts'; Whynes and Bean, *Policing and Prescribing;* Strang and Gossop, *Heroin Addiction.*

83 SFUA, JHSF #57.

84 SFUA, JHSF #74.

Chapter 7

1 Letter from C.H.L. Sharman to Dr. Procter, 19 March 1930, National Archives of Canada (hereafter NAC), RG 29, vol. 236, file 324-1-2, Part 3.

2 See Horn, *The Dirty Thirties*, 398–552.

3 'Treatment for Drug Addicts,' *Winnipeg Tribune*, 17 March 1937, in NAC, RG 29, vol. 237, file 324-1-2.

4 Acker, *Creating the American Junkie*, 125–55; White, *Slaying the Dragon*, 122.

5 Castel and Lovell, *The Psychiatric Society;* Gleason, *Normalizing the Ideal;* Rose, *Inventing Our Selves;* Rose, *Governing the Soul;* Giddens, *Modernity and Self-Identity;* Gordon, *Heroes of their Own Lives;* Valverde, *Diseases of the Will.*

6 Letter from W.W. Cross to Paul Martin, 13 March 1953, NAC, RG 29, Acc. 1983–84/118, vol. 4, file 321-4-4.

7 Letter from F.W. Cowan to Gilbert Agar, 16 February 1925, NAC, RG 29, vol. 605, file 325-4-7, Part 1.

8 Letter from J.J. Heagerty to B.T. McGhie, 18 October 1938, NAC, RG 29, vol. 604, file 395-3-6, Part 1.

9 Canada, *Report of the Royal Commission to Investigate the Penal System of Canada,* 159–61.

10 Steeves, *The Compassionate Rebel;* and UBC Special Collections, Angus MacInnis Memorial Collection, E.E. Winch Personal Papers, Box 76, file 8.

11 Strang and Gossop, *Heroin Addiction.*

12 Adams, *The Trouble with Normal;* Iacovetta, 'Gossip, Contest and Power'; Sangster, *Regulating Girls and Women.*

13 'Sordid Drug Traffic Bared in Court by Teen-Age Girls,' *Vancouver Sun,* 16 July 1952, 1.

14 'Teen-Age Girls Tell of Dope Orgies: Youthful Logger Accused of Supplying Narcotics,' *Vancouver Sun,* 24 July 1952, 2.

15 'Face Drug Problem Squarely,' *Vancouver Sun,* 11 August 1952, 4.

16 Greenfield, 'The Hopheads Are Ahead,' 13.

17 Donaldson, 'Our Losing Battle with Dope: Part 1,' 43.
18 Vancouver Community Chest and Council, 'Drug Addiction in Canada: The Problem and Its Solution,' 30 July 1952, reprinted in Stevenson, *Drug Addiction* as Appendix A.
19 'Drug Reform Vital,' *Vancouver Sun*, 30 July 1952, 4; 'The Fruit of Greed,' *Vancouver Province*, 30 July 1952, 4.
20 'Ottawa Set to Give Dope Grants to B.C.,' *Vancouver Sun*, 30 December 1952, 2; Canada, Parliament, *House of Commons Debates*, 8 May 1953, 5000–1.
21 Stevenson, *Drug Addiction*, 156–7.
22 Ibid., 157.
23 Ibid., 569.
24 Stevenson, 'Arguments For and Against the Legal Sale of Narcotics,' *Bulletin of the Vancouver Medical Association*, 31 (January 1955): 177–86, reprinted in Stevenson, *Drug Addiction* as Appendix H.
25 Canada, Senate, *Proceedings and Report of the Special Senate Committee on the Traffic in Narcotic Drugs in Canada*, xvi–xxii.
26 'Drug Addiction Myths Still Obscure Established Facts,' *Vancouver Sun*, 15 March 1958, 6.
27 Memorandum from Charles G. Stogdill to K.C. Hossick, 13 January 1951, NAC, RG 29, vol. 604, file 325-3-2.
28 Technical Advisory Committee Meeting on Drug Addiction, *Minutes*, 23 September 1954, NAC, RG 29, vol. 604, file 325-3-2.
29 See Davie Fulton's speech at the beginning of the second reading of the Bill. Canada, Parliament, *House of Commons Debates*, 7 June 1961, 5984–8.
30 R.S.S. Wilson, 'Drug Clinic Plan Opposed in Canada,' in Canada, Senate, *Proceedings and Report of the Special Senate Committee on the Traffic in Narcotic Drugs in Canada*, Appendix B, originally published in the *Vancouver Province*, 16 August 1952, 378.
31 Canada, Senate, *Proceedings and Report of the Special Senate Committee on the Traffic in Narcotic Drugs in Canada*, 44.
32 An Act to Provide for the Control of Narcotic Drugs, Statutes of Canada 1960–61, c. 35, part II.
33 Canada, Parliament, *House of Commons Debates*, 30 June 1960, 5611.
34 Ibid., 12 June 1961, 6211. See K.R. Vaughan Lyon, President John Howard Society to the Honourable David Fulton, 14 June 1961, Simon Fraser University Archive, John Howard Society of British Columbia Papers, file F-1-1-1-10.
35 Canada, Parliament, *House of Commons Debates*, 12 June 1961, 6213.
36 Stevenson, *Drug Addiction*, 555–6.
37 Erickson, *Cannabis Criminals*, 23.

38 Lynn McDonald, 'The Matsqui Institution,' Commission Research Paper, Royal Commission of Inquiry into the Non-Medical Use of Drugs, unpublished paper, pp. 1–17.
39 Canada, Dominion Bureau of Statistics, *Annual Report of Statistics of Criminal and Other Offences for the Calendar Year 1960* (Ottawa: Queen's Printer, 1962); and Canada, *Cannabis*, 322.
40 Canada, *Cannabis*, 249.
41 Canada, *Final Report of the Commission of Inquiry into the Non-Medical Use of Drugs*, 850.

Conclusion

1 City of Vancouver, 'Four Pillars Drug Strategy,' http://www.city.vancouver.bc.ca/fourpillars.
2 'North American Opiate Medication Initiative (NAOMI) Project Backgrounder,' http://www.ofcmhap.on.ca/addiction north_american_opiate_medication.htm.
3 Boyd, *Mothers and Illicit Drugs*.

Appendix

1 Personal correspondence with Cathy Bailey, the archivist responsible for this accession at the National Archives of Canada. A few studies by the Narcotic Addiction Foundation in the 1960s appear to have examined the Division of Narcotic Control files for contemporary research. They include Ingeborg, *A Comparative Study of Long-Term and Short-Term Withdrawal*; and Henderson, *An Exploration of the Natural History of Heroin Addiction*.
2 Stevenson, *Drug Addiction*, 414. Stevenson's study tried to determine how many drug users there were who did not come to the attention of narcotic authorities. The RCMP and city police officers believed that there were few such users. Doctors across the province were surveyed, and the results did not reveal a significant number of 'secret' drug users. The high cost of drugs, the relatively small amount of drugs seized by police, as well as the significant overlap between drug users known to social workers and police officers all lend support to the theory that it was fairly difficult to be a long-term drug user in the post-war period and not be known to police. Today, of course, when drug use is extremely widespread, the situation is very different. For the difficulties of measuring drug use today, see Zimring and Hawkins, *The Search for Rational Drug Control*.
3 Reaume, 'Portraits of People with Mental Disorders,' 93–125.

4 The most famous of these debates is Gordon and Scott. Book review by Joan Scott of Linda Gordon's *Heroes of Their Own Lives*, 848–52; Response to Joan Scott by Linda Gordon, 852–3; Book review by Linda Gordon of Joan Scott's *Gender and the Politics of History*, 853–8; Response to Linda Gordon by Joan Scott, 859–60.
5 Strange, 'The Historian and the Capital Case File,' 27.
6 For a discussion, see Iacovetta and Mitchinson, 'Introduction' in their *On the Case*, 3–24.

Bibliography

Archival Sources

National Archives of Canada
  RG 13 'Justice': Files to do with the Opium and Narcotic Drug Act 1911–61
  RG 18 'Royal Canadian Mounted Police': Files to do with policing under the
    Opium and Narcotic Drug Act 1920–61
  RG 29 'National Health and Welfare': All files from the Division of Narcotic
    Control 1920–61
  RG 76 'Immigration': Files to do with the deportation provision of the Opium
    and Narcotic Drug Act 1922–61
  MG30-D346 Robert Anderson Fonds
British Columbia Archives
  GR-0602 'Vancouver Lock-Up Charge Books'
  GR-1327 'Coroner's Inquests'
  GR-1975 'British Columbia County Court (Penticton) Criminal Case Files
    Originals 1922-1945'
  GR-2335 'Supreme Court (Vancouver) Originals 1946–9'
  GR-2788 'Prince George County Court Criminal Case Files Originals 1914–49
  GR-2812 'Vancouver County Court – Conviction and Acquittals: Vol. 1'
Provincial Archives of Alberta
  Acc. 72.26 'Criminal Case Files 1915–28'
  Acc. 76.347 'Attorney General: Department of General Administration'
City of Edmonton Archives
  Emily Murphy Papers MS.2
City of Metro Toronto Archives
  Series 100, Files 2041 and 2043 'Alcoholism, Drug Addiction, and Vice:
    Mental Health 1935-19–59'

City of Vancouver Archives
  Gordon Scott Papers MSS 289
  H.H. Stevens Papers MSS 69
  United Way of the Lower Mainland MSS 849 and MSS 849-2
  Vancouver Police Department Fonds
    Series 201 'Information bulletins,' 1960
  Vancouver Police Court
    Series 182 'Court calendars, 1889–1929'
    Series 184 'Court calendars of indictable offences, 1929–61'
City Social Service Department Fonds
  Series 450 'Narcotic Addiction'
Simon Fraser University Archives
  John Howard Society Papers
University of British Columbia Archives
  Chinese Canadian Research Collection
  Angus MacInnis Memorial Collection, E.E. Winch Fonds
  Alexander Manson Fonds

Other Sources

Aaron, Paul, and David Musto. 'Temperance and Prohibition in America: A Historical Overview.' In *Alcohol and Public Policy: Beyond the Shadow of Prohibition*, edited by Mark H. Moore and Dean R. Gerstein. Washington: National Academy Press, 1981.

Acker, Caroline. *Creating the American Junkie: Addiction Research in the Classic Era of Narcotic Control.* Baltimore: Johns Hopkins University Press, 2002.

Adams, Mary Louise. *The Trouble with Normal: Postwar Youth and the Making of Heterosexuality.* Toronto: University of Toronto Press, 1997.

Adler, Patricia A. *Wheeling and Dealing: An Ethnography of an Upper-Level Drug Dealing and Smuggling Community.* New York: Columbia University Press, 1985.

Agar, Michael. *Ripping and Running.* New York: Seminar Press, 1973.

Akers, Ronald L. 'Addiction: The Troublesome Concept.' *Journal of Drug Issues* 21, no. 4 (1991): 777–94.

Anderson, Earl. *Hard Place to Do Time: The Story of Oakalla Prison.* New Westminster, BC: Hillpointe Publishing, 1993.

Anderson, Kay. *Vancouver's Chinatown.* Montreal: McGill-Queen's University Press, 1993.

Backhouse, Constance. *Colour-Coded: A Legal History of Racism in Canada.* Toronto: University of Toronto Press, 1999.

Bailey, Beth L. *From Front Porch to Back Seat: Courtship in Twentieth Century America.* Baltimore: Johns Hopkins University Press, 1988.

Beaudoin, Marie-José, and Alain Stanké. *La Rage des 'Goof-Balls.'* Montreal: Éditions de l'homme, 1962.

Becker, Howard. *The Outsiders: Studies in the Sociology of Deviance.* New York: Free Press, 1963.

Bennett, John Sutton. *History of the Canadian Medical Association, 1954–1994.* Ottawa: The Canadian Medical Association, 1996.

Ben-Yehuda, Nachman. *The Politics and Morality of Deviance: Moral Panics, Drug Abuse, Deviant Science and Reversed Stigmatization.* New York: State University of New York Press, 1990.

Berridge, Virginia. *Opium and the People: Opiate Use and Drug Control Policy in the 19th and Early 20th Century.* London and New York: Free Association Books, 1999.

– 'Professionalization and Narcotics: The Medical and Pharmaceutical Professions and British Narcotic Use, 1868–1926.' *Psychological Medicine* 8 (1978): 361–72.

Bewley-Taylor, David. *The United States and International Drug Control, 1909–1997.* London: Pinter, 1999.

Biernacki, Patrick. *Pathways from Heroin Addiction: Recovery without Treatment.* Philadelphia: Temple University Press, 1983.

Blackwell, Judith Stephenson. 'Drifting, Controlling and Overcoming: Opiate Users Who Avoid Becoming Chronically Dependent.' *Journal of Drug Issues* (Spring 1983): 219–35.

Bliss, Michael. *The Discovery of Insulin.* Toronto: McClelland and Stewart, 1982.

Booth, Martin. *Opium: A History.* New York: St. Martin's Press, 1998.

Bourgois, Philippe. *In Search of Respect: Selling Crack in El Barrio.* Cambridge and New York: Cambridge University Press, 1995.

Boyd, Neil. 'The Origins of Canadian Narcotics Legislation: The Process of Criminalization in Historical Context.' *Dalhousie Law Journal* 8, no. 1 (January 1984): 102–37.

Boyd, Susan. *Mothers and Illicit Drugs: Transcending the Myths.* Toronto: University of Toronto Press, 1999.

Brasset, Edmund. *A Doctor's Pilgrimage.* Philadelphia and New York: J.P. Lippincott Company, 1951.

Brock, Deborah R. *Making Work, Making Trouble: Prostitution as a Social Problem.* Toronto: University of Toronto Press, 1998.

Brown, Claude. *Manchild in the Promised Land.* New York: Macmillan, 1965.

Brown, Wenzell. *Monkey on My Back.* New York: Greenberg Publisher, 1953.

Bruun, Kettil. 'International Drug Control and the Pharmaceutical Industry.' In *Social Aspects of the Medical Use of Psychotropic Drugs*, edited by Ruth Cooperstock, 1–8. Toronto: Alcoholism and Drug Addiction Research Foundation of Ontario, 1974.

Bruun, Kettil, Lynn Pan, and Ingemar Rexed. *The Gentlemen's Club: International Control of Drugs and Alcohol*. Chicago: University of Chicago Press, 1975.

Bryden, P.E. *Planners and Politicians: Liberal Politics and Social Policy, 1957–1968*. Montreal and Kingston: McGill-Queen's University Press, 1997.

Campbell, Robert. *Sit Down and Drink Your Beer: Regulating Vancouver's Beer Parlours, 1925–1954*. Toronto: University of Toronto Press, 2001.

Canada. *Cannabis: A Report of the Commission of Inquiry into the Non-Medical Use of Drugs*. Ottawa: Information Canada, 1972.

– *Final Report of the Commission of Inquiry into the Non-Medical Use of Drugs*. Ottawa: Information Canada, 1973.

– *Proceedings of the Special Committee on the Traffic in Narcotic Drugs in Canada*. Ottawa: Edmond Cloutier, 1955.

– *Report of the Royal Commission to Investigate the Penal System of Canada*. Ottawa: J.O. Patenaude, 1938.

Canada, House of Commons. 'Report on the Need for the Suppression of the Opium Traffic in Canada.' *Sessional Papers of Canada*, 3 July 1908, paper 36b.

Canada, Royal Commission on Chinese Immigration. *Report of the Royal Commission on Chinese Immigration*. Ottawa, 1885.

Canada, Senate. *Proceedings and Report of Special Senate Committee on the Traffic in Narcotic Drugs in Canada*. Ottawa: Edmond Cloutier, 1955.

– *Report of the Standing Senate Committee on Legal and Constitutional Affairs Parole in Canada*. Ottawa: Information Canada, 1974.

Canning-Dew, Jo Ann, ed. *Hastings and Main: Stories from an Inner City Neighborhood*. Vancouver: New Star Books, 1987.

Carstairs, Catherine. 'Innocent Addicts, Dope Fiends and Nefarious Traffickers: Illegal Drug Use in 1920s English Canada.' *Journal of Canadian Studies* 33, no. 3 (Fall 1998): 145–62.

Castel, François, and Anne Lovell. *The Psychiatric Society*. Translated by Arthur Goldhammer. New York: Columbia University Press, 1982.

Chaiken, Marcia, ed. *Street-Level Drug Enforcement: Examining the Issues*. Washington: U.S. Department of Justice, 1988.

Chan, Anthony. *Gold Mountain: The Chinese in the New World*. Vancouver: New Star Books, 1983.

Chapman, Terry. 'The Anti-Drug Crusade in Western Canada, 1885–1925.' In *Law and Society in Canada in Historical Perspective*, edited by D. Bercuson and L. Knafla, 89–116. Calgary: University of Calgary, 1979.

- 'The Drug Problem in Western Canada.' MA thesis, University of Calgary, 1976.
- 'Drug Usage and the Victoria Daily Colonist: The Opium Smokers of Western Canada.' In *Canadian Society for Legal History Proceedings*, edited by L.A. Knafla. Toronto: Canadian Society for Legal History, 1977.
Chein, Isodor. *The Road to H: Narcotics, Delinquency and Social Policy*. New York: Basic Books, 1964.
Chenier, Elise. 'Tough Ladies and Troublemakers.' MA thesis, Queen's University, 1995.
Clow, Barbara. *Negotiating Disease: Power and Cancer Care, 1900–1950*. Montreal and Kingston: McGill-Queen's University Press, 2001.
Coburn, David. 'Canadian Medicine: Dominance or Proletarianization.' *Millbank Quarterly* 66, no. 2 (1988): 92–116.
Coburn, David, George M. Torrance, and Joseph M. Kaufert. 'Medical Dominance in Canada in Historical Perspective: The Rise and Fall of Medicine?' *International Journal of Health Services* 13, no. 3 (1983): 407–32.
Cohen, Stanley. *Folk Devils and Moral Panics: The Creation of the Mods and Rockers*. Oxford: Martin Robertson, 1980.
Coleclough, A., and Lloyd G. Hanley. 'Marijuana Users in Toronto.' In *Deviant Behavior in Canada*, edited by W.E. Mann, 257–91. Toronto: Social Science Publishers, 1968.
Comack, Elizabeth A. 'The Origins of Canadian Drug Legislation: Labelling vs. Class Analysis.' In *The New Criminologies in Canada: Crime, State and Control*, edited by Thomas Fleming, 65–86. Toronto: Oxford University Press, 1985.
Cook, Sharon Anne. '*Through Sunshine and Shadow*': The WCTU, Evangelicalism and Reform in Ontario, 1874–1930. Montreal and Kingston: McGill-Queen's University Press, 1995.
Cook, Tim. '"More a Medicine than a Beverage": "Demon Rum" and the Canadian Trench Soldier of the First World War.' *Canadian Military History* 9, no. 1 (Winter 2000): 6–22.
- 'Wet Canteens and Worrying Mothers: Alcohol, Soldiers and Temperance Groups in the Great War.' *Histoire sociale/Social History* 35, no. 70 (2002): 311–30.
Coomber, Ross, ed. *The Control of Drugs and Drug Users*. Amsterdam: Harwood Academic Publishers, 1998.
Cooper, Robert Alan. 'Ideas and Their Execution: English Prison Reform.' *Eighteenth-Century Studies* 10, no. 1 (Autumn 1976): 73–93.
Copp, Terry, and Bill McAndrew. *Battle Exhaustion: Soldiers and Psychiatrists in the Canadian Army, 1939–1945*. Montreal: McGill-Queen's University Press, 1990.

Courtwright, David. *Dark Paradise: Opiate Addiction in America*. Cambridge: Harvard University Press, 2001.

– 'The Prepared Mind: Marie Nyswander, Methadone Maintenance and the Metabolic Theory of Addiction.' *Addiction* 92 (1997): 257–65.

Courtwright, David, Herman Joseph, and Don Des Jarlais. *Addicts Who Survived: An Oral History of Narcotic Use in America, 1923–1965*. Knoxville: University of Tennessee Press, 1989.

Coutts, Dorothy Mae. 'Social Structure of the Women's Unit at Oakalla.' MA thesis, University of British Columbia, 1961.

Creese, Gillian. 'Exclusion or Solidarity? Vancouver Workers Confront the "Oriental Problem."' *BC Studies* 80 (Winter 1988-89): 24–51.

Dawson, Michael. *The Mountie from Dime Novel to Disney*. Toronto: Between the Lines, 1998.

– '"That Nice Red Coat Goes to My Head Like Champagne": Gender, Antimodernism and the Mountie Image 1880–1960.' *Journal of Canadian Studies* 32, no. 3 (1997): 119–39.

Dikotter, Frank, Lars Laamann, and Zhou Xun. *Narcotic Culture: A History of Drugs in China*. Chicago: University of Chicago Press, 2004.

Donaldson, Gordon. 'Our Losing Battle with Dope: Part 1.' *Saturday Night* (21 June 1958): 10–11, 42–3.

Dorn, Nicholas, Jorgen Jepsen, and Ernesto Savono, eds. *European Drug Policies and Enforcement*. Houndmills, England: Macmillan Press, 1996.

Dubinsky, Karen. *Improper Advances: Rape and Heterosexual Conflict in Ontario, 1880–1929*. Chicago: University of Chicago Press, 1993.

Duffin, Jacalyn. 'The Guru and the Godfather: Henry Sigerist, Hugh MacLean, and the Politics of Health Care Reform in 1940s Canada.' *Canadian Bulletin of Medical History* 9 (1992): 191–218.

Dummitt, Chris. 'Finding a Place for Father: Selling the Barbecue in Postwar Canada.' *Journal of the Canadian Historical Association* 9 (1998): 209–23.

Ehrenreich, John. *The Altruistic Imagination: A History of Social Work and Social Policy in the United States*. Ithaca, NY: Cornell University Press, 1985.

Erickson, Patricia. *Cannabis Criminals*. Toronto: Addiction Research Foundation, 1980.

Erickson, Patricia G. and Bruce Alexander. 'Cocaine and Addictive Liability.' *Social Pharmacology* 3, no. 3: 249–70.

Erickson, Patricia G., Diane N. Riley, Yuet Cheung, and Patrick W. O'Hare. *Harm Reduction: A New Direction for Drug Policies and Programs*. Toronto: University of Toronto Press, 1997.

Ericson, Richard. *Reproducing Order*. Toronto: University of Toronto Press, 1982.

Ericson, Richard, and Kevin D. Haggerty. *Policing the Risk Society.* Toronto: University of Toronto Press, 1997.

Estievenart, Georges. *Policies and Strategies to Combat Drugs in Europe: The Treaty on European Union: Framework for a New European Strategy to Combat Drugs?* Dordrecht: Martinus Nijhoff Publishers, 1995.

Faderman, Lillian. *Odd Girls and Twilight Lovers: A History of Lesbian Life in Twentieth Century America.* New York: Penguin, 1992.

Faupel, Charles. *Shooting Dope: Career Patterns of Hard-Core Heroin Users.* Gainesville: University of Florida Press, 1991.

Finkel, Alvin. 'Origins of the Welfare State in Canada.' In *The Canadian State: Political Economy and Political Power,* edited by Leo Panitch, 344–70. Toronto: University of Toronto Press, 1977.

Fischer, Benedikt. 'Prescriptions, Power and Politics: The Turbulent History of Methadone Maintenance in Canada.' *Journal of Public Health Policy* 21, no. 2 (2000): 187–210.

Foucault, Michel. *The History of Sexuality,* Vol. 1. New York: Vintage Books, 1990.

Frankau, Lady Elizabeth. 'Experience with Canadian Addicts in Treatment in Britain.' Narcotic Addiction Conference, Niagara Falls, ON, 22–4 February 1963.

Fraser, Nancy. 'Foucault on Modern Power: Empirical Insights and Normative Confusions.' In *Social Control: Aspects of Non-State Justice,* edited by Stuart Henry. Aldershot: Dartmouth Publishing Company, 1994.

Giddens, Anthony. *Modernity and Self-Identity: Self and Society in the Late Modern Age.* Stanford: Stanford University Press, 1991.

Gidney, R.D. and W.P.J. Millar. *Professional Gentlemen: The Professions in 19th Century Ontario.* Toronto: University of Toronto Press, 1994.

Giffen, P.J., Shirley Endicott, and Sylvia Lambert. *Panic and Indifference: The Politics of Canada's Drug Laws.* Ottawa: Canadian Centre on Substance Abuse, 1991.

Gleason, Mona. *Normalizing the Ideal: Psychology, Schooling and the Family in Postwar Canada.* Toronto: University of Toronto Press, 1999.

– 'Psychology and the Construction of the "Normal" Family in Postwar Canada, 1945–1960.' *Canadian Historical Review* 78, no. 3 (September 1997): 442–77.

Goode, Erich, and Nachman Ben-Yehuda. *Moral Panics: The Social Construction of Deviance.* Oxford: Blackwell, 1994.

Gordon, Linda. Book review of Joan Scott's *Gender and the Politics of History,* and response to Joan Scott's review of Gordon's *Heroes of their Own Lives. Signs* 15. no. 4 (Summer 1990): 853–8, 852–3.

– 'Family Violence, Feminism and Social Control.' *Feminist Studies* 12, no. 3 (Fall 1986): 452–78.

– *Heroes of Their Own Lives: The Politics and History of Family Violence.* New York: Penguin Books, 1988.
– *Pitied but Not Entitled: Single Mothers and the History of Welfare, 1890–1935.* New York: Free Press, 1994.
Graham, John. 'A History of the University of Toronto School of Social Work.' PhD dissertation, Social Work, University of Toronto, 1996.
Green, Melvyn. 'A History of Canadian Narcotics Control: The Formative Years.' *University of Toronto Faculty of Law Review* 37 (1979): 42–80.
Greenfield, T.E.E. *Drugs (Mostly).* Meaford, ON: Knight Press, 1976.
– 'The Hopheads Are Ahead.' *Maclean's* (15 November 1948): 12–13, 65–8.
Grob, Gerald. *From Asylum to Community: Mental Health Policy in Modern America.* Princeton: Princeton University Press, 1991.
Groth, Paul. *Living Downtown: The History of Residential Hotels in the United States.* Berkeley: University of California Press, 1994.
Gusfield, Joseph. *Contested Meanings: The Construction of Alcohol Problems.* Madison: University of Wisconsin Press, 1996.
Hagan, John, and Bill McCarthy. *Mean Streets: Youth Crime and Homelessness.* Cambridge: Cambridge University Press, 1997.
Haggerty, Kevin D., and Richard V. Ericson. 'The Military Technostructures of Policing.' In *Militarizing the American Criminal Justice System,* edited by Peter Kraska, 233–55. Boston: Northeastern University Press, 2001.
Hall, Stuart, Chas Critcher, Tony Jefferson, John Clarke, and Brian Roberts. *Policing the Crisis: Mugging, the State, and Law and Order.* London: Macmillan, 1978.
Hanley, Lloyd G. 'Functions of Argot among Heroin Addicts.' In *The Underside of Toronto,* edited by W.E. Mann, 294–307. Toronto: McClelland and Stewart, 1970.
Hanson, Bill, George Beschner, James M. Walters, and Elliot Bovelle, eds. *Life with Heroin: Voices from the Inner City.* Lexington: D.C. Heath and Company, 1985.
Harvison, Clifford. *The Horsemen.* Toronto: McClelland and Stewart, 1967.
Hathaway, Andrew D. 'Marijuana and Lifestyle: Exploring Tolerable Deviance.' *Deviant Behavior: An Interdisciplinary Journal* 18 (1997): 213–32.
Haywood, A.K. 'Vice and Drugs in Montreal.' *Public Health Journal* 14, no. 1 (January 1923), 1–18.
Hebdige, Dick. *Subculture: The Meaning of Style.* London and New York: Methuen and Company, 1979.
Henderson, G. Irwin. *An Exploration of the Natural History of Heroin Addiction.* Vancouver: Narcotic Addiction Foundation, 1970.
Heron, Craig. *Booze: A Distilled History.* Toronto: Between the Lines, 2003.

Heron, Craig, and Robert Storey, eds. *On the Job: Confronting the Labour Process in Canada*. Kingston and Montreal: McGill-Queen's University Press, 1986.

Hewitt, Steve. 'The RCMP's War on Drugs: The Early Years 1920–1939.' Paper presented at the Canadian History Association annual meeting, Edmonton, 2000.

– *Spying 101: The RCMP's Secret Activities at Canadian Universities*. Toronto: University of Toronto Press, 2002.

– '"While Unpleasant It Is a Service to Humanity": The RCMP's War on Drugs in the Interwar Period.' *Journal of Canadian Studies* 38, no. 2 (Spring 2004): 80–104.

Horn, Michiel, ed. *The Dirty Thirties: Canadians in the Great Depression*. Toronto: Copp Clark, 1972.

Howell, Colin. 'Elite Doctors and the Development of Scientific Medicine: The Halifax Medical Establishment and Nineteenth Century Medical Professionalism.' In *Health, Disease and Medicine: Essays in Canadian History*, edited by Charles G. Roland, 105–22. Toronto: University of Toronto Press, 1983.

– 'Medical Professionalization and the Social Transformation of the Maritimes, 1850–1950.' *Journal of Canadian Studies* 27 (Spring 1992): 5–20.

– *Northern Sandlots*. Toronto: University of Toronto Press, 1995.

– 'Reform and the Monopolistic Impulse: The Professionalization of Medicine in the Maritimes.' *Acadiensis* 11, no. 1 (Autumn 1981): 3–22.

Iacovetta, Franca. 'Gossip, Contest and Power in the Making of Suburban Bad Girls: Toronto, 1945–1960.' *Canadian Historical Review* 80, no. 4 (December 1999): 585–623.

– 'Making "New Canadians": Social Workers, Women and the Reshaping of Immigrant Families.' In *Gender Conflicts*, edited by Franca Iacovetta and Mariana Valverde. 261–303. Toronto: University of Toronto Press, 1992.

– *A Nation of Immigrants: Women, Workers and Community in Canadian History, 1840s–1960s*. Toronto: University of Toronto Press, 1998.

– *Such Hardworking People: Italian Immigrants in Postwar Toronto*. Montreal and Kingston: McGill-Queen's University Press, 1992.

Iacovetta, Franca, and Wendy Mitchinson. *On the Case: Explorations in Social History*. Toronto: University of Toronto Press, 1998.

Iacovetta, Franca, and Mariana Valverde, eds. *Gender Conflicts: New Essays in Women's History*. Toronto: University of Toronto Press, 1992.

Ingeborg, Paulus. *A Comparative Study of Long-Term and Short-Term Withdrawal of Narcotic Addicts Voluntarily Seeking Comprehensive Treatment*. Vancouver: Narcotic Addiction Foundation, 1966.

Jackson, Charles O. 'The Amphetamine Inhaler: A Case Study of Medical

Abuse.' *Journal of the History of Medicine and Allied Sciences* 26, no. 2 (April 1971): 187–96.

Johnson, Bruce, Paul Goldstein, Edward Preble, James Schmeidler, Douglas S. Lipton, Barny Spunt, and Thomas Miller, eds. *Taking Care of Business: The Economics of Crime by Heroin Abusers.* Lexington: D.C. Heath and Company, 1985.

Johnson, Victor. *Before the Age of Miracles.* New York: Paul S. Erickson, 1972.

Jonnes, Jill. *Hep-Cats, Narcs, and Pipe Dreams: A History of America's Romance with Illegal Drugs.* New York: Scribner, 1996.

Josie, Gordon H. *A Report on Drug Addiction in Canada.* Ottawa: Edmond Cloutier, 1948.

Kealey, Gregory S. and Reginald Whitaker. *RCMP Security Bulletins.* Vols. 1–5. St. John's, NF: Canadian Committee on Labour History, 1989–97.

Keane, Helen. *What's Wrong with Addiction?* Mebourne: Melbourne University Press, 2002.

Kennedy, Elizabeth Lapovsky, and Madeline Davis. *Boots of Leather, Slippers of Gold: The History of a Lesbian Community.* New York: Penguin Books, 1993.

Kerr, Robert B. *History of the Medical Council of Canada.* Ottawa: Medical Council of Canada, 1979.

Kinsman, Gary. '"Character Weakness" and "Fruit Machines": Towards an Analysis of the Anti-Homosexual Security Campaign in the Canadian Civil Service.' *Labour/Le Travail* 35 (Spring 1995): 133–61.

– *The Regulation of Desire: Sexuality in Canada.* Montreal: Black Rose Books, 1987.

Kinsman, Gary, Dieter K. Buse, and Mercedes Steadman. *Whose National Security? Canadian State Surveillance, and the Creation of Enemies.* Toronto: Between the Lines, 2000.

Kleiman, Mark A.R. *Against Excess: A Drug Policy for Results.* New York: Basic Books, 1992.

Kleiman, Mark A.R. and Kerry D. Smith. 'State and Local Drug Enforcement: In Search of a Strategy.' In *Drugs and Crime,* edited by Michael Tonry and James Q. Wilson. Chicago: University of Chicago Press, 1990.

Kohn, Marek. *Dope Girls: The Birth of the British Drug Underground.* London: Lawrence and Wishart, 1992.

Kunzel, Regina. *Fallen Women, Problem Girls: Unmarried Mothers and the Professionalization of Social Work 1890–1945.* New Haven: Yale University Press, 1993.

Lacasse, Danielle. *La Prostitution féminine à Montréal.* Montreal: Boréal, 1994.

Ladd-Taylor, Molly. *Mother-Work: Women, Child Welfare and the State, 1890–1930.* Urbana and Chicago: University of Illinois Press, 1994.

Lai, David Chuenyan. 'Chinese Opium Trade and Manufacture in British Columbia, 1858–1908.' *Journal of the West* 38, no. 3 (1999): 21–6.

Larner, Jeremy, and Ralph Tefferteller, eds. *The Addict in the Street*. New York: Grove Press, 1966.

Leavitt, Judith Walzer. *The Healthiest City: Milwaukee and the Politics and Health Reform*. Princeton: Princeton University Press, 1982.

Lerner, Barron H. *Contagion and Confinement: Controlling Tuberculosis along the Skid Road*. Baltimore: Johns Hopkins University Press, 1998.

Levine, Harry Gene. 'The Discovery of Addiction: Changing Conceptions of Habitual Drunkeness in America.' *Journal of Studies on Alcohol* 39, no. 1 (1978): 143–73.

Lewis, D. Sclater. *The Royal College of Physicians and Surgeons of Canada 1920–1960*. Montreal: McGill University Press, 1962.

Li, Peter S. *The Chinese in Canada*. Toronto: Oxford University Press, 1988.

Lindesmith, Alfred R. *The Addict and the Law*. Bloomington: Indiana University Press, 1965.

Little, Margaret. *No Car, No Radio, No Liquor Permit: The Moral Regulation of Single Mothers in Ontario, 1920–1997*. Toronto: Oxford University Press, 1998.

Lodwick, Kathleen. *Crusaders against Opium: Protestant Missionaries in China, 1874–1917*. Lexington: University Press of Kentucky, 1996.

Lynch, Timothy, ed. *After Prohibition: An Adult Approach to Drug Policies in the 21st Century*. Washington: CATO Institute, 2000.

Maartman, Ben. *The Strange Thing about Miracles & Other Stories*. Errington, BC: Fogduckers Press, 1990.

MacCoun, Robert, and Peter Reuter. *Drug War Heresies: Learning from Other Vices, Times and Places*. Cambridge: Cambridge University Press, 2001.

MacDermot, H.E. *History of the Canadian Medical Association*. Vol. 2. Toronto: Murray Printing and Gravure, 1958.

Macdonald, Ian, and O'Keefe, Betty. *The Mulligan Affair: Top Cop on the Take*. Surrey, BC: Heritage House Publishing Company, 1997.

MacInnes, Tom. 'The Futile Fight against Dope.' *Saturday Night* (3 October 1925): 1, 3, 5.

MacLeod, R.C. 'The RCMP and the Evolution of Provincial Policing.' In *Police Powers in Canada: The Evolution and Practice of Authority*, edited by R.C. MacLeod and David Schneiderman, 44–56. Toronto: University of Toronto Press, 1994.

MacPherson, Kate, Cecilia Morgan, and Nancy Forestell, eds. *Gendered Pasts: Historical Essays on Femininity and Masculinity in Canada*. Don Mills, ON: Oxford University Press, 1999.

Malarek, Victor. *Merchants of Misery*. Toronto: Macmillan, 1989.

Malleck, Dan. '"Its Baneful Influences Are Too Well Known": Debates over Drug

Use in Canada, 1867–1908.' *Canadian Bulletin of Medical History* 14 (1997): 263–88.

– 'Refining Poison, Defining Power: Medical Authority and the Creation of Canadian Drug Prohibition Laws, 1800–1908.' PhD dissertation, Queen's University, 1998.

Mander, Christine. *Emily Murphy: Rebel.* Toronto: Simon and Pierre, 1985.

Manion, R.J. *Life Is an Adventure.* Toronto: Ryerson Press, 1936.

Manning, Peter. *The Narc's Game: Organizational and Informational Limits on Drug Law Enforcement.* Cambridge, MA: MIT Press, 1980.

Manning, Peter K., and Lawrence John Redlinger. 'Working Bases for Corruption: Organizational Ambiguities and Narcotics Law Enforcement.' In *Drugs, Crime and Politics,* edited by Arnold Trebach, 60–89. New York: Praeger, 1978.

Marquis, Greg. 'The Police as a Social Service in Early 20th Century Toronto.' *Social History/Histoire sociale* 25, no. 5 (1992): 335–58.

– 'Police Unionism in Early 20th Century Toronto.' *Ontario History* 81, no. 2 (1989): 109–28.

– *Policing Canada's Century: A History of the Chief Constables' Association of Canada.* Toronto: University of Toronto Press, 1993.

– 'The Technology of Professionalism: The Identification of Criminals in Early 20th Century Canada.' *Criminal Justice History* 15 (1994): 165–88.

– 'Towards a Canadian Police Historiography.' In *Law, Society and the State: Essays in Modern Legal History,* edited by Louis A. Knafla and W.S. Binnie, 477–95. Toronto: University of Toronto Press, 1995.

– 'Vancouver Vice: The Police and the Negotiation of Morality, 1904–1935.' In *Essays in the History of Canadian Law: British Columbia and the Yukon,* edited by Hamar Foster and John McLaren. Toronto: University of Toronto Press, 1995.

– 'Working Men in Uniform: The Early 20th Century Toronto Police.' *Social History/Histoire sociale* 20, no. 40 (1987): 259–77.

Massing, Michael. *The Fix.* New York: Simon and Schuster, 1998.

May, Elaine Tyler. *Homeward Bound: The American Family in the Cold-War Era.* New York: Basic Books, 1988.

May, Herbert A. 'The International Control of Narcotic Drugs.' *International Conciliation* 441 (May 1948): 324–33.

Maynard, Steven. 'Through a Hole in the Lavatory Wall: Homosexual Subcultures, Police Surveillance and the Dialectics of Discover, Toronto, 1890–1930.' *Journal of the History of Sexuality* 5, no. 2 (1994): 207–42.

McAllister, William B. *Drug Diplomacy in the Twentieth Century.* London and New York: Routledge, 2000.

McCormick, Lindsay. 'Group Living for Drug Addicts: An Assessment of the Narcotic Drug Addiction Research and Treatment Unit at Oakalla Prison Farm 1956–60.' MA thesis, University of British Columbia, 1960.

McCoy, Alfred W. *The Politics of Heroin: CIA Complicity in the Global Drug Trade.* Brooklyn, NY: Lawrence Hill Books, 1991.

McKim, A. *The Canadian Newspaper Directory.* Montreal: A. McKim, 1922.

McLaren, Angus. *Our Own Master Race.* Toronto: McClelland and Stewart, 1990.

McLaren, John, Robert Menzies, and Dorothy E. Chunn. *Regulating Lives: Historical Essays on the State, Society, the Individual, and the Law.* Vancouver: UBC Press, 2002.

McNab, Elizabeth. *A Legal History of Health Professions in Ontario: A Study for the Committee on the Healing Arts.* Toronto: Queen's Printer, 1970.

McPherson, Kathryn. *Bedside Matters: The Transformation of Canadian Nursing, 1900–1990.* Don Mills, ON: Oxford University Press, 1996.

McPherson, Kathryn, Cecilia Morgan, and Nancy Forestell. *Gendered Pasts: Historical Essays on Femininity and Masculinity in Canada.* Don Mills, ON: Oxford University Press, 1999.

McRobbie A., and S. Thornton. 'Rethinking "Moral Panic" for Multi-Medicated Social Worlds.' *British Journal of Sociology* 46, no. 4 (1995): 559–74.

Meyer, Kathryn, and Terry Parssinen. *Webs of Smoke: Smugglers, Warlords, Spies and the History of the International Drug Trade.* Oxford: Rowman and Littlefield Publishers, 1998.

Miles, Robert. *Racism after 'Race Relations.'* London: Routlege, 1993.

Miller, J.R. *Skyscrapers Hide the Heavens: A History of Indian-White Relations in Canada.* Toronto: University of Toronto Press, 1989.

Moore, Mark Harrison. *Buy and Bust: The Effective Regulation of an Illicit Market in Heroin.* Lexington, MA: Lexington Books, 1977.

– 'Supply Reduction and Drug Law Enforcement.' In *Drugs and Crime*, edited by Michael Tonry and James Q. Wilson, 109–58. Chicago: University of Chicago Press, 1990.

Morrison, Alexander B. 'Regulatory Control of the Canadian Government over the Manufacturing, Distribution and Prescribing of Psychotropic Drugs.' In *Social Aspects of the Medical Use of Psychotropic Drugs*, edited by Ruth Cooperstock, 9–20. Toronto: Alcoholism and Drug Addiction Research Foundation of Ontario, 1974.

Morton, Desmond, and Glenn Wright. *Winning the Second Battle: Canadian Veterans and the Return to Civilian Life, 1915–1930.* Toronto: University of Toronto Press, 1987.

Morton, Suzanne. *At Odds: Gambling and Canadians, 1919–1969.* Montreal and Kingston: McGill-Queen's University Press, 2003.

Mosher, Clayton. *Discrimination and Denial: Systemic Racism in Ontario's Legal and Criminal Justice System, 1920–1961.* Toronto: University of Toronto Press, 1998.

– 'The Legal Response to Narcotic Drugs in Five Ontario Cities, 1908–1961.' PhD dissertation, University of Toronto, 1992.

Mosher, Clayton, and John Hagan. 'Constituting Class and Crime in Upper Canada: The Sentencing of Narcotics Offenders, circa 1908–1953.' *Social Forces* 72, no. 3 (March 1994): 626–9.

Murphy, Emily. *The Black Candle.* Toronto: Thomas Allen, 1922.

– 'Fighting the Drug Menace.' *Maclean's* (15 April 1920): 11–12.

– 'The Grave Drug Menace.' *Maclean's* (15 February 1920): 1, 10–11.

– 'The Underground System.' *Maclean's* (15 March 1920): 12–13, 55.

Murray, Glen. 'Cocaine Use in the Era of Social Reform: The Natural History of a Social Problem in Canada, 1880–1911.' *Canadian Journal of Law and Society* 2 (1987): 29–43.

– 'The Road to Regulation: Patent Medicines in Canada in Historical Perspective.' In *Illicit Drugs in Canada*, edited by Judith C. Blackwell and Patricia Erickson, 72–87. Scarborough: Nelson Canada, 1988.

Musto, David. *The American Disease: The Origins of Narcotic Control.* Oxford: Oxford University Press, 1999.

Myers, Tamara. 'Women Policing Women: A Patrol Woman in Montreal in the 1910s.' *Journal of the Canadian Historical Association* 4 (1993): 229–45.

Nadelmann, Ethan. 'Commonsense Drug Policy.' *Foreign Affairs* 77, no. 1 (1998): 111–26.

– 'Drug Prohibition in the United States: Costs, Consequences and Alternatives.' *Science* 245 (September 1989): 939–47.

National Film Board of Canada. *The Drug Addict.* 1948.

– *Forbidden Love: The Unashamed Stories of Lesbian Lives.* 1992.

– *Pay-Off in Pain.* 1948.

Naylor, David. 'The CMA's First Code of Ethics: Medical Morality or Borrowed Ideology?' *Journal of Canadian Studies* 17, no. 4 (Winter 1982–3): 20–32.

– *Private Practice, Public Payment: Canadian Medicine and the Politics of Health Insurance 1911–1966.* Montreal and Kingston: McGill-Queen's University Press, 1986.

– 'Rural Protest and Medical Professionalism in Turn of the Century Ontario.' *Journal of Canadian Studies* 21, no. 1 (Spring 1986): 5–20.

Newman, R.K. 'Opium Smoking in Late Imperial China: A Reconsideration.' *Modern Asian Studies* 29, no. 4 (1995): 765–94.

Noel, Jan. *Canada Dry: Temperance Crusades before Confederation.* Toronto: University of Toronto Press, 1995.

Owram, Doug. *The Government Generation: Canadian Intellectuals and the State 1900–1945.* Toronto: University of Toronto Press, 1986.

Palmer, Bryan. *Working-Class Experience: Rethinking the History of Canadian Labour 1800–1991.* Toronto: McClelland and Stewart, 1992.

Palmer, Howard. *Patterns of Prejudice: A History of Nativism in Alberta.* Toronto: McClelland and Stewart, 1982.

Parr, Joy. *Domestic Goods: The Material, the Moral and the Economic in the Postwar Years.* Toronto: University of Toronto Press, 1999.

– *Labouring Children: British Immigrant Apprentices to Canada, 1869–1924.* Toronto: University of Toronto Press, 1994.

Parr, Joy, ed. *A Diversity of Women: Ontario, 1945–1980.* Toronto: University of Toronto Press, 1995.

Parr, Joy, and Mark Rosenfeld, eds. *Gender and History in Canada.* Toronto: Copp Clark, 1996.

Parssinen, Terry. *Secret Passions, Secret Remedies: Narcotic Drugs in British Society 1820–1930.* Philadelphia: Institute for the Study of Human Issues, 1983.

Paulus, Ingeborg, and Robert Halliday. 'Rehabilitation and the Narcotic Addicts: Results of a Comparative Methadone Withdrawal Programme.' *Canadian Medical Association Journal* 96 (18 March 1967): 655–9.

Pearson, Geoffrey. *Hooligan: A History of Respectable Fears.* London: Macmillan Press, 1983.

– *The New Heroin Users.* Oxford: Blackwell, 1987.

Perry, Anne Anderson. 'The Dope Traffic in Canada.' *Western Home Monthly* (August 1929): 5–6, 34, 36.

Peters, Dolores. 'The British Response to Opiate Addiction in the 19th Century.' *Journal of the History of Medicine* 36, no. 4 (October 1981): 455–87.

Phillips, Sandra S. *Police Pictures: The Photograph as Evidence.* San Francisco: San Francisco Museum of Modern Art, 1997.

Piovesana, Roy H. *Robert J. Manion: Member of Parliament for Fort William 1917–1935.* Thunder Bay, ON: Thunder Bay Historical Museum Society, 1990.

Pon, Madge. 'Like a Chinese Puzzle: Constructions of Chinese Masculinity in Jack Canuck.' In *Gender and History in Canada,* edited by Joy Parr and Mark Rosenfeld, 88–100. Toronto: Copp Clark, 1996.

Preble, Edward, and John Casey Jr. 'Taking Care of Business – The Heroin User's Life on the Street.' *International Journal of the Addictions* 4, no. 1 (1969): 1–24.

Price, H.F. 'The Criminal Addict.' In *Annual Report of the RCMP for the Year Ended March 31, 1946,* 73–82. Ottawa: Edmond Cloutier, 1946.

Reagan, Leslie. *When Abortion Was a Crime: Women, Medicine, and Law in the United States, 1867–1973.* Berkeley: University of California Press, 1997.

Reaume, Geoffrey. 'Portraits of People with Mental Disorders in English Canadian History.' *Canadian Bulletin of Medical History* 17, no. 1/2 (2000): 93–125.

Reins, T.O. 'Reform, Nationalism and Internationalism: The Opium Suppression Movement in China.' *Modern Asian Studies* 25, no. 1 (1991): 101–42.

Rice, John Steadman. *A Disease of One's Own: Psychotherapy, Addiction and the Emergence of Co-Dependency.* New Brunswick, NJ: Transaction Publishers, 1996.

Richards, A.R. 'Medical and Legal Aspects of Drug Addiction.' *Canadian Public Health Journal* (February 1928): 66–74.

Richmond, Guy. *Prison Doctor.* Surrey, BC: Nunaga Publishing, 1975.

Roberts, Julian. 'Sentencing Trends and Sentencing Disparity.' In *Making Sense of Sentencing,* edited by Julian Roberts and David P. Cole. Toronto: University of Toronto Press, 1999.

Robinson, Daniel J., and David Kimmel. 'The Queer Career of Homosexual Security Vetting in Cold War Canada.' In *Gender and History in Canada,* edited by Joy Parr and Mark Rosenthal. Toronto: Copp Clark, 1996.

Rose, Nikolas. *Governing the Soul: Shaping of the Private Self.* London: Routledge, 1990.

– *Inventing Our Selves: Psychology, Power, and Personhood.* Cambridge: Cambridge University Press, 1998.

Rosenbaum, Marsha. *Women on Heroin.* New Brunswick, NJ: Rutgers University Press, 1981.

Ross, Becki. 'Destaining the (Tattooed) Delinquent Body: The Practices of Moral Regulation at Toronto's Street Haven, 1965–1969.' *Journal of the History of Sexuality* 7, no. 4 (1997): 561–95.

– '"Down at the Whorehouse?" Reflections on Christian Community Service and Female Sex Deviance at Toronto's Street Haven, 1965–1969.' *Atlantis* 23, no. 1 (Fall/Winter 1998): 48–59.

Roy, Patricia. *The Oriental Question: Consolidating a White Man's Province.* Vancouver: UBC Press, 2003.

– *A White Man's Province: British Columbia Politicians and Chinese and Japanese Immigrants.* Vancouver: UBC Press, 1989.

Rudolph, R.D. 'Narcotic Addiction in Canada.' *Canadian Medical Association Journal* 22, no. 3 (March 1930): 431–2.

Sanders, Byrne Hope. *Emily Murphy: Crusader.* Toronto: Macmillan, 1945.

Sangster, Joan. *Regulating Girls and Women: Sexuality, Family and the Law in Ontario, 1920–1960.* Don Mills, ON: Oxford University Press, 2001.

Schaler, Jeffrey A., ed. *Drugs: Should We Legalize, Decriminalize or Deregulate.* New York: Prometheus Books, 1998.

Scott, Joan. Book review of Linda Gordon's *Heroes of Their Own Lives: The Politics and History of Family Violence,* and response to Linda Gordon's review of Scott's *Gender and the Politics of History. Signs* 15, no. 4 (Summer 1990): 848–52, 859–60.

Sharp, Elaine B. *The Dilemma of Drug Policy.* New York: Harper Collins College Publishers, 1994.

Shortt, S.E.D. 'Physicians, Science and Status: Issues in the Professionalization of Anglo-American Medicine in the 19th Century.' *Medical History* 27, no. 1 (1983): 51–68.

Single, Eric. *Canadian Community Epidemiological Network on Drug Use: Overview Report 2000.* Ottawa: Canadian Centre of Substance Abuse, 2000.

Small, Shirley. 'Canadian Narcotics Legislation, 1908–1923: A Conflict Model Interpretation.' In *Law and Social Control in Canada*, edited by William K. Greenaway and Stephen L. Brickley, 28–41. Scarborough: Prentice Hall of Canada, 1978.

Solomon, Robert. 'Drug Enforcement Powers and the Canadian Charter of Rights and Freedoms.' *University of Western Ontario Law Review* 21, no. 2 (1983): 219–63.

Solomon, R., and Green, M. 'The First Century: The History of Nonmedical Opiate Use and Control Policies in Canada, 1870–1970.' *Illicit Drugs in Canada: A Risky Business.* Scarborough: Nelson Canada, 1988.

Spillane, Joseph. *Cocaine: From Medical Marvel to Modern Menace in the United States, 1884–1920.* Baltimore: Johns Hopkins University Press, 2000.

Starr, Paul. *The Transformation of American Medicine.* New York: Basic Books, 1982.

Steeves, Dorothy. *The Compassionate Rebel: Ernest E. Winch and His Times.* Vancouver: Boag Foundation, 1960.

Stein, S.D. *International Diplomacy, State Administrators and Narcotics Control: The Origins of a Social Problem.* Aldershot, Hampshire, England: Published for the London School of Economics and Political Science by Gower, 1985.

Stevens, Richard. *The Street Addict Role: A Theory of Heroin Addiction.* New York: State University of New York Press, 1991.

Stevenson, George H. 'Drug Addiction in British Columbia.' Unpublished manuscript, University of British Columbia, 1956.

Stoddart, Kenneth. 'The Enforcement of Narcotics Violations in a Canadian City: Heroin Users' Perspectives on the Production of Official Statistics.' *Canadian Journal of Criminology* 24(4): 425–38.

Strang, John, and Michael Gossop, eds. *Heroin Addiction and Drug Policy: The British System.* Oxford: Oxford University Press, 1994.

Strange, Carolyn. 'The Historian and the Capital Case File.' In *On the Case: Explorations in Social History*, edited by Franca Iacovetta and Wendy Mitchinson, 25–48. Toronto: University of Toronto Press, 1998.

– *Toronto's Girl Problem: The Perils and Pleasures of the City, 1880–1930.* Toronto: University of Toronto Press, 1995.

Strong-Boag, Veronica, Sherrill Grace, Avigail Eisenberg, and Joan Anderson, eds. *Painting the Maple: Essays on Race, Gender and the Construction of Canada.* Vancouver: UBC Press, 1998.

Stroud, Charles. *The Blue Wall: Street Cops in Canada.* Toronto: McClelland and Stewart, 1983.

Struthers, James. *The Limits of Affluence: Welfare in Ontario, 1920–1970.* Toronto: University of Toronto Press, 1994.

– *No Fault of Their Own: Unemployment and the Canadian Welfare State, 1914–1941.* Toronto: University of Toronto Press, 1983.

Sutter, Alan. 'Worlds of Drug Use on the Street Scene.' In *Delinquency, Crime and Social Process*, edited by Donald R. Cressey and David A. Ward, 802–29. New York: Harper and Row, 1969.

Talbot, C.K., C.H.S. Jayewardene, and T.J. Juliana. *Canada's Constables: The Historical Development of Policing in Canada.* Ottawa: Crimcare, 1985.

Taylor, Arnold H. *American Diplomacy and the Narcotics Traffic, 1900–1939: A Study in International Humanitarian Reform.* Durham, NC: Duke University Press, 1969.

Taylor, Malcolm G. *Health Insurance and Canadian Public Policy: The Seven Decisions that Created Canada's Health Insurance System and their Outcomes.* 2nd ed. Kingston and Montreal: McGill-Queen's University Press, 1987.

Terry, Charles E. and Mildred Pellens. *The Opium Problem.* Montclair, NJ: Patterson Smith, 1970. First published in 1928.

Thornton, Sarah. *Club Cultures: Music, Media and Subcultural Capital.* Cambridge: Polity Press, 1995.

Tonry, Michael, and James Q. Wilson, eds. *Drugs and Crime.* Chicago: University of Chicago Press, 1990.

Topping, C. Wesley. 'The Rise of the New Penology in British Columbia, Canada.' *British Journal of Delinquency* 5, no. 3 (January 1955): 180–90.

Trasov, G.E. 'History of Opium and Narcotic Drug Legislation in Canada.' *Criminal Law Quarterly* 4 (1961–2): 274–84.

Trocki, Carl. *Opium, Empire and the Global Political Economy: A Study of the Asian Opium Trade 1750–1950.* New York: Routledge, 1999.

Tupper, R.H. *Final Report of the Vancouver City Police Force Inquiry.* Vancouver, 1956.

– *Interim Report of the Vancouver City Police Force Inquiry.* Victoria, 1955.

Uchida, Craig D., and Brian Forst. 'Controlling Street-Level Drug Trafficking: Professional and Community Policing Approaches.' In *Drugs and Crime: Evaluating Public Policy Initiatives*, edited by Doris Layton MacKenzie and Craig D. Uchida, 77–94. Thousand Oaks, CA: Sage Publications, 1994.

Valverde, Mariana. *Diseases of the Will: Alcohol and the Dilemmas of Freedom.* Cambridge: Cambridge University Press, 1998.

– ed. *Studies in Moral Regulation.* Toronto: Centre of Criminology and Canadian Journal of Sociology, 1994.

Van Solinge, Tim Boekhout. 'Dutch Drug Policy in a European Context.' *Journal of Drug Issues* 29, no. 3 (1999): 511–28.

– *The Swedish Drug Control System: An Indepth Review and Analysis.* Amsterdam: Uitgeverij J. Mets, 1997.

Walden, Keith. *Visions of Order.* Toronto: Butterworths, 1982.

Waldorf, Dan. 'Natural Recovery from Opiate Addiction: Some Preliminary Findings.' *Journal of Drug Issues* 11, no. 1: 61–74.

– 'Natural Recovery from Opiate Addiction: Some Social-Psychological Processes of Untreated Recovery.' *Journal of Drug Issues* 13, no. 2 (Spring 1983): 237–80.

Waldorf, Dan, Craig Reinarman, and Sheigla Murphy. *Cocaine Changes: The Experience of Using and Quitting.* Philadelphia: Temple University Press, 1991.

Walker, William O. *Drug Control in the Americas.* Albuquerque: University of New Mexico Press, 1989.

Walkowitz, Daniel. *Working with Class: Social Workers and the Politics of Middle-Class Identity.* Chapel Hill: University of North Carolina Press, 1999.

Ward, Hilda Glynn. *The Writing on the Wall.* Toronto: University of Toronto Press, 1974. First published in 1921.

Ward, Peter. *White Canada Forever.* Montreal and Kingston: McGill-Queen's University Press, 1978.

Warling, Thomas. 'Canada's Greatest Menace.' *Canadian Home Journal* (August 1930): 8, 61.

Warsh, Cheryl Krasnick. *Moments of Unreason: The Practice of Canadian Psychiatry and the Homewood Retreat, 1883–1923.* Montreal and Kingston: McGill-Queen's University Press, 1989.

– 'Stephen Lett.' In *The Canadian Encyclopedia,* 2nd ed. Edmonton: Hurtig Publishers, 1988.

Weaver, John. *Crime, Constables and Courts: Order and Transgression in a Canadian City, 1816–1970.* Montreal and Kingston: McGill-Queen's University Press, 1995.

Whitaker, Reginald, and Gary Marcuse. *Cold War Canada: The Making of a National Insecurity State, 1945–57.* Toronto: University of Toronto Press, 1994.

White, William L. *Slaying the Dragon: The History of Addiction Treatment.* Bloomington, IN: Chesnut Health Systems, 1998.

Whynes, David K. and Bean, Philip T. *Policing and Prescribing: The British System of Drug Control.* Houndmills: Macmillan, 1991.

Wickberg, Edgar, Harry Con, Ronald J. Con, Graham Johnson, and William E. Willmott. *From China to Canada: A History of the Chinese Communities in Canada.* Toronto: McClelland and Stewart, 1982.

Willis, Paul. *Learning to Labor: How Working Class Kids Get Working Class Jobs.* New York: Columbia University Press, 1977.

Wills, Gale. *A Marriage of Convenience: Business and Social Work in Toronto 1918–1957.* Toronto: University of Toronto Press, 1995.

Wilson, R.S.S. *Undercover for the RCMP.* Victoria: Sono Nis Press, 1986.

Wilton, Jean. *May I Talk to John Howard: The Story of J.D. Hobden – A Friend to Prisoners.* Vancouver: J.B. Wilton, 1973.

Winks, Robin W. *The Blacks in Canada: A History.* Montreal and Kingston: McGill-Queen's University Press, 1997.

Worden, Robert E., Timothy S. Bynum, and James Frank. 'Police Crackdowns on Drug Abuse and Trafficking.' In *Drugs and Crime: Evaluating Public Policy Initiatives,* edited by Doris Layton MacKenzie and Craig D. Uchida, 95–113. Thousand Oaks, CA: Sage Publications, 1994.

Yee, Paul. *Saltwater City: An Illustrated History of the Chinese in Vancouver.* Vancouver: Douglas and McIntyre, 1988.

Zhou, Yongming. *Anti-Drug Crusades in Twentieth-Century China: Nationalism, History, and State Building.* Lanham, MD: Rowman and Littlefield, 1999.

Zimring, Franklin E., and Gordon Hawkins. *The Search for Rational Drug Control.* Cambridge: Cambridge University Press, 1992.

Zinberg, Norman. *Drug, Set and Setting: The Basis of Controlled Intoxicant Use.* New Haven, CT: Yale University Press, 1994.

Index

STUDIES IN GENDER AND HISTORY

General editors: Franca Iacovetta and Karen Dubinsky